Dismantling America

Also by Susan J. Tolchin and Martin Tolchin

To the Victor: Political Patronage from the Clubhouse to the White House

Clout: Womanpower and Politics

SUSAN J. TOLCHIN AND MARTIN TOLCHIN

Dismantling America

The Rush to Deregulate

Houghton Mifflin Company   Boston   1983

Portions of chapter 2 have appeared in different form in the
New York Times magazine and *Regulation* magazine.

Library of Congress Cataloging in Publication Data

Tolchin, Susan.
   Dismantling America.

   Bibliography: p.
   Includes index.
   1. Administrative procedure — United States.
2. Administrative agencies — United States.   3. Consumer protection — Law and legislation — United States.
4. Trade regulation — United States.   5. Law and
politics.   I. Tolchin, Martin.   II. Title.
KF5407.T64   1983   342.73'066   83-10840
ISBN 0-395-34427-1   347.30266

PRINTED IN THE UNITED STATES OF AMERICA

D 10 9 8 7 6 5 4 3 2 1

Book design by Ann Schroeder

Contents

To Mickey and David Bazelon

Acknowledgments

Regulation has been a fact of life since Babylonian times, when the Code of Hammurabi fixed weights and measures, limited interest rates, and otherwise attempted to bring order to everyday commerce. This gave rise to the first anguished cries of those who wanted to "get the government off the backs of the people." Over the course of history, this strife intensified, as increased regulation begat growing resentment. This recurring struggle captured our interest at the onset of the 1980s, when the question of the legitimacy of government intervention loomed large on the political landscape.

To better understand the nature of this conflict, we drew liberally from many disciplines in addition to our own, namely, business administration, law, economics, sociology, and management science. We are deeply grateful to our friends and colleagues from those fields, as well as to those from our own professions of journalism and public administration. To the scores of regulators, White House aides, lobbyists, business leaders, environmental and consumer advocates, and members of Congress and their staffs whom we interviewed for this book, we express our special thanks. Their perspectives were invaluable in leading us through the intricacies of the regulatory process; this is as true of those who disagree with our premise as of those who agree with our views.

Interviews were conducted throughout the research and writing of the book, and took place from 1980 to 1982. All direct quotes in the text that are not cited in the footnotes are taken from these interviews.

We are especially indebted to Tom Hart, our editor at Houghton Mifflin, who nurtured this project and provided both a critical eye and moral support. The final product reflects his editorial skill and his insight. Robie Macauley, senior editor at Houghton Mifflin, guided the book through its final stages. We also thank Helena Bentz, chief copy editor, for the considerable patience, care, and skill with which she shepherded the book to completion.

This book originated with an article for *Regulation* magazine

Acknowledgments

on President Carter's attempt to reduce the burdens of regulation through White House efforts. For her early encouragement and editorial help, we thank Anne Brunsdale, managing editor of the journal.

We also acknowledge an intellectual and personal debt to David L. Bazelon, whose judicial decisions as Chief Judge (and now Senior Judge) of the U.S. Court of Appeals for the District of Columbia reflect his essential humanity, as well as his courage and foresight in the field of regulatory law. He and his wife, Mickey, critiqued portions of the manuscript and were continually supportive throughout the writing of the book.

We also gratefully acknowledge the extensive research and writing support provided by George Washington University. Norma Maine Loeser, dean of the School of Government and Business Administration, was particularly generous in allocating both staff and resources, which went toward the transcription of interviews, as well as typing and word processing of successive drafts of the manuscript. We also appreciate her constant encouragement, as well as her substantive suggestions in the field of airline deregulation.

The themes of the study were developed over a long period of time, and involved extensive discussions with our colleagues, many of whom read and critiqued portions of the manuscript. We would especially like to thank Astrid E. Merget of the Public Administration Department at George Washington University. She was consistently supportive throughout the project, and contributed her special expertise in cost-benefit analysis. We also thank Bayard L. Catron for his thought-provoking suggestions on the cotton dust chapter. David S. Brown read the manuscript, and was most generous in offering his criticism and encouragement throughout the duration of the project. Others who contributed their thoughts were Stephen R. Chitwood, Kathryn Newcomer, and Michael M. Harmon.

We are indebted to many other colleagues at George Washington University who read and critiqued portions of the manuscript: from the Business Administration Department, we thank Ben Burdetsky, Daniel Kane, Charles Shepherd, Guy Black, and John Lobuts. William Halal of the Management Science faculty gave the manuscript a detailed reading and offered incisive criticisms. University Professor Amitai Etzioni, who read portions of the man-

viii

uscript, also made many helpful suggestions on both theory and content.

We are also grateful to members of the Washington Bureau of the *New York Times* for their insights, encouragement, and substantive criticisms of the manuscript. Especially helpful were Bill Kovach, John W. Finney, Philip Shabecoff, Robert Pear, and Steven V. Roberts. David Burnham was a constant source of expertise, advice, and criticism.

Other colleagues throughout the country and in Washington added their considerable background and knowledge to the book. Herbert Kaufman, of The Brookings Institution, gave the manuscript a meticulous reading, sharing with us the benefit of his vast knowledge of administration, as well as his lively intellect. We also thank A. Lee Fritschler, also of Brookings, for his thoughtful critique of the book. For their thoughtful help and constructive suggestions, we also thank Miriam Ershkowitz, of Temple University; Martha Minow, of Harvard Law School; Nan Aron, of the Alliance for Justice; Mark Nadel, of the Battelle Institute; Barbara Greenfield; Dorothy Goldsmith; Rick Neustadt, of the law firm of Kirkland & Ellis; Joseph Perpich, of the Genex Corporation; Michael Pertschuk of the Federal Trade Commission; Robin Schwartzman, formerly of the Department of Commerce; and Fran Dubrowski, of the Natural Resources Defense Council.

Ralph Nader, a pioneer in the field of regulatory justice, was generous with his insights and criticism.

We are indebted to Kathleen Corry, of the Department of Public Administration, who typed the initial draft of the book; her efficiency and fine humor were in constant evidence, and we thank her for taking on this prodigious task. We are also grateful to Vale Dry and Michael Lewis, of the Office of Continuing Professional Education at George Washington University, who were responsible for putting the manuscript on a word processor. They both performed with speed, accuracy, and precision, not to mention unfailing grace under the pressure of deadlines. We also thank their supervisor, John F. McCarthy, director of that office, who made their time available, and whose management skill facilitated the book's speedy completion.

Over the course of the last two years, considerable research

Acknowledgments

assistance was made available to us through the Public Administration Department's Graduate Teaching Fellows program. We thank Beth Craig and Van Ellet, both of whom contributed enormous amounts of time to checking facts, researching, and performing the myriad tasks that go into writing a book. They probably became more familiar with the *Federal Register* and *Code of Federal Regulations* than they ever dreamed possible, and we thank them for their thoroughness, patience, and research skill.

Our agents, Mort Janklow and Anne Sibbald, were most helpful to us throughout the last two years, and we thank them both.

The greatest source of strength and inspiration to us are our children, Karen and Charles, who help us keep our sense of humor and perspective.

So many people helped us along the way, with their generous concern, as well as intellectual and moral support. We thank them all.

Dismantling America

1

Silent Partner
The Politics of Deregulation

I don't know anybody who believes in dirty air or dirty water.
— Irving Shapiro, former chairman of the board of the Du Pont Company

Regulation is the key to civilized society.
— The late Jerry Wurf, president of the American Federation of State, County, and Municipal Employees

CENTURY-OLD ANACONDA, MONTANA, in the foothills of the well-named Bitterroot Range of the Rocky Mountains, became an instant ghost town on a crisp September morning in 1980. With little warning to its fifteen hundred employees, some of whose fathers and grandfathers had worked for the company, the Anaconda Copper Company closed the smelter that was as old as the town itself, and its reason for existence. The smelter had processed the copper ore mined in Butte, twenty-eight miles southeast, and the smelted copper was then sent by rail to a refinery in nearby Great Falls. The refinery was also closed soon afterward.

Dismantling America

The company announced that because of the high cost of complying with government regulations, it would henceforth ship its copper to Japan, where it would be refined and smelted before being returned to the United States, a round trip of about fourteen thousand miles. Anaconda had recently been acquired by the ARCO Oil Company, which claimed that compliance with federal and state standards would cost between $300 and $400 million. At a press conference called to announce the closing, the president of the company explained that the decision was reached after "exhausting every option available" to bring the smelter into compliance with environmental, health, and work place regulations, but the costs of compliance were "prohibitive."

It was part of a pattern in which overregulation was blamed for reducing the United States to an underdeveloped nation, whose minerals were taken by industrialized nations that in turn sent back finished products. This was a reversal of the industrial imperialism that had sent America and other industrial powers roaming the world for natural resources, exploiting their less-developed neighbors and intervening in their internal political and fiscal affairs. The emergence of a potent Japanese lobbying effort in the nation's capital, and its influence on legislation and regulation, is testimony that the United States is considered by some ripe for the picking, and on the verge of joining the industrial have-nots. Like the closing of the steel mills in Youngstown, Ohio, Anaconda highlighted a new trend that has disturbing implications for the national defense, as well as an estimated total nationwide cost of $125 billion in lost production and more than two million jobs.

Skeptics, and there were many, contended that the closing was really triggered by a costly labor dispute preceded by decades of poor management, when technological improvements were shunned in favor of the pursuit of profits. These skeptics cited a short-term approach, in which managers were encouraged to regard their positions as stepping stones to more prestigious and lucrative appointments, rather than developing long-term loyalties to institutions and rejecting immediate profits in favor of capital investments and long-term growth. As early as 1972, *Forbes* magazine observed that "Anaconda's problems seem to have stemmed directly from its corporate style of life; its patrician stance, its attitude of affluence."[1]

A major corporate blunder had been the company's failure to foresee the nationalization of its extensive copper mines in Chile by the government of Salvador Allende, which marked the beginning of a steady decline in Anaconda's fiscal fortunes. "The company was making so much money in Chile that they let their domestic operations go a little flat," said L. R. Mecham, vice president of Anaconda.

Mecham added that labor troubles were a major factor in the closings. The plant had been idle since July, due to a nationwide strike against the copper industry. "Montana was notorious for having some of the worst labor practices in the country," he said.

The ranks of the skeptics also included government regulators, who argued not only that the costs of complying with regulations were far lower than the company's figures, but that they were willing to negotiate flexible timetables for meeting those standards. Challenging Anaconda's figures, the federal Environmental Protection Agency (EPA) put the price tag at about $140 million; the Occupational Safety and Health Administration (OSHA) added another $3 million to the estimate. Roger Williams, a regional administrator of EPA, said the finality of the decision came as a "complete surprise" to him because of Anaconda's earlier commitment to retrofit its existing facilities to meet air pollution requirements. "The company's past failure to investigate options with EPA," he wrote, "coupled with the company's ability to quickly secure profitable contracts with foreign industry piques my interest, and I'm sure the public's, in knowing the reasons behind the company's decision." [2]

The real reasons, that is. For regulation had become the national whipping boy, and it was easier to lay the blame at the feet of faceless bureaucrats in Washington than on mismanagement, the greed of organized labor, the worldwide decline of the copper industry, or the fact that copper smelting's most valuable by-product — sulfuric acid — had become virtually unmarketable in the United States. "They have used the closing as a political tool, to send a message to Congress about the Clean Air Act," said Steve Rovig, an aide to Senator Max Baucus, Democrat of Montana.

In the years following the Anaconda closing it became even clearer that factors other than regulation were responsible for the industry's problems, namely, a worldwide slump in copper prices. In Arizona, which produced more than two-thirds of the nation's copper, mine after mine had closed, its workers joining the thirty thousand unemployed copper miners. The United States found itself in a noncompetitive position in the world market, not because of the Clean Air Act, but because its labor costs were much higher than those in countries like Zaire, and because, unlike many foreign competitors, the United States government did not subsidize the copper industry to sustain it in periods of decline.[3]

The Anaconda closing also echoed the steel industry's complaint that between 1968 and 1975, dozens of steel mills were forced to shut down because they could not afford to comply with costly environmental regulations. But here, too, the suspicion lingered that the closings — and the perilous state of the steel industry — were more related to the antiquated state of the steel mills themselves and the industry's inclination to diversify by putting its money into unrelated industries rather than investing in the technological improvements that had become standard features of steel mills in Western Europe and Japan. As in Anaconda, questions were also raised about the industry's estimates of the cost of compliance. Did the figures represent the true cost of meeting regulatory standards, or did they incorporate the cost of retooling plants to beat back their competitors?

Similarly, the American automobile industry blamed its precipitous decline, not on its high prices, oversized cars, or shoddy products, but on the raft of government regulations intended to improve the safety and fuel efficiency of the vehicles and perhaps make them more marketable. No matter that Japan overcame its long-standing reputation for shoddy production by applying rigorous standards of quality control, standards that were abandoned during the same period by Detroit. And how do the steel, copper, and auto industries reconcile their tendency to make regulations the scapegoat with the cold fact that their foreign competitors, most notably Japan, also live with stiff regulations, particularly in the environmental field?

By the late 1970s, complaints of excessive regulation had become management's all-purpose cop-out. Were profits too low? Blame regulation. Were prices too high? Blame regulation. Were

4

inadequate funds and manpower earmarked for research and development? Blame regulation for sapping both funds and manpower. Was American industry unable to compete with foreign competitors? Blame regulation.

In a highly technological society such as ours, the need for increased regulation is manifest. It is inconceivable to think of "lessening the regulatory burden," as some put it, at a time when private industry has the power to alter our genes, invade our privacy, and destroy our environment. A single industrial accident in the 1980s is capable of taking a huge toll in human life and suffering. Only the government has the power to create and enforce the social regulations that protect citizens from the awesome consequences of technology run amuck. Only the government has the ability to raise the national debate above the "balance sheet" perspective of American industry. This is not to dismiss the many socially conscious businessmen who are concerned with the public interest, but, unfortunately, they do not represent the political leadership of the business community. After all, the "bottom line" for business is making a profit, not improving the quality of the environment or the work place. Its primary obligation is to its shareholders, not to the community at large.

Complaints against regulation have become a standard lament of American business, not without some justification. Horror stories abound. Federal bureaucrats were designing everything from toilet seats to university buildings. Small companies complained that they were drowning in paperwork and were being "regulated out of business." Douglas Costle, a former administrator of the Environmental Protection Agency in the Carter administration, estimated that his agency's regulations alone increased the Consumer Price Index by four-tenths of one percent each year; while estimates of the total cost of regulation exceeded $100 billion a year.

The complaints focused on what are known as social regulations, regulations not geared to a specific industry but to the general public. Regulations falling into this category included those whose benefits were designed to provide clean air and water, safety in the work place, product safety, pure food and drugs, and protection for the consumer in the marketplace. Their goals were ambitious, but expensive to implement.

5

Dismantling America

Individual companies began calculating the costs of social regulation, and publicizing the results. The Dow Chemical Company assigned a ten-man task force to this chore, which reported that in one year alone the company spent $147 million on compliance with federal regulations. Of the total figure, Dow considered $87 million "appropriate" in terms of the normal costs of doing business; $50 million as "excessive"; and $10 million as "questionable." The regulations assigned to the "excessive" category included 41 percent of the health and safety regulations and 31 percent of the environmental regulations.[4]

Studies like Dow's added fuel to the antiregulatory campaign, striking a responsive chord among thousands of businesses and their Washington representatives. "Is excessive government regulation strangulating your business?" asked a U.S. Chamber of Commerce brochure, publicizing the chamber's Regulatory Action Network. "If federal 'red tape' has your hands tied, we can help." Thousands of unnecessary regulations offering "no visible benefit to society" had gotten "so out of hand," the brochure alleged, that "government regulation now threatened to squeeze the very life out of our free enterprise system."

A media blitz reflecting this point of view during the 1980 presidential campaign linked federal regulation to declining productivity and a worsening balance of trade with other nations. Cover stories on reindustrialization in *Newsweek, Business Week,* and *U.S. News & World Report* vied with each other to make the case against regulation, alleging a conflict between regulatory practices and the nation's economic survival.

Business Week contended that the drug industry had been especially victimized. "Once a technological trailblazer, that industry is now well on the way to becoming a producer of standard products, since the task of bringing a new drug to market, made arduous by regulation, has reduced considerably the payoff from innovation."[5]

Ironically, the drug industry was to plead for government regulation in the fall of 1982, after the "Tylenol" murders, when a madman placed cyanide inside Tylenol capsules. As a result, Tylenol sales plummeted, and the manufacturers of other patent medicines began to fear that the public's growing anxiety could destroy their sales. They requested, and received, government regulations

6

that required new devices to secure the medicine bottles and make them "tamper-proof." Instead of the months and even years normally required to produce new regulations, the government announced these in a matter of weeks. It was a classic case of industry turning to the government to restore public confidence in their products — a much overlooked function of government regulation.

Long a silent partner in the corporate board rooms, where its initial function was to help industries and later smaller businesses, regulation became a dirty word when it served the public's interests and compelled industry to spend large sums of money for clear air, clean water, and other objectives not directly related to its profits. Those who had been indifferent to complaints that regulatory agencies had become the captives of industry grew apoplectic when they saw some of those agencies had become the captives of consumer and environmental groups. By 1980, the business community had framed a major presidential campaign issue: "get the government off our backs." They contended that regulation threatened to strangle the steel and automobile industries, had raised the price of consumer items, was a major factor in the inflation that had reached double digits, and was responsible for the high interest rates that had virtually destroyed the housing industry and had made it impossible for young families to purchase homes. Critics linked regulation with America's declining productivity and industrial growth, and claimed that regulation created an uncertainty that discouraged investors. In the declining steel industry, the uncertainty of escalating regulations prevented the construction of new mills since investors were unwilling to risk large amounts of capital without knowing if the plants would meet federal requirements when they were completed.

This view was echoed later by Anaconda executives in explaining their action. "In deciding to close the Montana facilities," said Ralph Cox, president of Anaconda, "our investigations and research disclosed that no option to retrofit or build a new smelter combined both essential requisites — economic feasibility and compliance with the environment, health, and safety laws."[6]

Critics of regulation ranged from those who contended that it was a major cause of most of what is wrong with the American economy to those who regarded it as a petty nuisance. One businessman, tired of filling out forms at the expense of running his business, vented his frustration on an Equal Employment Opportunity Commission questionnaire, which asked, "How many employees do you have, broken down by sex?" "None," he responded. "Our problem here is alcohol."

Former regulators pondered how to counter the public's negative images as they struggled to find jobs in the midst of an increasingly unfriendly environment. "I was actually told by somebody at a job interview that I had three strikes against me," said a former assistant at the Consumer Product Safety Commission. "I was a Democrat, I was a regulator and I was a woman." She was not consoled when a friend told her she could change two things about herself, but she would always be a regulator.[7]

Not limited to the business community, public impatience was also reflected in a 1981 Pulitzer Prize–winning cartoon by Mike Peters of the *Dayton Daily News*. The cartoon depicted a gun, labeled as the killer of nine thousand Americans a year, placed alongside a saccharin package identified as the killer of four white rats. The caption read: "Can you guess which one's been banned?" The reference was to one of the most highly publicized and unpopular examples of what is known as "zero-risk regulation," the Delaney amendment, which instructs the Food and Drug Administration to ban all food additives known to cause cancer in laboratory animals.

The Peters cartoon, buttressed by a raft of newspaper articles, demonstrated anew that whoever succeeds in formulating an issue considerably improves his chances of victory in the public arena. The regulators clearly lost ground by permitting the critics of regulation to shape the debate almost exclusively in terms of excessive government interference — the view that government is an unchecked and unwanted business partner whose demands needlessly drive up the cost of doing business and place the private sector at a severe disadvantage compared to foreign competitors.

Zero-Risk Regulation

Regulators and their supporters watched helplessly as the horror stories began to mount, dramatizing allegations that government was driving business out of existence through onerous regulation. It was government's traditional role to aid business, to protect it against all enemies foreign and domestic. A healthy business economy was crucial to the nation's economic success, they said, and that fact was amply demonstrated by Japan and the Western democracies, which used every opportunity to strengthen their domestic industries.

As the economic consequences of social regulation came to dominate policy making, other rationalities faded, and adversarial patterns dominated a scene that showed winners and losers battling over such difficult choices as jobs versus safety, clean air versus productivity, health versus the balance of trade. When the United States began to industrialize, there were no such options. Government's task was clearly perceived as aiding the fledgling industries. The nation needed coal and steel, and could not afford to worry about the human costs. Building a transcontinental railroad was an overriding priority, which took precedence over the safety and welfare of those building it. The giant meat-packing plants fed a nation that needed a quantity of food more than it needed quality in food, an accident-free work place, or antitrust laws. Industry owned government, both figuratively and literally. Legislators came to the state houses to be bought, said Lincoln Steffens.

Eventually, however, the prosperity and arrogance of American industry led to widely publicized scandals, then to a wave of reforms, prompted by the Upton Sinclairs and Ida Tarbells. Indeed, the Food and Drug Act of 1906, passed in response to Sinclair's classic exposé of the meat industry, *The Jungle,* created the first regulatory process designed to serve a wider constituency. But the role of the regulators remained essentially the same: to help industry.

In the last decade, however, the public interest movement has made some advances of its own, leading to the creation of agencies such as the Environmental Protection Agency (EPA) and Occupational Safety and Health Administration (OSHA) in 1970, the Consumer Product Safety Commission (CPSC) in 1972, and a reinvigorated Federal Trade Commission (FTC) in 1974. These agencies came alive during the presidency of Jimmy Carter, who appointed aggressive administrators to protect the public interest. In the process, these regulators were accused of being insensitive to businesses, which bore the brunt of the costs of escalating public protections.

Many businesses came to feel they were victims of overregulation, and their partnership with the government now meant an unequal distribution of burdens, imposed because of the new regulators' zero-risk objectives: totally pure air and water, a safe work place guaranteed to all workers — to name two of the most controversial mandates accorded to regulators in the Clean Air and Clean Water acts (which governed EPA regulatory policy) and in the enabling legislation for OSHA.

To White House economists, whose sympathies often paralleled those of the business community, these objectives were impossible to implement. "If we had an ambulance waiting on every street corner, response times in the event of an accident would be cut to zero, and there would be many fewer traffic fatalities," wrote Charles L. Schultze, chairman of the Council of Economic Advisers under President Carter. "Why don't we do it? . . . Because . . . we implicitly recognize that reducing risks to zero is impossible, and trying to do so would impose unbearably large losses in our living standards. . . . Zero risk is simply an unrealistic goal."[8]

In the pendulum movement so typical of American politics, public opinion began to swing inexorably toward the private sector, in sympathy with its case against regulation: the uncertainty; the high costs of paperwork; the unnecessary delays; the inequities; and the negative impact on the market position of individual industries in the world economy.

To a certain extent, the case was well founded. Critics objected to the exponential growth of the regulatory agencies, as well as to the arrogance and open hostility to business demonstrated by many regulators, who also displayed a rigid unwillingness to factor costs into their decisions. It was soon clear that the campaign against regulation orchestrated by the Chamber of Commerce, the Business Roundtable, and numerous trade associations representing the business community had succeeded in becoming part of the mainstream and was no longer identified exclusively with the private sector lobbying in its own interest.

The general public began to link America's declining economy with regulation, and to identify with the plight of industries like the drug industry, which claimed it had lost its competitive strength in the international market through overregulation. The results, said drug company spokesmen, were evident in their trade imbalance: from 27 percent of the world market in 1962 to 15 percent in 1980. Drug companies pointed to the slow approval process of the Food and Drug Administration — it takes up to seven years to bring a drug to market — as an example of the overregulation that imposes excessive costs on companies struggling to recapture the market.[9]

The drug companies echoed a complaint made throughout the industrial sector: the diversion of capital. Instead of spending more than one-tenth of all new capital formation on compliance with government regulations, the money could be better spent on research, more aggressive marketing, new equipment, and retooling outmoded plants. Economists, both liberal and conservative, joined the chorus against the new partnership between business and government, labeling government as the albatross. "The revolt against regulation that we're experiencing is also a revolt against government compulsion and meddling," said Alfred Kahn, an economist, when urging his colleagues in the Carter administration to "do its best to keep the hand of government as invisible as possible."

But regulation is necessarily coercive, in that it directs private parties — from companies to consumers to citizens to towns and counties — to spend their money for public purposes. The business community, which feels it has carried the lion's share of the economic burden, has reacted most vociferously, on the grounds that it was picking up the tab for decisions over which it felt it had very little control. Why should industry — and ultimately the consumer — bear the brunt of what is termed "social regulation," in which value choices are translated into public policy: a safe work place, health, clean air and water, and product safety? Not surprisingly, the agencies in charge of implementing those "public goods" have been the ones on the firing line of the antiregulatory movement, slowly watching their mandates and their budgets disintegrate. Polls show widespread agreement with the regulators' goals, but consensus is lacking on the extent to which these goals should be implemented.

"I don't know anybody who really believes in dirty air or dirty water,'' said Du Pont board chairman Irving Shapiro, illustrating this dichotomy. ''I don't know anyone who believes that you ought not to have safety in your plants.''

The issue, he continued, was that regulation too often diverted capital and manpower from more productive uses, particularly striking in Du Pont's case, ''where the water that comes out of our plants . . . in many cases . . . is purer than the water that came from the river before we used it.''[10]

Regulation as an Ally of Business

Regulatory agencies were not always on the defensive. Indeed, today few recall the origins of this highly organized system of government intervention: to protect business from the vagaries of the marketplace. That was the initial purpose of agencies such as the Federal Trade Commission, the Interstate Commerce Commission, and the Federal Communications Commission, and the basis for the more popularly accepted form of regulation known as ''economic regulation'' — regulation geared to benefit a specific industry. For although the corporate world regularly proclaimed its devotion to the free enterprise system, it looked to the government for protection against competition, both foreign and domestic. Even today, Lee Iacocca, chairman of the Chrysler Corporation, who has frequently assailed the burdens of regulation, argues just as forcefully on the other side, in favor of stricter regulations in the area of foreign trade to exclude Japanese automobiles from the American market. Similarly, the deregulation of the airlines and the trucking industry was initially opposed by the leading companies in both industries, who also advocated the risks of marketplace competition for everyone but themselves.

More recently, the advertising industry has petitioned the Federal Trade Commission not to relax its rules requiring that advertisers substantiate their advertising claims, once again demonstrating how regulation protects the status quo. The established merchants fear that unscrupulous competitors may make wholly fictitious claims whose appeal could drive the more legitimate merchants out of business. If an unscrupulous tire manufacturer could claim, for instance, that his tire would travel two hundred thousand miles with only ordinary wear, or a patent medicine manufacturer could claim that a particular pill relieves everything from headaches to dandruff and ingrown toenails, the reputable manufacturers would suffer.[11] Regulation serves many masters, but, ideally, it should serve them all at once, like a traffic light controlling the flow without showing preference for any one group or individual.

Indeed, the antiregulatory fervor that has swept the business community appears rather selfish in light of the original purpose of regulation, whose mission — the protection of business — has only recently expanded to include the protection of the public. Industry complains that it is picking up a disproportionate share of the costs while the benefits are spread among many. But specific responsibilities of business toward the public are notably absent from these discussions.

When regulation protected business from the vagaries of the marketplace, it enjoyed a high level of support. The complicated antitrust enforcement functions shared today by the Federal Trade Commission and the Justice Department originated in the late nineteenth century, when the "free market" created giant monopolies that prevented other businesses from entering the marketplace and kept prices artificially high. Even at the height of the antiregulatory campaign, when David A. Stockman, President Reagan's budget director, sought to eliminate the antitrust function from the FTC in the spring of 1981, the business community — particularly the small business community — raised enough of a protest to stop the action in its tracks.

Numerous other regulatory agencies were created for the purpose of protecting business, and — despite occasional skirmishes — have consistently worked in the interest of companies, sometimes to the point of absurdity. The Department of Agriculture's federal marketing orders, which set the price of certain agricultural commodities to protect growers from crop uncertainty, forced the Sunkist company to leave mountains of oranges rotting in the California sun in 1980. One grower who distributed his surplus to the poor was heavily fined, on the grounds that he could open the way for other growers to reduce their prices and flood the market. In a cooperative agreement, legal but somewhat collusive, the growers themselves set the prices, which are virtually rubber-stamped by the same federal officials who are responsible for enforcing these orders. This is a prime example of a smoothly conceived partnership between business and government, ideal in every way except for the exclusion of consumers from the process.

On the state level, licensing requirements regulate entry into thousands of occupations, ostensibly to protect the public from unqualified practitioners. This is understandable in the case of physicians, lawyers, and other professionals. But barbers? As anyone who has tried to become a barber in Arizona has found out, the extent of the restrictions gives rise to suspicions that limiting entry serves to keep fees artificially high.[12]

Those in danger of losing their regulatory protection fight hard to maintain it, despite all arguments to the contrary. And the arguments sound remarkably familiar. They should. They are the same arguments used to advocate the lifting of social regulations: closing the trade gap, increasing productivity, lowering consumer prices, and fighting inflation. But the loss of regulatory protection means the loss of millions of dollars to industries, a high stakes struggle that is nowhere more apparent, for example, than in the communications industry. On this front, the newspapers have mobilized for a losing battle against the encroachment of the telecommunications industry, which they fear seeks to eventually replace the print media with home computers and other technologies that deal with electronically transmitted information. The two giant industries stand pitted against each other: the newspapers, jealously guarding their turf, are fighting to maintain the status quo, while the American Telephone and Telegraph Company, equally feisty and gaining ground since the Justice Department dropped its antitrust suit in January 1982, plots its moves into the business of information distribution.

The newspaper publishers argue that the massive resources of A.T. & T., both technical and financial, give that industry such an enormous advantage over their own industry that it would only be a matter of time before they would be driven out of business. A.T. & T., a $51 billion a year empire, counters with the argument that it must either expand or perish.[13] The scenario is predictable.

Each industry operates in its own self-interest in deciding how much regulation to reject or accept. The Bell System advocates the free market approach, popular with deregulation proponents, because they would emerge as the victors. Many of the nation's newspapers, whose editorials often support the free market over government regulation, find themselves in the paradoxical position of advocating the free market approach for others and regulatory protection for themselves.

Against the backdrop of a growing negative environment, it is important to recall that virtually the entire regulatory system was built in response to the needs of the business community. Bursts of regulatory activity can be directly related at each point in history to pressures related to stabilizing the uncertainties of the marketplace. The Interstate Commerce Commission, the nation's first regulatory agency, was created in 1887 to force the railroads to discontinue their practice of extracting unfairly high prices from farmers and manufacturers. At the turn of the century, the antitrust laws began to challenge the monopolies of oil and steel. Newly created regulatory commissions controlled the electrical power and railroad monopolies. The goal: to protect certain segments of the business community — particularly those being disadvantaged by the economic power of the monopolies. During the New Deal, a number of agencies were created with the purpose of protecting the business community from running the risk of another depression. The Securities and Exchange Commission, for example, was created in 1934 to protect businesses and investors by regulating the stock market; its task of eliminating the unscrupulous sellers and monitoring the practices of others helped rebuild public confidence in the market by assuring investors that the risks of investment were cushioned by government protection. By the end of the New Deal, there was general agreement that the marketplace alone could not deal with the complexities of the twentieth century and that government was the natural vehicle for regulating the nation's economy. To the extent that a consensus was reached, it was generally agreed that the role of government was to be minimal: protective, supportive, and concerned primarily with maintaining economic stability.

The shared values on which the regulatory agencies functioned ensured their relatively peaceful development, unimpaired by the controversy and turmoil characterizing their later circumstances. The primary reason for the agencies' unimpeded progress was the relationship they enjoyed with the business community, a relationship so cozy that many agencies were soon accused of having become "captives" of the industries they were supposed to regulate. Indeed, what conflicts these agencies did encounter occurred among industries competing within the same jurisdiction. The Interstate Commerce Commission, long the captive of the railroad industry, eventually succumbed to the superior political skills of the trucking industry, which became active in the 1920s and eventually preempted the railroads as the dominant power over agency decisions. Conflict was restricted to clashes among the vested interests, in the course of which agencies, like the ICC, merely exchanged captors, while the criticism, mainly academic, was leveled at the ease with which agencies identified with the very interests they were regulating.

Regulators as Adversaries

In the past several decades, smaller businesses increasingly availed themselves of the same kind of government protection previously given the corporate giants. Encouraged by the success of small businesses, the public at large accelerated its demands on the government for protection against the excesses of business, large and small. The cutting edge was an aggressive campaign waged by public interest groups that resulted in a plethora of regulations intended to improve the environment, guarantee employees' health and safety, ensure consumer rights, and end discrimination on the basis of sex and race.

The regulatory process also grew from a lack of other kinds of government involvement, common to other countries, such as government ownership of private industry or more direct government control over the private sector. In Japan, where industry depends very heavily on the Bank of Japan, a government-owned bank, the government can issue orders to stop air pollution without issuing detailed regulations specifying how to achieve this goal. Industries that do not comply, according to economist Lester Thurow, will have trouble with their "friendly 'neighborhood banker.' "[14] The same sort of cooperation exists in many European countries where government owns major industries that, in turn, depend on government for their capital.

As life grew more complex so did the regulatory system, as a necessary accompaniment to the increasing problems of industrialization and social change. In view of the enthusiasm with which the Reagan administration plunged into dismantling the regulatory process, it is ironic that it was during a Republican administration that three of the most "despised" regulatory agencies were created — the Environmental Protection Agency, Occupational Safety and Health Administration, and the Consumer Product Safety Commission — while the fourth, the Federal Trade Commission, got a new lease on life when then FTC chairman Caspar W. Weinberger exhorted the agency to discard its image as the "Little Old Lady of Pennsylvania Avenue" and begin protecting the consumer. Congress also strengthened the FTC's consumer mandate, in 1974, with passage of the Magnuson-Moss Act, which expanded the agency's power to make rules for entire industries.[15]

The regulators, initially the handmaidens of large and small businesses, thus became more clearly identified with the public interest. The agencies began to concentrate on social regulation, policies intended to benefit all citizens equally. Clean air and water, public health, worker safety, and consumer protection were indivisible —if one person benefits, all persons benefit — as opposed to the more traditional "economic regulation," which focused on special interests. Although only a handful of the 116 regulatory agencies were involved in the task of "social regulation," regulation itself became synonymous with social reform and was soon labeled antibusiness. The leading offenders, the EPA, OSHA, CPSC, and FTC, all shared the same political albatross: instead of protecting business as enforcers, they were there to take something away from business, namely, its capital resources and managerial freedom.

Just as the old regulatory agencies were often captives of business, the new agencies were closely identified with their public interest constituencies. To their adversaries, their power was intolerable, and so was their arrogance. Imbued with a missionary zeal, many of these regulators were oblivious to the financial burdens their policies imposed on hard-pressed industries. To many, their role was no longer marginal. As their power grew, so in the minds of many did their arrogance, and their excesses prompted a public outcry that, in a previous age, had been directed at the excesses of private enterprise.

The social regulators operated within an adversarial framework that reflected much of the antiestablishment spirit of the late 1960s and early 1970s. The "us against them" posture stimulated resistance in those they sought to persuade, and armed their critics with the argument that the regulators were unreasonable and insatiable. Even when the regulators and the regulated were in initial agreement, their relationship became so adversarial that it often seemed as if 90 percent of their energies were expended in unproductive conflict. The Ford Motor Company's experiment with inflatable air bags is a case in point.

In 1970, the Ford Motor Company considered installing air bags in a line of luxury cars to test their effectiveness and consumer appeal. As originally designed, these devices would automatically inflate on impact, creating a giant, inflated barrier between the driver and the steering wheel. For those who forgot or neglected to use seat belts, this new safety feature could mean the difference between life and death, permanent injury and minor whiplash, particularly in "high speed" crashes of over thirty-five miles per hour.

At the same time that Ford was studying the air bag, safety officials at the Department of Transportation were also reflecting on its virtues. Their method of testing the waters? A proposed rule to require air bags in both the front and rear seats of all lines of automobiles.

Stunned Ford officials quickly abandoned their experiments. For the next twelve years, automobile industry lawyers and lobbyists pressed their case in Washington, arguing that air bags and other safety devices were unnecessarily costly and would undermine their trade war with the Japanese. Regulators and lobbyists spent the entire time locked in unproductive combat, with no end in sight.

The insurance industry, consumers, and air bag suppliers joined the National Highway Traffic Safety Administration (NHTSA) in supporting the use of air bags while the three major automobile companies hardened their opposition.

"They bullshit all the time," said former NHTSA head Joan Claybrook, referring to her former adversaries, the lobbyists for General Motors. "They say the air bag costs $1,100 now, but that's only if you manufacture fifty thousand of them. If you make two million, it only costs $185."

"They did the same thing with fuel economy standards," she continued. "In September 1978, GM said it couldn't meet the fuel economy standards. We said we don't believe you, because Ford had shown the figures were cost effective. After they found out about GM, they [Ford] quickly changed their figures."

Eventually, the issue was addressed at the White House level during the first year of the Reagan administration. Acceding to their pressures, President Reagan rescinded thirty-four regulations affecting the automobile industry, including the proposed air bag rule. Ralph Nader, who is regarded as the father of many of the automobile safety rules, complained that the "regulation rollbacks are going to kill a lot of people and ruin the health and environment for others." The Supreme Court later ruled the administration had exceeded its authority.

The air bags case stands as a striking example of a typical regulatory stalemate. For today air bags remain unavailable in most current automobile models, and the public is missing out on the benefits of this potentially life-saving invention. An experiment that started out as a constructive, exploratory venture, with laudable and progressive objectives, deteriorated into a political war with very high stakes and very hard choices: safety versus jobs and profits. The stakes, which were economic, and the choices, which were philosophical, soon became hopelessly enmeshed, as government and industry focused on the confrontation instead of the issue.

The tragedy of the air bag story was that the outcome could have been different if Ford and the regulators had been able to operate differently from the beginning and cooperate with each other. Instead, both sides hardened their positions quickly, became more extreme than necessary, and used their energies in the hearing rooms instead of on the drawing boards. Ultimately, the issue ended up in the courts.[16] In the end no one benefited, neither the consumer nor the affected industries; no one, that is, but an army of lawyers and lobbyists who benefit from the increasingly adversarial posturing that dominates the regulatory process.

If the solutions to regulatory problems remain so unsatisfying, it is because they often reflect the *modus operandi* of the lawyers who dominate the process: they seek minor adjustments rather than comprehensive solutions; delay as much as they can; and frequently lay the groundwork for future conflict (which ensures future business for themselves). The adversarial relationship, which underlies our legal system, is therefore part and parcel of the regulatory process.

But what is the alternative? The business community is naturally reluctant to expend large sums of money unless compelled to do so. In other words, industry seldom responds to the gentle nudges of government, especially when millions of dollars are involved. Government is therefore forced to initiate adversarial proceedings if it seeks to change industry's behavior. Quiet persuasion seldom leads to social change. Factories ringing the Great Lakes were turning them into cesspools until the Clean Air and Clean Water acts produced regulations that forced them to stop. The regulators had no choice but to assume an adversarial posture in the face of industry's opposition. In that case they won a short-lived victory, returning to the fray when the lobbyists began chipping away at the Clean Air and Clean Water acts. More often than not, the battle never reaches that stage. Instead, the regulators and their adversaries spend their time and resources locked in a stalemate, in effect a victory for those fighting against constructive solutions.

Taking Charge of Regulation

The long simmering battle against regulation finally found a champion during the 1980 presidential campaign. Ronald Reagan, en route to the White House, needed little prodding. Once a television host and lecturer for the General Electric Company, he had made a political career of championing the virtues of free enterprise, and had vowed during the campaign to ''get the government off the backs of the people.'' Responding to this deeply bipartisan anti-regulatory mandate, the new President initiated a crusade against government regulation and quickly laid the groundwork for the direction of regulation in the 1980s. To Reagan and his allies, the future lay in deregulation, or the removal of regulations from the books wherever possible in order to allow market forces to operate in their stead. Barely a week after his election, Ronald Reagan promised to dismantle existing regulations, and to freeze all new rules for at least a year after his inauguration. In living up to the spirit of his campaign promises, Reagan gave the American people a chance to see for themselves what life would be like without the onerous hand of big government.

The President's appointment of Murray Weidenbaum to chair the Council of Economic Advisers was an important choice, both substantively and symbolically, in the President's war against the regulators. A well-known economics professor at Washington University in St. Louis, Weidenbaum's major distinction was his philosophic opposition to the excesses of regulation. ''The encroaching of government power in the private sector in recent years has been massive [and] self-defeating,'' he wrote prior to his appointment.[17] Afterward, he frequently exhorted federal regulators: ''When you have nothing to do, undo.''

There is no question, of course, that a President and a Congress can change regulatory priorities. The question is whether such changes are in the interests of a highly technological society, in which private industry has the power to inflict widespread damage to life and health. Additional questions of particular relevance to President Reagan concern administrative procedures. While a President is empowered to change these procedures, with the help of Congress, questions have been raised about whether President Reagan adhered to traditional procedure governing the regulatory process, and the extent to which ''undoing regulation'' through procedural change has acted to the detriment of society.

The new President was so successful in capitalizing on his public relations victory over regulation that the system virtually reeled from its impact. Environmental protection became a thing of the past, as the EPA studiously ignored the laws and regulations dealing with clean air and water, as well as hazardous waste. Mine

Dismantling America

deaths shot up as regulations governing the safety of the mines were slowly dismantled through budget cuts and lack of enforcement. Through a program of consistent neglect, worker safety followed a similar path, victim of a more relaxed OSHA. No area of social protection was left untouched by White House efforts to unravel the regulations, the agencies, and the process. Even the nuclear regulators were encouraged to speed up the permit-granting process for nuclear plants by"streamlining" safety regulations.

What had taken years to build was dismantled in the first twelve months of the Reagan administration. Following the dictum that the marketplace could better evaluate the public's needs than government, Reagan trusted his friends in the business community to determine air quality, public safety, and a variety of other social questions far outside their realm of expertise. But the nation had become too complex for a return to this version of nineteenth-century laissez-faire capitalism, as became all too apparent early in the deregulation program. Nobody said anything about dead miners when discussing the burdens of regulation; no one reminded the public that not all industrialists would voluntarily clean up the local waterways and air without big government's interference. More than likely, the midnight dumpers were too busy finding new landfills for their illegal toxic wastes to make speeches about overregulation; now, with lax enforcement, they could probably operate in broad daylight.

It soon became apparent that in dismantling regulation, the President was dismantling America. Regulation is the connective tissue, the price we pay for an industrialized society. It is our major protection against the excesses of technology, whose rapid advances threaten man's genes, privacy, air, water, bloodstream, lifestyle, and virtual existence. It is a guard against the callous entrepreneur, who would have his workers breathe coal dust and cotton dust, who would send children into the mines and factories, who would offer jobs in exchange for health and safety, and leave the victims as public charges in hospitals and on welfare lines. "The child labor laws or the abolition of slavery would never have passed a cost-benefit test," said Mark Green, a public interest advocate, referring to the theory that now dominates regulatory decision making.

Silent Partner

Regulations provide protection against the avarice of the marketplace, against shoddy products and unscrupulous marketing practices from Wall Street to Main Street. They protect legitimate businessmen from being driven out of business by unscrupulous competitors, and consumers from being victimized by unscrupulous businessmen. "Regulation is the key to civilized society," said the late Jerry Wurf, president of the American Federation of State, County, and Municipal Employees. The extent to which we take regulations for granted in our daily lives is reflected by the confidence with which we drink our water, eat our food, take our medication, drive our cars, and perform hundreds of other tasks without thought of peril. This provides a striking contrast to the situation in many Third World nations, devoid of regulations, where those tasks can be performed only with extreme care. (Indeed, there is evidence that some of those countries adhere to United States regulations in the absence of their own government protections. The Squibb representative in Egypt, for example, said in 1979 that he could not market his company's drugs in that country unless they had been cleared by the United States Food and Drug Administration.)

In responding so agreeably to the critics of regulation, the politicians so quick to deregulate forgot that it was the very same process that prevented thalidomide — a tranquilizer prescribed to pregnant women that caused birth defects — from reaching the United States marketplace. A conscientious FDA medical officer, Frances Kelsey, spotted the drug and held it up, unimpressed with the fact that it had already been approved by the West German regulators. Critics also forget that regulations have helped to restore the Great Lakes, which ten years ago were on their way to a polluted oblivion, and have brought the nation more breathable air by reducing sulfur emissions by 17 percent since 1972. And although the Anaconda Copper Company complained bitterly about EPA regulations, lung disease in western Montana declined significantly after the copper company took its first steps toward compliance with air quality standards.

When social regulation works, its benefits are invisible. It is hardly newsworthy, or even noticeable, that the nation's air and water have become considerably cleaner over the last decade, a regulatory development that could be viewed as a stunning success.

So could the Consumer Product Safety Commission's regulations that changed the design of cribs and significantly reduced the number of crib deaths by strangulation.

The problem is that those who breathe and those whose lives were saved by a safer crib have no trade association to applaud the unseen and unheralded benefits of the regulatory process — when it is working well. They have no Political Action Committee to reward politicians who support the regulatory system, or to punish those who attack it. Indeed, most people are unaware that regulations play any role in their well-being. No constituency with significant power has developed over the years to bolster, promote, reinforce, and expand these "public goods." Yet this is another reason the regulatory process was created in the first place: to protect those public goods and those who benefit from them. Indeed, ever since the first United States Congress gave the President the power to make rules for trading with the Indians, regulation has grown geometrically, often with the enthusiastic support of Congress and the President, because it represented a system that held the promise of protecting the public against the incursions of more narrowly focused interests. "We created the regulatory agencies to do what we don't have time to do," said the late Sam Rayburn, when he was Speaker of the House.

But it is not only a lack of time. It is also the inability of its members to agree fully on comprehensive legislation that leads Congress to leave the details to the regulators. Hard-fought legislative battles often result in ambivalent legislation. Congress created the Occupational Safety and Health Administration, for example, for the purpose of protecting the work place "so far as possible." Through this clause Congress covered all bases. It could point to regulation by OSHA but also control the extent of regulation by contending that various regulations were beyond the scope of the legislation because they were not feasible. Meanwhile, the regulators who interpret these laws find themselves in the untenable position of being attacked each time they exercise their own judgment; whatever they do, they find themselves out on a limb. If they interpret the law strictly and issue rigorous regulations, segments of the business community may accuse them of operating with too much discretion. On the other hand, if they are flexible, too generous in extending compliance deadlines or in delaying the writing of regulations, they may be vulnerable to lawsuits from public interest groups, as well as to attacks from angry congressional committees.

Political factors ultimately take precedence over all other variables, and explain the almost revolutionary direction in which deregulation is heading. If anything, the process has become harsher as the President and Congress become increasingly involved in the management of regulation. Their choice of an initial target, the social regulatory agencies — primarily EPA, OSHA, CPSC, and the FTC — reflects the vulnerability of these agencies, and the extent to which they shoulder a disproportionate share of the attack on government that has become so epidemic in our times.

The social regulatory agencies have become the government's orphans, attacked by both management and labor. Management contends that the cost of compliance will erode profits, while labor fears that it could cost jobs and lead to the destruction of entire industries. In an increasing number of cases, management and labor have joined forces to fight the regulatory agencies, producing formidable alliances. In one successful effort, the grain millers union fought side by side with management against the FTC's antitrust efforts to break up the giant cereal companies. In cases like this, who is left to provide the support network and the constituency so necessary to an agency's effective survival?

In this harsh political climate, it is no wonder that leadership on all fronts is in short supply. When President Carter claimed credit for returning salmon to the Columbia River, few applauded his efforts in cleaning up that once polluted waterway. When he attempted to intervene to cut the cost of environmental regulation, he was quickly branded an "enemy of the environment" by an army of critics. Nor did he find many friends among members of the business community, who faulted him for not moving fast enough to dismantle the regulatory process.

Both Congress and President Reagan learned the political lessons of the past, finding it was much easier to correct regulatory "excesses" by dismantling an agency, by reducing its budget to a point that renders it virtually ineffective, than to address the issue at hand.

25

Dismantling America

Throwing the baby out with the bath water became a familiar pattern. It was guaranteed to stop an agency that had failed to work efficiently, that was perhaps working too efficiently, or that was working against the interests of a powerful industry. When certain members of Congress began receiving complaints against the FTC, they mounted such a successful campaign to hold up its appropriations that the agency was forced to close down for a few days in the spring of 1980. By 1981, another consumer agency, the Consumer Product Safety Commission, less vigorous than the FTC but equally offensive to business interests, fought valiantly to stay alive, even on its paltry budget of $40 million a year.

Congress regards its interventions as part of its legitimate oversight function to monitor the regulatory agencies. This has more than a grain of truth to it. A closer look reveals, however, that Congress bears considerable responsibility for the current state of siege that confronts the agencies, as well as for the volatility of regulatory politics in general. With its ambiguous mandates, increasingly detailed legislation, vulnerability to special interests, and increased involvement in the budget process, Congress has reinforced the uncertainty surrounding regulation and done little to improve its troubled future.

What few citizens realize is that all regulation stems from a statutory base. Agencies do not regulate on the basis of whim. OSHA did not initiate the guarantee of a safe work place for every worker; Congress wrote the enabling legislation that created the agency and gave it that far-reaching mandate. It was also Congress that set the goals for air quality standards, not the EPA, although both Reagan and Congress eleven years later threatened to reduce the EPA's power during the renewal of the Clean Air Act — essentially penalizing the agency for doing its job.

Under the guise of responding to pressures, Congress is acting out a charade. The members bask in the applause when they are crediting with giving the nation clean air and a safe work place, but recoil from the anger of those who must bear the brunt of the high cost of regulation.

The greatest charade of all was acted out through the legislative veto. Frustrated with the limitations on controlling the regulatory agencies through the appropriations process alone, Congress had succeeded in writing a legislative veto into more than two hundred bills, giving itself the power to veto selected regulations after they had been promulgated by the regulatory agencies. Congress had given itself the veto to keep control over the broad mandates that it had given the regulatory agencies during the explosion of social legislation of the 1970s. A blanket legislative veto covering all regulations came closer to victory every year, with its chief sponsor, Rep. Elliot Levitas (Democrat, Georgia), claiming 254 cosponsors. Contending that this would give Congress executive as well as legislative power, both Presidents Carter and Reagan strongly opposed the legislative veto as a usurpation of their constitutional prerogatives.

The courts, so far, have indicated support for this position. The Supreme Court ruled in 1983 that the veto was an unacceptable intrusion into the powers of the executive branch and independent agencies. Although many regulators initially hailed the decision, it quickly became apparent that, without the veto, Congress would seek to rescind the broad delegation of authority and relegate the agencies to advisory commissions. Within days of the Supreme Court decision, the House of Representatives approved legislation that would eviscerate the Consumer Product Safety Commission.[18]

The power that Congress exerted through the congressional veto or through the budget process was essentially a negative power. Members of Congress may be able to prevent an agency from pursuing a given area of activity — as they did with the FTC and children's television advertising — but their creative powers are far more limited. Most of the time, they must content themselves with conducting hearings, which are increasingly adversarial in nature, as well as limited in terms of their positive results. Often in the harsh glare of publicity, the agency head is called on the carpet by committee members, who have less and less control over the agency's budget and its priorities. Agency heads find the responsibilities of testifying more and more burdensome as more time is taken away from running the agency. Douglas Costle, former EPA administrator, said he testified before Congress scores of times in his last year in office. "How can I run an agency at the same time?" he asked.

Most important, congressional power over the agencies was further reduced by President Reagan. In the past, Congress could frighten agencies into submission by threatening to cut their budgets. Since 1981, this no longer remained a viable threat. By cutting regulatory budgets to the bare bones, Reagan removed Congress's most effective influence over the agencies.

Eventually, Congress rebounded to seize back some of its oversight power. Although its budget powers were more limited, Congress still retained the capability of drawing considerable media attention to issues through highly publicized hearings, as when six of its committees focused their attention on the EPA throughout the winter of 1982–83. The investigations produced revelations that described how Reagan administration appointees, under White House direction, were systematically dismantling the agency and its regulatory powers. The information literally poured out, showing in vivid detail agency officials being wined and dined by corporate polluters, being advised by corporate representatives hired as agency consultants while they excluded environmental groups, and even allowing lobbyists to revise agency documents — documents accusing them of disgorging toxic wastes — in order to show their companies in a more favorable light.

The EPA scandal knocked the economic crisis off page one in the newspapers, and dominated the network evening news shows. Finally, the President was forced to request the resignation of Anne (Gorsuch) Burford, the agency's director; Rita Lavelle, the administrator in charge of toxic wastes; and a host of top aides. Most important, it showed that Congress could still play a creative role in regulatory oversight, for the congressional outcry generated enough public pressure to make White House leaders think twice about the political wisdom of continuing to unravel regulatory protections in the environmental area.

Government after the Fact

In this rush to deregulate, dominant elements in the White House and Congress have downgraded the role of the agencies, eager to reinforce the negative perceptions of government that have proved so politically attractive to the public. Soon government itself began to bend toward this negative view in addressing regulatory problems; after all, it seemed incapable of helping many businesses out of their long-term predicaments and unable to restore the public's confidence in the benefits of positive government involvement.

All of these factors combined to reinforce government's reluctance to become involved until it was too late. The actions of Congress and the executive branch in the Anaconda case are a typical example of what has become a recurring pattern of government intervention rendered impotent by late, after-the-fact timing. There was no way the government could prevent Anaconda from closing down its refinery or its smelter, despite the intense involvement of the state's two senators and two representatives. Indeed, these legislators were so surprised by the company's decision that Senator Max Baucus, Democrat of Montana, likened the move to the "economic equivalent of Pearl Harbor Day for thousands of Montanans" and "ARCO's economic raid on Montana."[19] Baucus and his colleagues attempted to persuade the company to change its decision, promising regulatory relief of all kinds as inducements. "We have been guaranteed cooperation from every appropriate federal agency from the White House to the Environmental Protection Agency and the Occupational Safety and Health Administration," said Baucus in testimony before the Montana Senate Committee on Economic Problems.[20]

Regrettably, their offers were rebuffed; the company's decision was irrevocable. Although company officials blamed regulation, they were unwilling to join with their government counterparts to reform what it was about regulation that was driving them out of the country. "Our company does not advocate changes in these environmental and health laws and regulations, or seek preferential treatment for our operations in Montana," said Ralph Cox, president of the Anaconda company.[21] Clearly, the company did not want to come out against regulation, which by that point had proved its value with a marked decrease in lung disease not only among copper workers but also among their families and neighbors.

Failing in their efforts at quiet persuasion, Baucus and his colleagues went public, reminding the company of its past commitments. In a letter to Mike Mansfield, a former Montana senator and majority leader, then ambassador to Japan, urging his support in persuading the White House to intervene, Baucus pointed out that during merger proceedings before the Federal Trade Commission in 1976, ARCO promised to make investments of up to $1 billion in the Anaconda company.[22] Of course, the company never said this money would be invested in its Montana operations, but many felt this was the implied commitment. More than implied was an earlier letter to Baucus from Ralph Cox, in which Cox explicitly said that "Atlantic Richfield Company merged with Anaconda because we felt the long-term future for copper was exciting and Montana operations, in particular, had a great potential. We still feel this way and our actions in the past couple of years since the merger demonstrate this. I also think the future for copper operations in Montana will meet our original expectations." Cox concluded his letter by saying that he "looked forward to working with you, the rest of the Montana congressional delegation, the governor, the state legislature and the people of Butte, Anaconda, and Great Falls in making Montana and the Anaconda Company a competitive and significant part of the long-term copper industry."[23]

Barely one and a half years later, the company closed down its Montana operations, with no warning to the battery of political leaders whose participation the company so warmly invited. Why did ARCO not "take advantage of provisions in the Clean Air Act that extended the deadline for compliance with sulfur dioxide standards until January 1988?" asked Baucus.[24] Both Baucus and OSHA officials also argued that the parent company, ARCO, earned ample funds to sustain Anaconda, as indicated by the company's own report of its third quarter earnings of 1980 — released barely a month after the Anaconda closing — which revealed a 22 percent rise from the previous year's level. As early as 1979, officials at OSHA flatly stated that either ARCO, with its operating income of $2.4 billion, or Anaconda, with profits of $179 million, had more than adequate resources to comply with the $2.8 million worth of arsenic control improvements required by the agency, improvements, they said, that would rid the smelter of its lead problem as well.[25]

For its part, the company argued that ARCO, Anaconda's parent company, had no obligation to sustain "a plant or a mine or processing operation that becomes uneconomic," even if it meant preserving jobs. "The economic strength of the company is diluted and diluted very quickly," said an official statement released by Anaconda's Washington office, if such a policy is pursued. "Every unit of ARCO must stand on its own two feet, and in this case Anaconda Copper cannot afford such losses."[26]

EPA official Roger Williams also attempted to challenge the ARCO decision by conducting his own investigation and issuing a report documenting that the closing was not due solely to the cost of regulation. "One is tempted to blame this closure on the Clean Air Act," he said, "but EPA's investigation clearly revealed that other factors were more important."[27]

"The smelter was a marginal operation," he continued, adding such other factors as high operating costs associated with an energy-intensive smelting process, the cost of modernization, and underutilization of the smelter's capacity. To his credit, Williams attempted to broaden the discussion beyond the Anaconda smelter to include the problems of the copper industry in general, reminding everyone of the incentives offered by other governments to offset not only the costs of regulation but also the rigors of foreign competition. "In Japan, for instance, where environmental requirements are more stringent than in the U.S., the government aids its industry with greater tax benefits, protective tariffs, and low interest loans that allow the Japanese copper industry to effectively compete in world markets."[28]

In the final analysis, despite the best efforts of the legislators, there was little Congress or the White House could do. They were able to get minor forms of impact aid to the ghost towns of Montana, and to persuade the regulators to adopt patterns of flexible enforcement, but they were unable to attract the full attention of President Carter, then preoccupied with his bid for reelection. Theirs was merely a mop-up operation; they were totally unsuccessful in their attempts to influence corporate decision making, and had to content themselves eventually with maximizing the delivery of government resources to those who were hurt by the closing. Anaconda eventually dismantled the copper mine in Butte, so that by mid 1983 almost all Anaconda copper operations in Montana were suspended. In a final ironic twist, Anaconda's fifteen hundred workers were denied aid from the Office of Trade Adjustment Assistance —

aid granted workers whose jobs are lost due to foreign competition — while four employees laid off from their jobs with a Butte Chevrolet dealership were successful in obtaining TAA relief.

Government involvement after the fact does nothing to address the real problem or prevent its recurrence. In effect, government operates almost at cross-purposes with itself by getting involved in protecting the public's health, safety, and environment, but failing to deal with the very serious problems caused by industrial failure. Regulation had virtually nothing to do with the problems of the copper industry, yet government could have exercised a more positive role much earlier, by offering the same kinds of assistance other countries relied on to sustain their industries. In that way, regulation could not be used as a scapegoat, and problems could be addressed before they reached the crisis stage, when they are often too severe to be resolved.

After Anaconda:
Congress's Abdication to the President

In the absence of constructive remedies, Congress increasingly finds itself on the side of the deregulators, dismantling regulation while refusing to accept any responsibility for its reconstruction. Even when Congress makes a mistake, even when it makes specific requests of an agency and the agency's subsequent actions prove politically unpopular, the agency stands alone in facing the criticisms for decisions that originated with its legislative overseers.

Occasionally, you can even see the smoking gun. At Congress's urging, for example, the FTC pursued investigations into children's television advertising and the insurance industry. When the FTC's policies backfired, the political pressures intensified, and Congress quickly melted into the background, leaving the FTC to fend for itself. Congress manifested its disapproval by substantially reducing the agency's budget and issuing strict instructions minimizing its future activities.

The Clean Air Act offers another example of well-intentioned but misapplied congressional intervention. Acting in what they believed to be the public interest, lawmakers enacted a very detailed law specifying an inordinate number of guidelines, timetables, and chemical formulas that left administrators very little latitude — what they called wiggle room — within which to negotiate. Fearful of the Nixon administration, Congress purposely boxed in the administrators; but at the same time that they were trying to insulate the EPA from the White House, they overlooked other consequences of their acts.

"Congress never asked scientists how long it would take to implement the law," said an official with the Chemical Manufacturers Association. "When the statutes got into technical areas, where the science is extremely soft, they held very few hearings, and deferred the hard science to administrators, who then made political judgments."

When administrators at EPA attempted to regulate according to the letter of the Clean Air and Clean Water acts, they found themselves buffeted from all sides. In some instances, the law gave them only 180 days to issue air or water quality standards; when they exceeded these deadlines, they found themselves being taken to court by any one of a number of environmental groups. "We have to litigate to maintain our credibility," explained Jonathan Lash, an attorney with the Natural Resources Defense Council. "Otherwise industry would never take us seriously." Similarly, when EPA proceeded to implement the laws against what the business community felt was in its best interests, the agency confronted more litigation from that quarter.

When political decisions become controversial, as they invariably do, the agency, not Congress (or the White House), is transformed into the lightning rod for political discontent. Arguing that "a strong EPA [Environmental Protection Agency] is good for us," the representative of the Chemical Manufacturers Association advocated more consistent and vigorous congressional involvement over the long term: "Congress has no interest after the laws are passed. . . . It is like a postpartum depression. The trauma is so great after the laws are passed [that] there is very little oversight."

Agencies can bank on congressional oversight, however, when organized constituent complaints start flowing in, as agencies like the Federal Trade Commission discovered. "If you wanted to alienate every prominent citizen in every major town, you couldn't have done a better job, Wendell Ford [Democratic senator from Kentucky] told us," recalled FTC commissioner Mike Pertschuk, referring to the commission's initiatives affecting car dealers, real estate brokers, doctors, lawyers, insurance salesmen, dentists, and funeral directors, among others. "If the commission had chosen to get everybody up in arms, it did exactly the right thing."

The FTC learned its lesson, and its responses were quick and sure. By the spring of 1981, the agency made more news by the initiatives it withdrew from circulation than by those it began, a far cry from its heyday following the passage of the Magnuson-Moss Act in 1974. The pattern was set in January 1979 in a memo from Robert Reich, of the Policy Planning Division, to Pertschuk, entitled "FTC's Humility Update," which listed nine major rules the commission had considered and rejected.[29]

Even the Consumer Product Safety Commission, not known for stepping on too many toes, struggled valiantly in the face of Reagan's budget cutbacks and deregulatory initiatives to stave off efforts to relocate it in the Department of Commerce, where, editorialized the *New York Times,* it would surely be "strangled by hostile hands."[30]

"The politics of regulatory reform is focused on who's in charge," said Richard Wegman, former staff counsel to the Senate Governmental Affairs Committee. The three branches of government, each controlling a piece of the regulatory process, display great confusion in the growing number of areas of technical uncertainty, where scientific judgment and economic viability clash repeatedly. Only sparse statutory guidance remains for deciding urgent questions. The Administrative Procedure Act of 1946, designed to insulate the regulators from political interference, remains the only guide; its inadequacies are clear from the power vacuum that has developed in recent years.

The very legitimacy of the regulatory agencies is being challenged by Congress and by the President, with the appropriations process substituting for a more straightforward confrontation on policy issues. Another dimension has appeared in the form of direct presidential intervention in individual regulations, which both Presidents Carter and Reagan have defended in terms of their legitimate executive power and America's economic crisis. The courts, which in the past have tended to uphold the judgments of the agencies, now question their own role in regulatory decision making, as well as the adequacy of the scientific data on which they must base their judgments.

In the wake of these conflicts come decisions that are characterized primarily by their piecemeal and political nature. With the institutions of government competing against one another, the tendency is to reject either the rules or the agency, without much thought of what is to follow. To correct the excesses of the FTC, Congress reduced its budget and established a pattern of regularly intervening in its policy-making actions on an issue-by-issue basis. To check EPA on air quality standards for coal-fired plants, the midwestern and eastern senators under the leadership of Senator Robert C. Byrd, Democrat of West Virginia, united to influence the writing of the regulations. To no one's surprise, the resulting standards benefited the "dirty coal" interests by forcing western coal producers to put unnecessary scrubbers in their plants; this kept eastern coal competitive with western coal, and the prices for this source of energy higher for everyone.[31] Presidential and legislative intervention in the area of economic deregulation, particularly trucking, banking, and airline deregulation, also has led to uncertain outcomes: large airlines appear to have suffered in favor of smaller airlines; banks find themselves in a condition of increased uncertainty; and only trucking seems to have survived so far without too much of an upheaval, perhaps due to the snail's pace of its deregulation.[32]

Who Benefits and Who Loses?

The most serious consequence of the trend to deregulate is the dismantling of the social regulations, which provide a connective tissue between the needs of the public and private sectors. Private industry is entitled to make a profit, but its employees are entitled to their health and safety, their consumers are entitled to safe and well-made products, and the public is entitled to have its air, water, and quality of life safeguarded.

The rapid pace of technological advances has given industry awesome tools with which to alter our genes, invade our privacy, and even destroy our lives. It is difficult, therefore, to regard the current dismantling of regulation as anything but an aberration, a trend that will soon be reversed. One can thus expect increased pressures on government for protection against forces over which individuals have less and less control. And one would certainly expect those forces to be resisted by the affected industries. That conflict will be resolved in the political arena, which will be the ultimate arbiter in the current attempt at dismantling America.

Deregulation — a code word for dismantling the regulatory process — is clearly not the answer; for around the next corner lurks a series of potential disasters — a nuclear "incident," an increase of cancer directly attributable to a chemical spill, babies born with drug-related birth defects — any or all almost certain to accompany life in a society with an untended regulatory system. A better approach is to be more selective: to eliminate regulations that are truly harmful to business and to consumers, and to identify those that work and make them work better; to eliminate government as an obstacle course and make it a true partner in managing the growth of the country as well as in the protection of its citizens.

In sorting out the regulatory problems, a more genuine effort could be made to spread the burdens; if society makes the choice, for example, to improve its air and water quality, then society through its government should bear the responsibility for assuming a fair share of the costs of that decision. In this way, the burden would fall directly rather than indirectly on those making the decision, the taxpayers. They would decide just how clean they wanted the air and water within the limits of the public purse. The political burdens would also be eased by defusing industry's accusations that they have been driven out of existence by the regulatory strangle hold.

It all comes back to the partnership between business and government, and to the nature of that partnership. In the Reagan administration, government has been relegated to minority status as an unwanted partner, a subservient partner existing only to offer help without receiving anything in return.

36

Is government more like a subsidiary of the private sector, a mere supplier or subcontractor as in the old days, to be controlled and manipulated in the best interests of the corporation? Or is it the dominant partner, using its massive resources to harass or to subsidize, to decide which industries live or die, and which populations it will protect or neglect?

Or, optimally, should government at least be an equal partner, enforcing the law within the limits of its own expertise and judgment? At this stage, the regulators have been relegated to minor roles while the private sector takes over their functions. As before, choices are being made every day about pollution and safety, but these decisions are being made without public participation, and without public knowledge. Who should decide on the quality of the air we breathe? Who should set the standards for the pills we take, the food we eat, and the cars we drive? Only industry? Only government? A mix of the two? The dismantling of regulations means the dismantling of a political and social fabric that took two hundred years to construct. How long will it take to rebuild?

2
Capturing the Regulators
Presidential Power over the Administrative Process

We hit the ground running. . . . We knew what we were doing the minute we came in. Stockman let me loose, and said "be tough."
— James C. Miller III, chairman of the FTC

Everyone is extremely cautious about anything they let through that would upset industry. . . . It's true these things are deadly or carcinogenic, but the economy's a mess and that takes precedence.
— An official from the Food and Drug Administration

FEW PRESIDENTS HAVE ENTERED the White House with more well-defined or ambitious goals than those of Ronald Reagan. His objective was nothing less than a reversal of the direction of government, a repeal of much of the New Deal, a reduction in both the size and scope of government. A major part of that objective was the scaling back of the regulatory agencies, under the rubric of "getting the government off the backs of the people." But the prime targets were those agencies that sought to protect consumers and workers and to improve the air, water, and work place. They were the agencies, in effect, that tried to get industry off the backs of the people. President Reagan's antiregulatory stance was thus perceived as pro-business and antipublic, and fueled the fairness issue that was to haunt this presidency.

The new President lost little time converting his philosophy into reality. Nine days after his inauguration, he imposed a sixty-day freeze on all new regulations. A conservative, business-oriented politician, the new President placed a high priority on the dismantling of social regulations, which he considered excessive, inflationary, and counterproductive.[1]

He was familiar with the horror stories, and believed in a more laissez-faire approach to the problems of the environment and the work place; indeed, his replacement of Harry S. Truman's portrait in the White House with one of Calvin Coolidge said it all. Promising the American people speedy regulatory relief, he initiated the most comprehensive overhaul of the regulatory process in the history of the Republic.

No one told him it would be easy. A Carter administration official, Rick Neustadt, drew on his Navy experience to describe presidential efforts at regulatory management: "It's like steering a supertanker," he recalled. "You may put the wheel over hard, but it's still not going to turn on a dime." White House regulation experts who served under Presidents Nixon and Ford agreed with Neustadt that it was unrealistic to expect dramatic changes from regulatory reform, largely because of the overwhelming political and legal barriers. Change would only come, they warned, through slow, gradual improvements, introduced carefully at moderate intervals.

But when Reagan, an avid deregulator, took office, he disagreed. Taking the helm of the supertanker, he changed its course and glided over obstacles that had seemed insurmountable to his predecessors. A change in political climate helped, as did the fact that the basic design of regulatory reform was already in place, thanks to reforms already implemented by Presidents Carter, Ford, and Nixon. What helped most of all was the presence of a political vacuum. Where regulation was concerned, Reagan confronted virtually no unified opposition, only confusion and uncertainty from the three branches of government. Congress kept delaying its regulatory reform bill; the courts sent mixed signals; and the regulatory agencies, stung by public criticism, seemed to capitulate almost completely to the new President's challenge. As for legal obstacles? These too were crushed by the presidential juggernaut, lightly dismissed by the men in charge of regulatory reform.

The key to Reagan's regulatory policy was a three-pronged attack, consisting of a regulatory rollback, budget cuts, and the appointment of key personnel dedicated to the Reagan philosophy of "getting the government off the backs of the people." Massive budget cuts left regulatory agencies bereft of resources, and struggling to maintain a minimum level of operation. Severe reductions in force (RIFs) curtailed their services and guaranteed that the agencies would need years, if not decades, to train the experts needed to do the job. Managers who remained faced a new set of bosses, Reagan appointees, who shared their President's commitment to reduce regulatory burdens and did not hesitate to quash regulations despite professional staff advice, or the number of years it took to develop those rules. "All of our appointees have religion," remarked James C. Miller III, a burly, fast-quipping former economics professor who headed the Office of Management and Budget (OMB) regulatory reform effort before going on to chair the Federal Trade Commission (FTC). "We want to make sure OSHA is no longer a four-letter word."

These changes, along with Reagan's Executive Order 12291 — granting OMB superagency status over regulations and mandating economic analysis from the agencies — created a new regulatory landscape, a still life actually, with the presidential agencies fearful of issuing new regulations, or introducing too many new initiatives. White House regulatory policy also had a chilling effect on the "independent" regulatory agencies — the headless fourth branch of government, so called because they are technically accountable to Congress, which has traditionally ceded them wide discretion. Their discretion is limited, however, by the President's power to appoint the commissioners, and by the trend toward more direct White House intervention into their day-to-day policy activities. The independent agencies find themselves further constrained by the sensitivity of their leaders to public opinion, and by the winds of presidential and congressional change.[2]

41

Dismantling America

Through its power to monitor the regulatory performance of the executive agencies, OMB kept the agencies so busy with requests for additional information that it held *de facto* control of their agendas as well as their output. After a while, OMB could relax, when it was evident the message had filtered down to the agency level. One midlevel management official at the Food and Drug Administration (FDA) described his agency's new approach by recalling a meeting held in the spring of 1981.

"We were meeting with the director of the Bureau of Drugs, on a drug we had been studying for over a year, and whose toxic effects included cancer and bladder trouble. The biggest concern from everyone was 'who's upset?' — meaning which industry would be upset. Everyone is extremely cautious about anything they let through that would upset industry. It's not that they're not proconsumer, but they're realists. They're sensitive to Reagan. They know he's there to represent business, and they're terrified. The result is that things are operating at a snail's pace. We're just doing busywork. Unless somebody's on our tail, like Ralph Nader, nothing gets done. The administration's point of view is that we're just slowing things down. We're just taking a closer look at everything. It's true these things are deadly or carcinogenic, but the economy's a mess and that takes precedence."

Scarcely two months after that meeting, the FDA, as expected, proposed eliminating its plan to require "patient package inserts," informational brochures inserted into ten widely used prescription drugs detailing each drug's benefits as well as possible harmful side effects. Among the ten drugs covered were Darvon, a painkiller, and Valium, a tranquilizer that is the most frequently prescribed drug in the country. The recall was applauded by the Pharmaceutical Manufacturers Association and many drug companies, who feared the business losses that could result after patients learned about the dangers and refused to buy these drugs. Consumer groups denounced the move.

Conservatives are usually concerned about individual rights and government intrusions that could affect biological functions. In this case, however, a conservative administration moved to deprive the individual of the information needed to make an informed judgment about certain drugs whose ingestion could be dangerous in some cases.

Indeed, it took a conservative President turning activist to put the brakes on regulation, using the most potent instruments of presidential power: budget, personnel, and executive fiat. The results were manifest well before the end of the first year of the Reagan presidency. But the Reagan program raised more questions than it answered, and cast an unsettling pall over the process itself. Was the executive order constitutional? Legal? Did it subvert the guarantees of the Administrative Procedure Act, passed in 1946 to protect the executive branch agencies from political interference?[3] Was the secrecy inherent in OMB's activities ultimately in the public interest? And, finally, did presidential dominance over the regulatory process really address the problem of overcoming the adversarial relationship between business and government? Or did it lay the groundwork for future conflict by appearing to serve primarily the interests of the business community, while excluding other segments of the public from the new partnership? It appeared that under Reagan's version of regulatory management, the agencies were reverting to their former mode, when they were accused of being "captives" of the industries they were supposed to regulate. Only now, they answered to another captor: the President.

Origins of Presidential Intervention

Andrew Jackson was the first President to argue that the President controls the actions of cabinet officers and agencies. Angered by the refusal of two consecutive Treasury Department secretaries to obey his orders to remove deposits from the Second Bank of the United States, Jackson fired them both, and announced that he would continue to hire and dismiss secretaries until he found one who would do his bidding. "A secretary," he said, "is merely an executive, an agent, a subordinate."[4]

Firing cabinet secretaries, however, represented a blunderbuss approach, surely not a viable management tool for the volume of regulation that had begun to surface by the early 1970s. Until that time, almost all regulations were issued by the independent agencies, and were primarily economic. The White House did not exert much influence, except through appointments to the commissions, and there is not much evidence to suggest that Presidents were able to make substantial inroads despite periodic attempts — including recommendations from various blue-ribbon panels — to bring these agencies closer to the executive branch. Moreover, there had not yet appeared any ground swell of concern on the part of interest groups, who had developed their own relationships with the agencies and saw regulation primarily in the context of their own individual transactions.

By 1970, it had become clear that regulation had a considerable social and economic impact on society, and that some form of centralized oversight was needed. It also became apparent that the agencies were unable to coordinate their efforts — particularly in the area of environmental regulation — and the call for presidential intervention took on a new sense of urgency.

Richard Nixon became the first President to introduce a formal management system into the regulatory arena, a process known as the Quality of Life (QOL) review. The review required all agencies involved in health, safety, or environmental regulation to advise all other affected agencies of all conceivable impacts of a proposed regulation — economic, intergovernmental, and environmental. Involving mostly Environmental Protection Agency (EPA) regulations, these comments were sent to other agencies like Commerce, Interior, and the Army Corps of Engineers, with OMB in the role of mediating interagency conflicts. Agencies could appeal OMB decisions to the head of OMB, and theoretically to the President, but according to James Tozzi, who then headed the Quality of Life program as chief of the environmental branch of OMB, this occurred "only once in a blue moon."

To Tozzi, who is now the deputy administrator for information and regulatory affairs at OMB, the "guts of the program" rested on a review process, a portent of things to come, that for the first time made agencies accountable to the President for their actions. Since most of the affected regulations were environmental, EPA became the agency most involved in QOL reviews and, in the process of going through those reviews, developed an analytical capability that many, including Tozzi, believed far superior to that of all the other agencies. As inflation began to rise, along with congressional pressure, President Gerald Ford redirected regulatory management from an environmental to an economic focus, a pattern that was to continue under President Carter. Ford's Economic Impact Statements (EIS) affected all agencies, and OMB's enforcement and coordinating role was replaced by the newly formed Council on Wage and Price Stability (COWPS). With COWPS in charge of compliance, OMB was virtually removed throughout the late 1970s from the nucleus of regulatory power until the Reagan administration resurrected the agency's earlier role and gave it primary responsibility for regulating the regulators.

With OMB on the periphery and no one technically in charge, it was easy to ignore prior executive orders in the period immediately following President Carter's election. Although OMB director Bert Lance pressed for the continuation of QOL review, he soon became preoccupied with his own problems, and the agencies quickly stepped in to fill the vacuum. With the agencies again in full ascendancy, presidential management fell by the wayside. Under pressure from one segment of the Carter campaign and from EPA staff members who opposed QOL reviews, the deputy director of EPA unilaterally canceled the reviews. During the next two years, presidential oversight was moderated, until members of the Council of Economic Advisers urged the President to renew efforts at regulatory management. "Lack of performance of the executive branch," remarked Tozzi, "was the best argument for oversight."

In quick succession, the Regulatory Council and the Regulatory Analysis Review Group (RARG) were formed in 1978, establishing the basis for what was to follow under Reagan. Despite the reluctance of Reagan appointees to acknowledge the Carter legacy, there is no question about its importance in laying the foundation for Reagan's more comprehensive program. Carter's efforts represented the first strong move by a President to intervene directly in the day-to-day operations of regulatory agencies. Other Presidents consistently made the effort to intervene in both executive and independent regulatory agencies, but not until President Carter was there such a blatant, concerted effort to manage the entire process. Previous attempts were academic exercises compared with Carter's efforts to apply his own political muscle to the problems of regulatory management.

A dramatic example occurred one evening in early May 1979,

when Stuart Eizenstat, head of the White House domestic policy staff under President Carter, called the Office of the Federal Register and, in a highly unconventional move, stopped publication of interim regulations about to be issued by the Department of Energy. The regulations in question were designed to implement the coal conversion provisions of the Power Plant and Industrial Fuel Act of 1978. There was no disagreement between the White House and the Department of Energy on the underlying aim of the statute — to encourage industry to convert to alternate fuels, like coal, where the price of those fuels did not "substantially" exceed the cost of using imported oil. But there was disagreement between them, as it turned out, on the appropriate definition of the key term "substantially." Though the spread between their respective targets might have seemed minuscule, the extra costs involved, in aggregate, could have — in the view of the Carter White House — given a nudge to the economy's chronic high inflation.

Stuart Eizenstat stopped the regulations because they had not gone through what was known as the RARG process, the first serious attempt at presidential intervention in the regulatory arena initiated by the Carter administration. "They started to," said Eizenstat in an interview, "but the process had not been completed. When I was alerted to the inflationary potential of those regs, I wanted more of a chance to study them in detail."[5]

The incident illustrates how difficult it was to get the agencies to cooperate with the administration's political leadership, and the lengths to which President Carter was willing to go to bring them into compliance. For the RARG was really a front for the President to influence the regulatory process without appearing overly directive. It also indicated that the President took regulatory management seriously, by forcing the agencies to submit to presidential review despite the arguments of many officials that this represented a usurpation of their power. Carter knew that if he allowed Secretary of Energy James Schlesinger to circumvent the White House at this early stage, other agencies would follow suit and the program would have been doomed. (It was not entirely coincidental that several months later, in the summer of 1979, Schlesinger was among the first to be fired when Carter purged his cabinet.) For Carter also knew that any initiative mounted without a strong legislative mandate relied heavily on the President's continuing personal interest and his willingness to back up his advisers when confronted with the inevitable challenges from Congress, the agencies, and the special interest groups that direct their energies through the media and the courts.

In a foreshadowing of Reagan's strategy, Carter relied on an executive order (EO 12044) promulgated in March 1978. The order focused on the economic impact of regulation and added a stronger role for the President in reducing its costs. The Carter administration was waging a losing battle against inflation, and the high cost of regulation was frequently cited as a major factor — another example of regulation as an all-purpose scapegoat. Under Carter's edict, all executive agencies were required to conduct economic analyses of their proposed regulations whenever those regulations appeared to have a substantial impact on the economy. A selected group of economic advisers, the Regulatory Analysis Review Group (RARG), then reviewed the most inflationary of the regulations — those costing industry more than $100 million a year — presumably with the intention of mitigating their impact.

By any name, RARG was there to modify regulations, to relax them, and ultimately to make them less expensive for the business community and, to a lesser extent, for states and localities. This practice of modifying the impact of proposed regulations through executive power turned out to be the crux of a controversy that plagued both Presidents Carter and Reagan in their efforts to establish a presidential beachhead in the regulatory arena.

Although the executive order formally assigned OMB to the task of reviewing these economic analyses, the agency at that time was too fragmented — "like the Balkans before World War I," one White House staff member explained — to take on such a politically sensitive task. Instead, extensive reviews of about six regulations a year were conducted by RARG, which included representatives of all cabinet departments (except State, Treasury, and Defense) and top officials from OMB, the EPA, and the White House Office of Science and Technology Policy. In actual fact, RARG was run by an executive committee, chaired by Charles L. Schultze, the original architect of RARG and chairman of the President's Council of Economic Advisers (CEA).[6] The bulk of the analytical staff work was undertaken by economists from the Council on Wage and Price Stability (COWPS).

To avoid the political dangers of agency resistance, Carter had decided to draw the regulators themselves into the process by giving them a minor role in a body known as the Regulatory Council. Composed of top officials from the cabinet departments and the leading regulatory agencies, the council operated independently of RARG, but had far less power. Essentially a research and discussion group, its principal function was to coordinate common regulatory approaches among agencies with overlapping responsibilities, the role originally intended for OMB. Chaired by EPA administrator Douglas Costle, the council's chief responsibility was the publication of a semiannual calendar listing major forthcoming regulations, which RARG then used to help identify its own candidates for review.

Initially, the creation of the Regulatory Council increased the conflict between White House advisers and the regulators. The economists at COWPS and CEA objected to being excluded from the council, but they soon realized that if RARG were to function effectively, it needed at least the grudging support of key regulators; besides, it was hardly worth their effort if the council were to have such limited power. Bringing them formally into the process through the Regulatory Council seemed a good way to obtain the regulators' support while keeping them from infringing on the White House's power. The Regulatory Council and RARG were later abolished by President Reagan, who viewed them as a political threat to his own program, which placed OMB — no longer as Balkanized — in the role originally intended for it in the Carter executive order.

Clearly, RARG's existence depended almost entirely on President Carter's continuing personal interest and his willingness to exert political clout on its behalf. "The administration has found that the fact that RARG is there to monitor the quality of the analyses has helped to improve them," noted Charles Schultze in testimony before the Senate Judiciary Committee in May 1979. "This is especially true," he added, "because it is understood that the President personally authorized establishment of the program and is personally following its progress." In fact, White House aides sent the President a biweekly memo on the progress of the program.

Schultze's rule in the RARG process marked another turning point in presidential management of regulation: the ascendancy of economists over lawyers. Shaped by their own discipline, White House economists did not even bother to conceal their disdain for what they considered rigid, legalistic approaches adopted by many of the agencies, especially when they encountered opposition. "The first time an agency is 'RARGed,' it is like a cold shower," reported one CEA staff member in the Carter administration. "Many have never done cost-benefit analysis and OSHA, for example, had, at most, one economist in the whole agency."

"Economists don't like a lot of detail; they like looser performance standards," he continued. "Regulators, on the other hand, like detail. They like to design and fix means of compliance. They don't trust business. Sometimes it's impossible to design performance standards. How do you tell how much earth to dump in a crater?"

A sampling of quotes from other White House officials at the time reflected an almost universal contempt for agency regulatory habits:

- OSHA doesn't believe in costs. We had to teach them to do cost-benefit analysis.

- HEW is not very good at listing forthcoming regulations. We've got to go back over and over again.

- DOE is out of control. Schlesinger and his cadre are good bureaucratic infighters. They know how to get around the White House. The regulatory people in DOE are cut off from the mainstream of the department.

For their part, critics feared the effects of the new supremacy of economists, who, they felt, were bound by their discipline into a new rigidity in which "sound analysis" was equated solely with economic analysis. Capitulating to the RARG standards of balancing costs against benefits meant viewing regulatory policy strictly through the context of White House economists, and in that framework, they predicted, cost factors would invariably take precedence over social concerns. No one knew where other forms of analysis — political, demographic, scientific — would fit into this scheme, although many guessed that it would not take long before health and safety standards would be sacrificed to the needs of cooling the economy. Still others warned that cost-benefit analysis was often misleading by failing to include the costs of inaction, in terms of increased illness, for example, with its related costs in lowered productivity and increased medical expenses. In a letter sent to President Carter in 1978, and cosigned by over thirty environmental, health, and labor groups, Richard Ayres of the Natural Resources Defense Council charged that White House regulatory oversight had become a "serious threat to the interests of millions of Americans" by substituting the judgment of CEA and COWPS "on questions of work place and environmental health and welfare for the technical and legal judgment of agencies that Congress has explicitly created and directed to make such decisions."

The Tightrope of Regulatory Management

As a management system, RARG incorporated many commendable features. But as a political institution, it raised two major issues, both of which remained to haunt the Reagan administration's program: the scope of the President's authority over regulatory decision making within the executive branch, and the compatibility of White House intervention with the requirements of the most comprehensive law governing the regulatory process, the Administrative Procedure Act. Through RARG and the executive order, President Carter hoped to establish hegemony over the regulatory actions of disparate agencies while allowing agency heads to retain the formal responsibility for making decisions. By adding another layer between himself and the agencies, the President hoped to shield himself from the responsibility for unpopular decisions. But there was no place to hide. Carter learned the hard way how costly these decisions could be. His experience with the cotton dust rule in May 1978, when he interceded directly to relax standards imposed by Secretary of Labor Ray Marshall (acting on the basis of proposals from OSHA) for maximum permissible levels of cotton dust in textile mills, touched off a storm of protest. The new standard came under intense criticism from labor unions, health groups, and industry — and, not surprisingly, most of the anger was aimed at Carter himself.[7] Carter faced similar criticisms when he tried to intervene in rule making on strip mining, following the passage of the Surface Mining Control and Reclamation Act. This time, two legal challenges were immediately initiated, both questioning the formulation of strip-mining regulations. Initially, environmentalists unsuccessfully sought an injunction to stop closed, off-the-record meetings between Charles Schultze and Secretary of the Interior Cecil Andrus. In a subsequent case that sounded what was to become a recurrent theme, the plaintiffs alleged that off-the-record consultations between CEA officials and Interior Department officials significantly affected the decision-making process.[8] Faced with litigation and political opposition, Carter never again directly intervened in a regulatory issue without covering his tracks.

President Carter's experience showed why previous Presidents had shunned blatant, overt intervention in the regulatory process, and had limited themselves to behind-the-scenes maneuvering. On the other hand, some argue, the President is ultimately praised or blamed for the decisions of the regulatory agencies, because the public does not make the fine distinctions between those agencies and the President himself. That being the case, some believe that a President is in a no-win position and has little to lose in making his views public.

The issue, never clarified during the Carter years, continued to plague advocates of the Reagan executive order, with no legal resolution in sight. How far can the White House go to ensure that its policies are being carried out without violating the public comment provisions of the Administrative Procedure Act, which courts have interpreted as the prohibition of introducing new material in a regulatory proceeding after the public comment period has officially closed? Would not a President's intervention violate the prohibition against *ex parte* contacts — contacts made by private parties outside the official comment period? Or is it unfair to classify the White House as an outside party when it is communicating with its own executive branch?

Defenders of presidential intervention argued that RARG did

not go far enough, that its interventions ceased at the close of the comment period, when its report was filed and made part of the public record. But those who worked in the White House admitted that the President really did intervene through his economic advisers, and actually set regulatory policy.

"The real oversight occurs when RARG hammers out its report," said economist Tom Hopkins, who then worked for COWPS and now occupies a similar position at OMB. "However, further intervention by presidential advisers, such as the CEA or COWPS chairman [as distinct from RARG], is possible after the comment period."

"In the strip-mining case," continued Hopkins, "RARG ended its involvement after filing its report, but the CEA felt the issue was important enough to warrant a follow-through on the three or four issues RARG had identified. CEA staff then worked with Department of Interior staff in the interest of seeing that the final result was in keeping with the RARG report."

The nuances tended to obscure the realities: RARG was indeed an arm of CEA, staffed by COWPS, and there was no question that RARG took an active role after the comment period ended, despite its formal fade-out. White House officials claimed — and there was more than a germ of truth in their allegations — that before the review group was created, low-level bureaucrats were making decisions while the White House, as the readiest focal point for public dissatisfaction, was being blamed for the consequences. In establishing the President's right to direct the regulatory process, RARG laid the groundwork for increasing presidential authority over the implementation of the laws, at the same time that it shielded him from the worst of the political consequences.

Substantial support accompanied this remarkable shift in power, informally referred to during the Carter years as the "one big happy family" theory. This theory holds that the postcomment period need not be open to the public, because White House advisers and agency heads were all part of the same family; any attempts to differentiate them were purely artificial. Since all agency decisions are ultimately made behind closed doors, and since agencies not granted independent status by Congress are all part of the executive branch of government, what difference did it make whether the President interceded early or late in the process? After all, by intervening he was only fulfilling his continuing responsibility for executing the laws.[9]

As it happened, it made a lot of difference to interest groups, who did not object to the fact that these meetings were held as much as to the secrecy of the meetings. If CEA and EPA officials were discussing the Clean Air Act, for example, representatives from the whole spectrum of environmental groups wanted to know what happened at those meetings — what new considerations were introduced — so that they could determine whether or not to press for a reopening of the comment period and a full opportunity to respond. Moreover, they feared that legal challenges to the final decision would be much more difficult if all considerations that went into it were not on the record and available to the reviewing court. This is the basic reasoning behind the charge that such off-the-record meetings violated the standards of due process envisioned by the Administrative Procedure Act.

A different point was made by the Capitol Hill foes of RARG, who framed the dispute in terms of an overextension of presidential power. "The Constitution never envisioned the President as super-regulator. Yet, now the President is rewriting the laws, by deciding which ones are important and which are not," argued one legislative aide. "Should the President have the power to rearrange national objectives? Can he decide not to enforce the Clean Air Act because of inflation and unemployment?"

"Presidents who plead helplessness are not being entirely honest," said Jim Graham, a staff aide with the Senate Governmental Affairs Committee, in a statement prophetic of what was to follow under Reagan. "There are devices that enable the President to control the process. He can exert his influence through the budget or through hire-and-fire policy."

RARG's effectiveness also depended on the extent of agency cooperation, which varied according to the agency involved. In some cases, the mere awareness of White House interest seemed sufficient to influence a decision; in others, more solid brokering was necessary to influence the outcome; and in still others (as with the Department of Energy) RARG was ignored until a direct contest of power occurred.

Even agencies that were openly cooperative with RARG were quick to point out that White House influence was not as great as appeared. Roy Gamse, an EPA staff analyst, argued that although RARG flagged the ozone emission standards for review, the group had virtually no impact on EPA's final decision in January 1979, despite a widespread public perception to the contrary. "The environmentalists think we caved in to White House pressure," said Gamse, "but the decision was our own and was based on scientific data, not the RARG report." Still, the standard was relaxed in the end, and many people insisted that the economic concerns of the White House were responsible.

Buffeted by competing claims and political pressures, the RARG staff began to tone down the group's function, carefully using the words "review," "coordinate," and "analyze" to describe RARG's oversight of "inflationary" regulations. Strict cost-benefit analyses began to give way to less controversial forms of analysis, formulated in terms of the "most efficient" compromise, or policies with the "least risk" and the "least cost" method of achieving the administration's goals. In part, this reflected the technical difficulties in quantifying benefits and balancing the equation.[10] But it also helped deflect the criticism that decisions were dominated by cost factors at the expense of social concerns. The modifications in OSHA's exposure standards for acrylonitrile, a carcinogen used in the manufacture of acrylics, were a good example of RARG's modified approach. According to Bob Litan, who worked on this regulation at the CEA, OSHA had set an exposure standard that was as high as possible without posing a serious cancer risk. "We made the standard stricter," he said, "but used marketplace incentives and introduced flexibility so as to achieve the most cost-effective result."

The RARG experience highlighted the difficulties of regulatory oversight, and ultimately RARG itself had less and less influence on specific regulations as its political and legal vulnerabilities unfolded. "You have to realize that this is not a management or an engineering process but a political one," explained Peter Petkas, former executive director of the Regulatory Council. He was right, for in the short run it was the political difficulties that limited RARG's effectiveness as an oversight tool.

54

Capturing the Regulators

Some of the problems encountered by RARG reflected recent political trends, while others originated in long-established patterns in national politics. Throughout its short tenure, for example, RARG confronted the problems of congressional oversight. The sponsors of some of the newer regulatory statutes maintained a proprietary interest in the administrative or enforcement policies developed under "their" programs. Former Senator Edmund Muskie (Democrat, Maine), one of the authors of the Clean Air Act and several clean water statutes, continued for almost a decade to display a keen interest in the activities of EPA, often defending the agency against pressures for compromise. With Congress having the last word at that time on the budgets and legislative authorizations (or restrictions) of the regulatory agencies, leading figures on congressional oversight committees were often more influential than the White House. Agency staff soon learned that lesson, often fleeing to congressional patrons for sympathy and support when they disapproved of the direction toward which they were being prodded by the President's staff.

That hard political reality often forced prior administrations to engage in quiet bargaining with congressional committee chairmen when they wanted to effect a change in regulatory policy or to develop a new rule along particular lines. These efforts were not always successful, but defeat at least could be accepted without public humiliation in most cases. In recent years, however, with the rising potency of single-interest advocates and their ready access to the media, disagreements over regulatory policy have suddenly flared up into heated public controversies. Today, the setting within which the White House operates is clearly more inflammatory, harsher, and more public than it used to be, with the President wedged between the proverbial rock and a hard place. When President Carter pressed EPA to pay closer attention to economic costs, he was branded an "enemy of the environment." When he promoted himself as an environmentalist, as he did many times, he was attacked for adding to the country's runaway inflation. Many critics at the time insisted that Carter himself compounded these problems with his antiseptic and apolitical style of leadership.

Taken together, these factors created a political climate that led agency leaders to scrupulously avoid antagonizing special interest groups or key figures in Congress while, at the same time, trying to meet the suggestions of the President's economists. But avoiding controversy did not seem to help: the criticism continued in the same whipsaw fashion. The government continued to be sued by the environmental groups, and agencies like OSHA and EPA were regularly attacked for overzealousness or for selling out. The intensity of the debate on all sides reflected people's awareness of the stakes involved: the lives of millions of citizens and their health, safety, and welfare were being weighed against billions of dollars in dwindling economic resources.

To its credit, the gist of Carter's program survived its political difficulties and marked a turning point in the history of presidential control over agency regulatory behavior. From that time on, as reflected in Reagan's reform plan, agencies began, on a routine basis, to introduce cost-benefit analyses into their decision-making activities. Although many seemed to adopt and exaggerate this method of analysis without the necessary modifications, it still represented an important step forward in introducing the awareness of cost factors to agencies that had previously ignored them.

The Reagan Juggernaut

Ronald Reagan undertook the role of an activist President, playing Henry V to Carter's Hamlet, with a love of political battle reminiscent of Franklin Roosevelt. Not for him the politics of ambivalence, or the legal niceties that called for at least an appearance of respect for the independence of the agencies. In short order, he sought to place the independent agencies as well as the executive agencies under his own executive order, yielding only when the legal obstacles became apparent. He then requested that the independent agencies "voluntarily" comply with the order.

The Reagan administration reaped the benefits of Carter's regulatory initiatives and learned from his mistakes. "We bullet-proofed our executive order," said James C. Miller III, in the fall of 1981, referring to the legal protections of their program compared to the RARG. "RARG was an ordinary intervenor, with only a counseling capacity. RARG was analogous to someone writing an article for a professional journal, having to convince the editor it was worthwhile printing. Now we [OMB] are the editor; and we know we're being published. It's like being the editor of the *Federal Register*. Besides,'' he added, "our President is tough. Carter folded on his first big issue, cotton dust.''

Other officials echoed Miller in separating their program from Carter's efforts, which vice presidential assistant Boyden Gray also dismissed, in the spirit of partisanship, as a "step back.'' Carter circulated his executive order to the agency counsels, "who shook their heads and started writing in the margins,'' explained Gray. No such latitude was allowed by the Reagan task force, headed by the Vice President. "We sent the executive order straight to the agency chiefs. The counsels, many of them Carter holdovers, were still shaking their heads and writing in the margins, but it doesn't make any difference now.''

"We hit the ground running,'' continued Miller. "All the work was done in the transition period; we knew what we were doing the minute we came in. Stockman let me loose, and said, 'be tough.' Like the budget, when Stockman came in with his troops, Jim Miller also came in with his troops — but I was careful not to abuse that.''

No doubt, much of Reagan's success hinged on moving into the regulatory arena quickly, catching potential adversaries off guard, and insisting on White House hegemony over the process. Without this kind of mandate from the President, Miller was quick to point out, neither he nor other members of his team, whom he called the regulatory triumvirate, would have been able to push through their program. Lest they forget, all top members of the administration were constantly reminded of their mission, according to Miller, who said not a cabinet meeting went by without the President referring to "some regulatory horror story.''

To ensure a substantial return on the enormous amount of political capital invested in this venture, the President put the full force of his office behind the reform effort. The White House task force responsible for implementing the executive order was represented on an operating level by Richard Williamson, assistant to the President for intergovernmental affairs; the Office of Management and Budget by James C. Miller III; and the Vice President by

Boyden Gray. "Just like Meese, Baker, and Deaver were the Big Three, I called us the Little Three," quipped Miller.

As the formal leader of the task force, Vice President Bush kept a high profile on the subject of regulatory reform through his speeches and other well-publicized activities. OMB freely used the Vice President's influence to bring recalcitrant agency heads into line. One agency head called to tell Miller he wanted to go ahead anyway on a regulation that had been delayed by OMB. Miller said that was fine with him, but he would have to take it up with the Vice President. "I'm amazed at how fast the opposition withered," added Miller.

In his official capacity as chairman of the task force, Bush sent letters to thousands of businessmen, civic leaders, governors, and other political leaders, inviting them to submit their recommendations for regulatory reform. His letter to small businessmen urged "documentation of instances in which specific regulations could be changed in order to increase benefits or decrease costs . . . generating greater *net* benefits overall."

"We need your participation in this effort," continued the letter. "Your organization is comprised of many people who have direct experience with the effects of government regulation."[11]

Thousands of responses poured in, which OMB never bothered to analyze empirically. But acquiring a data base was not the intent of the Bush letter; the real goal was to convey to the business community the message that this administration was sincere in its intent to alleviate the burdens of excessive regulation. The message was reinforced in frequent subsequent communications, which substituted the word "relief" for "reform." This astute public relations strategy, coupled with the widely publicized executive order, resulted in giving the Reagan program its intended visibility.

The business community was assured in other ways as well that the Reagan administration meant to deliver regulatory relief by cutting red tape whenever possible. In a speech delivered to the Chamber of Commerce on April 10, 1981, Boyden Gray told businessmen not to be discouraged if they failed to get satisfaction from the agencies. That is what the White House is there for, he told them:

"If you go to the agency first, don't be too pessimistic if they

---

Capturing the Regulators

can't solve the problem there. . . . That's what the task force is for.

"We had an example of that not too long ago. . . . We told the lawyers representing the individual companies and the trade associations involved to come back to us if they had a problem.

"Two weeks later they showed up and I asked if they had a problem. They said they did, and we made a couple of phone calls and straightened it out. We alerted the top people at the agency that there was a little hanky-panky going on at the bottom of the agency, and it was cleared up very rapidly. The system does work if you use it as sort of an appeal. You can act as a double check on the agency that you might encounter problems with."[12]

The informal system worked very well, downgrading the professional role of the agencies while increasing through White House intervention the influence of the special interests. But as with Carter's intervention through RARG, the Reagan administration needed some kind of legal foundation to add legitimacy to its regulatory maneuvers. It produced its own variation of RARG, through Executive Order 12291, issued February 17, 1981.

The executive order gave OMB the power to oversee all major regulations promulgated by the executive branch agencies, excluding the twenty-two independent agencies that are legally under the jurisdiction of Congress.[13] The order also imposed formal requirements on the agencies that would guarantee their submission to the President's program, in order to increase "agency accountability for regulatory actions," provide for "presidential oversight, minimize duplication and conflict of regulations, and ensure well-reasoned regulations."[14]

Heavy emphasis was placed on cost-benefit analysis, with informational requirements spelled out in great detail, directing agencies to develop new regulations involving the "least net cost to society." Agencies were discouraged from taking regulatory action at all unless the "potential benefits to society . . . outweigh the potential costs to society." Another requirement asked the agencies to "set regulatory priorities," taking into account the condition of particular industries affected by the regulation, as well as the "condition of the national economy." Additional requirements mandated that the agencies submit regulatory impact analyses justifying their finding that the benefits exceeded the costs; regulatory reviews establishing that a proposed regulation fell within the agency's legal authority; and regulatory agendas to be published twice a year, in October and April, containing a summary of each rule being considered.

On the process questions that had plagued Carter the most, the task force adopted a forceful political strategy, the only realistic option while the legal issue remained in limbo. The task force managed the secrecy and *ex parte* issues, for example, by assuming a Dr. Jekyll and Mr. Hyde posture that initially appeared to work well. On one level, the process seemed perfectly clear-cut, with everything aboveboard and on the record. Boyden Gray said he sent everyone who petitioned him on a regulatory issue straight to the agencies, where their complaints were immediately entered on the record. Answering critics who charged that this meant the business community could change any regulation by simply going through the backdoor at the White House, Gray countered by saying that he had made a special effort to contact groups on the other side of the fence: "We contacted the environmentalists; they hadn't contacted us." In stressing the importance of entering everything on the record, Gray added that he had once sent an "interested party" to an agency and the agency had failed to enter the material in the record; an oversight that was quickly corrected by the Vice President's office.

OMB followed a similar procedure, according to James Tozzi, who said that all letters, reports, and assorted documents were sent directly to the agencies, with only Tozzi, Christopher DeMuth, and Tom Hopkins allowed to see outside groups.[15] "You have to be equally open," said Tozzi, a career civil servant, describing his evenhanded approach in dealing with outside groups. "The major complaint of the private sector was that they didn't have access. I see everyone. Nader is in to see me all the time. Sometimes we change the regs their way. PPIs [patient package inserts] are one example. We put one or two of them on a trial basis. Highway design is another. Nader wanted it revised and we did it." When asked about those meetings, Ralph Nader claimed he had never met with Tozzi at OMB: "I've never been in to see him, but one of our groups has been in to see him once or twice."

Miller also expressed his indignation at "all the accusations that we're operating in secret. If anyone talks to us, or comes in with information, I ask if they've gone to the agencies," he said. "We don't want to serve as conduits because of fairness and legal questions. In the past, the 'right people' would call. Here everything is up front. The process is up front. Here are the standards and the regulatory principles. We've minimized the number of times people have come to us."

As partial proof that his system worked, Miller recalled that he ended up being very popular with the agency heads. The "regulators were sorry to see me leave OMB," he remarked. "Many of them called when they heard I was going to the FTC."

Enter Mr. Hyde. The purity of the process all seems perfectly aboveboard until the role of OMB emerges. Although OMB was technically responsible for regulatory reform under Carter, the agency then was too ridden with internal strife to play any significant role. Its difficulties smoothed over, OMB today has assumed the role previously carved out by RARG and the President's economic advisers, intervening at all points in the regulatory process to ensure that the President's mandate is implemented. Its real goal, according to advocates of the process, is to eliminate the adversarial conflicts between business and government that have severely inhibited regulatory progress in the past. OMB can only do this by negotiating quietly, particularly at the beginning, as Boyden Gray explained, "before the train has left the station, when the polarizing begins — before the regs go to the *Federal Register.*"

The problem with OMB's efforts is that the benefits of public discussion, even when it turns into controversy, are neglected in the course of conducting business in secret. In order to avoid the inevitable controversies that surface following a proposed rule's publication, in the *Federal Register,* the agency insists it must operate in private, and with a great deal of discretionary power. The architects of this process argue that if all meetings were open at every stage, the logistical difficulties would be insurmountable, not to mention the political problems. "I would have to summarize this conversation with you," explained Tozzi during an interview in his office, to show the impossibility of an agency as small as OMB logging all meetings and conversations.

Dismantling America

"There's no reason why OMB's contacts should be on the record; desk officers don't meet with outside parties," continued Boyden Gray, who elaborated his analysis by analogizing OMB as an arm of the President. "It's not a theoretical matter. The public has no more right to know what a member of the President's staff says to an agency than a congressman who communicates privately with his staff. The Congress will never do it. Why should we?

"Also, it's a practical matter," he added. "You couldn't talk if you had to summarize everything. Why should the President be different?" And with echoes of the "happy family" theory, he said: "Besides, we're all one government."

OMB officials are quick to point out that the executive order was not meant to stop regulations but merely to flag potentially inflationary regulations in much the same way RARG and CEA identified trouble spots. But unlike RARG, which ultimately reviewed less than half a dozen regulations each year, OMB chose to operate on a much grander scale, identifying almost two thousand regulations for review within the first six months after the issuance of the executive order.

Although OMB cannot substantively alter or revise regulations, according to the executive order, the agency can delay regulations, send them back to the agency for reconsideration, or extend the time for review, all of which could potentially alter regulations. "We never use the word 'disapprove,' " explained an OMB examiner, but rather " 'return to the agency for reconsideration.' They don't have to change anything if they don't want to."

In 90 percent of the cases, the regulations are not questioned — or changed — in any substantive way. "That was the biggest surprise to me," said Miller, who estimated that "90 percent of the regs are rubber-stamped by us." Only a few, he added, were "troublesome," and only a few slipped past the scrutiny of OMB examiners.

One whose escape Miller regretted involved the "resuscitation of sea turtles. If a fisherman netted a sea turtle, he'd have to resuscitate it before he threw it back into the water. That's silly." Silly to Miller perhaps, and to several officials at OMB who also used this as an example of the ludicrous side to regulation. After all, how could this regulation possibly be enforced, since it affected only a few fishermen out in the middle of the ocean? But what about the semicomatose sea turtles who find themselves accidentally entangled with a shrimp trawler's daily catch?[16] Perhaps to them, and to those who care about protecting endangered species, it might be worth a try.

In the final analysis, the executive order imposed so many additional requirements on the agencies that it was bound to accomplish its original objective: deterring the writing and development of future regulations.

The Congressional Reaction

Even if 90 percent of the regulations passed OMB scrutiny unaltered, critics were still worried about the other 10 percent: troublesome regulations that were delayed by OMB, some never to see the light of day, unless a lawsuit or a newspaper story uncovered their existence. At this point, proving the disparities between what OMB said and what OMB did became easier, particularly to those attempting to follow up the progress of specific regulations. Fortunately, Congress does not for the most part operate in secret; its hearings and bill-drafting sessions are now conducted in public, a result of extending the principles of the sunshine laws to the legislature. It was through congressional oversight of this kind that OMB's regulatory activities were finally subjected to public scrutiny.

OMB maintained its right to secrecy before a congressional committee, the Subcommittee on Oversight and Investigations of the House Committee on Energy and Commerce, chaired by Rep. John Dingell, Democrat of Michigan. To obtain the most basic kinds of information, the committee was forced to subpoena OMB, going back repeatedly to the agency for basic data. OMB spokesmen claimed the agency did not keep logs of telephone calls or meetings, and that all business was conducted without much record keeping of any sort. The sketchy record finally compiled by the agency at the committee's request confirmed its suspicion that the mere fact that OMB was engaged in questioning a regulation struck

sufficient terror in the hearts of the agencies to bury that regulation
for good. "The record shows that from June to September 1981,
seven regulations were returned to the agencies. Six were never
resubmitted," said Patrick McLain, the committee staff member in
charge of regulation. "What we want to know is how many regulations are never submitted at all?"

Regulations referred to by McLain included two Federal Aviation Administration (FAA) regulations, both affecting air safety and
both involving minimal cost. The first dealt with the prohibition of
hang gliders from airspace around airports, the second with blood
alcohol rules for pilots. Since neither of these regulations imposed
significant costs on industry, it was difficult to determine why OMB
delayed them. OMB and White House sources refused to comment
on specific regulations when questioned; they would comment only
on the program as a whole.

OMB strategists had decided that it was against their interest
to cooperate immediately with the Dingell committee, and stalled
until they could establish some degree of discipline over the regulatory process. After several months, OMB finally produced a list
of meetings, responding only after the committee issued a subpoena
requesting such a list as well as information about what transpired
at those meetings. The list reads "like a list of the Fortune 500,"
remarked McLain, who also expressed his dismay at the vague gen-
eralities listed under the subject category. At a meeting listed on
January 29, 1981, for example, the Air Transport Association met
with OMB officials to discuss "progress and problems under airline
deregulation."[17] At another meeting, on February 18, 1981, the
American Mining Congress met with OMB officials to discuss
"support for regulatory relief"; the Chemical Manufacturers Association (CMA) met five days later to discuss the very same topic,
as did the National Association of Manufacturers, the Chamber of
Commerce, General Motors, the Eli Lilly Drug Company, the Sun
Oil Company, and a succession of others. Out of forty-one groups
visiting OMB to discuss regulatory relief, only two vaguely identified groups did not represent the business community: "Ralph Nader's organization" and a group of "Hispanic representatives"
meeting to discuss the President's "economic recovery program."[18]

64

Although OMB officials denied any cause and effect relationship between the visits and subsequent regulatory relief, the Dingell committee rejected OMB's descriptions of the meetings, calling them inadequate, too vague to be meaningful, and designed to conceal the real influence OMB wields over the Vice President's "hit list" of regulations. "What is really significant," said McLain, reflecting the position of several members of the committee, is "what it means to be on that list. What happens to the regs while they're on the list? Are they enforced while OMB is delaying them? Presupposing, of course, that they eventually get out of the agencies.

"Many of the regulations simply get withdrawn by the agencies," added McLain, answering his own question, "and that's really more significant, because neither the Congress nor the public has any idea what those regulations are that never see the light of day."

At an oversight hearing that June (1981), members of the Dingell committee tried to extract more information about OMB's activities. It soon became apparent, judging by the acerbic line of questioning, that the conflict represented a contest of power between the President and Congress, with allegiance to different political parties only an incidental factor. On what legal authority did witnesses James Miller and Boyden Gray base their effort to "hotwire the regulatory proceedings at the agencies?" queried Rep. Albert Gore, Democrat of Tennessee.[19] Gore was followed by Rep. Mike Synar, Democrat of Oklahoma, who accused Miller and Gray of "stepping on some very serious constitutional questions" when they controlled "all these guys who are your 'hired guns' . . . circumventing the whole process of administering the law . . . and the prohibitions against *ex parte* communications."

Synar was especially concerned about the question of public access to the regulatory process, guaranteed by the Administrative Procedure Act, but under the new system dependent only on OMB's good will. "Do all people have the right to call you," he asked Boyden Gray, "or just a select group of people?" Can "my mom and dad who are upset about something call directly to you?" he asked. Miller and Gray both said "absolutely," although Gray added that he hoped Synar's mom and dad would go to the agencies first with their complaints. After later hearing Rep. Gore read the subpoenaed list of businesses, Synar concluded to the general amusement of those attending the hearing that "it does not look as if my mom and dad are getting in there."[20]

Miller denied categorically any correlation between OMB's meetings with corporate representatives and the withdrawal of specific regulations:

MR. GORE: "You had a 20 minute meeting with the Chemical Manufacturers Association talking about regulatory relief a month before you asked to pull back the regulations on hazardous waste disposal, and you are telling me under oath that you did not even mention hazardous waste with the CMA?"

MR. MILLER: "I am telling you, to the best of my recollection, that topic did not come up."

MR. GORE: "What about February 18, 1981? You met with the American Mining Congress and discussed 'support for regulatory relief.' Isn't it more likely that you discussed their support for the postponement of the Interior Department's rule on extraction of coals, which has now been postponed indefinitely?"

MR. MILLER: "I cannot recall that particular meeting."[21]

Gore also asked whether Miller discussed pending air carrier certification, operating, and flight rules in a meeting with the Air Transport Association. Under oath, Miller denied discussing these issues, tempering his answers by reference to the limits of his own recollections.

Eventually, Gore charged that OMB's secret meetings circumvented established procedure, giving organized interest groups the opportunity to "bias the outcome" and persuade OMB leaders to "direct the results of regulatory proceedings under way."

Discontent was also growing in the Senate, even from those who supported an increase in presidential control over the regulatory process. Senator Carl Levin, Democrat of Michigan, after counting at least fifty-five regulations that failed to meet OMB's approval, called the process an "extraordinary but almost hidden centralization of power" that has "overturned some 35 years of practice under the Administrative Procedure Act." OMB's newly acquired power as superregulator, warned Levin, was "unchecked and unaccountable," subverting "Congress' appropriate oversight

66

role,'' as well as the public's "basic right to petition government effectively."[22]

The tug of war between Congress and the President ultimately reached a draw. In the meantime, OMB moved quietly ahead, unafraid of what amounted to empty challenges that the superagency was privately displacing the authority, discretion, and expertise of the agencies. "It's some GS–12 budget examiner imposing his or her judgment on whether these rules were good or not," noted one critic, in an ironic reversal of previous accusations that midlevel bureaucrats were making high level policy through the regulatory process. Only now those GS–12s come from OMB and act as representatives of the President.

"OMB needs to be the President's agent," countered Murray Weidenbaum, defending the agency. "It is the only agency with a broad array of concerns. If the U.S. Department of Agriculture could look at a farm bill from the point of view of the consumer, then I wouldn't have to get involved." But OMB also looks at the world through its own narrow perspective — fiscal policy. It is the government's fiscal watchdog, perforce not overly concerned with social needs such as public health and safety.

As yet, the question of OMB's legitimacy as a regulatory watchdog remains unresolved, although the legal and legislative foundations of the executive order have been reinforced through two laws preceding the order: the Regulatory Flexibility Act and the Paperwork Reduction Act.[23] The Paperwork Act gave OMB the power to pare down paperwork requirements, as well as other information-gathering burdens imposed by regulations; the Regulatory Flexibility Act, which mandated regulatory analysis in certain categories of rule making, supported OMB's efforts to impose cost-benefit analysis on the executive agencies.

To Reagan strategists, further affirmation for regulatory reform was indicated by a recent court of appeals decision, *Sierra Club v. Costle*.[24] This decision upheld the legality of "intra-executive contacts" between the President's staff and the agencies after the comment period had officially closed. Recognizing the need for the "President and his White House staff to monitor the consistency of executive agency regulations with administration policy," Judge Patricia Wald ruled that the government could not "function effectively or rationally if key executive policy makers were isolated from each other and from the Chief Executive.''[25]

The *Sierra* case gave the Reagan "reform" effort a new lease on life, as well as increased legitimacy. Immediately following the decision, OMB director David Stockman distributed a memo declaring that OMB's procedures will be consistent with the "holding and policies" discussed in the *Sierra* case. In actuality, however, some legal scholars argue that OMB has gone beyond the legal limits of the *Sierra* decision, especially since the decision never "endorsed the principle of *secret* White House contacts with private parties or with agency officials.''[26] During these secret meetings, OMB assumes the role of a "conduit contact," or a critical access point for outside pressure groups to influence the outcome of a rule-making proceeding, without the safeguard of a public record. The *Sierra* decision appears to indicate the reverse: "If oral communications are to be freely permitted after the close of the comment period, then at least some summary of them must be made in order to preserve the integrity of the rulemaking docket.''[27] The court, in its landmark decision, did not bar oral communications between the White House and the agency, but it did rule that relevant communications be recorded so as not to violate the provisions of the agency's enabling legislation, which in the *Sierra* case specifically stated that any information affecting the final rule be placed "on the docket."

In a report commissioned for the Dingell committee by the Congressional Research Service (CRS), legal expert Morton Rosenberg concluded that OMB had exceeded the *Sierra* decision, as well as its own constitutional mandate. Rosenberg argued that the executive order deprived "participants of essential elements of fair treatment required by due process. In particular, in view of the fact that the President's closest managerial agent is the operational head of this sensitive access point, there may be said to be an invitation to the President and White House aides to make their views known in an effective manner. Similarly, nongovernmental interests may attempt to utilize the White House or OMB as a conduit for their views and thereby covertly influence the agency.''[28]

Rosenberg's study specifically focused on the ways in which the executive order violated the Administrative Procedure Act by subordinating agency expertise to the judgment of the OMB director. Rosenberg went on to point out that the executive order also imposed uniform rule making at the expense of the flexibility guaranteed by the act. "Nothing has occurred legislatively to the APA since 1946 [when it was passed] which would support such presidential action," the report noted. On the contrary, laws enacted since the passage of the act have enhanced its safeguards, particularly those ensuring due process protection against secrecy. Amendments to the act, for example, have "reinforced the original scheme," and statutes like the Freedom of Information Act of 1966 (and its amendments) have expanded the public's right to information by imposing an obligation on executive agencies to grant access to agency records unless specifically exempted. Further guarantees against secret decision making were granted by the Sunshine Act of 1976, which required all multiheaded agencies, such as the Federal Communications Commission, to hold open meetings, and specifically prohibited *ex parte* contacts in formal rule making. All of these changes, said the report, were "consonant with the public participation and public disclosure themes evident in the original act" and "in no way support the substantive overhaul effected by Executive Order 12291."[29]

Members of the Reagan task force derided the CRS study. Presented with the results, along with the legal reasoning supporting the report, Miller responded: "Would you rather be defended by the Justice Department or the CRS?" He was referring to the Justice Department's defense of the executive order, which was based primarily on the *Sierra* decision and the *Myers* case, both of which supported the notion of executive hegemony in regulatory matters.[30]

OMB officials brushed off congressional oversight efforts as mere partisan harassment from a Democratic-controlled committee, noting it was time the White House made a permanent dent in the power of the congressional "barons" over the regulatory agencies. This was no mean feat, considering Congress's past power over the agencies, a relationship so strong it was termed the "iron triangle," a triad of interest groups, congressional committees, and the agencies, all revolving around their special issues — and all attempting to circumvent the White House. With OMB in control, these long-established patterns have receded, making it much more difficult for agency staff to flee to their congressional patrons for sympathy and support.

Within a five-month period, the President's executive order spelled out its own success in the context of its stated objective: to reduce the burden of federal regulation. A dramatic decrease occurred in the number of proposed and final regulations issued, with confirmation offered by the 33 percent reduction in the size of the *Federal Register;* there was a 50 percent reduction in the volume of proposed rule making compared with 1980 totals for the same period. At a press conference held on June 13, 1981, to announce the Reagan administration's achievements, Vice President Bush also reported that 180 regulations had been withdrawn, modified, or delayed, at an annual savings of $6 billion a year. Businesses, he added, would save $18 billion by not having to invest in equipment that would have been required as a result of those regulations. The regulatory "relief" negotiated in the White House without OMB intervention marked further presidential inroads into the regulatory process and indicated the direction of future reform. A year later OMB proudly issued a report documenting its achievements made under the provisions of the executive order. "None of the major rule makings issued in 1982 imposes substantial new regulatory burdens," concluded the report.[31] Benefits and protections lost in the process were not mentioned.

In the final analysis, Reagan was able to finish what Carter had originally planned: the legitimization of OMB as a regulatory manager. Anchored with the full weight of the President's clout, OMB could exert a degree of control over the agencies never achieved by previous Presidents.[32] In return, the agency deflected most of the inevitable controversy away from Reagan and onto a more diffuse target — a stroke of political acumen that made the regulatory reform program as effective as it was in terms of its own goals.

The new OMB also added another layer of bureaucracy to the already complex regulatory process — an ironic development in view of all the past criticism leveled at regulation for its delays and inordinate red tape. As OMB plunged deeper into the management of regulation, it added its own reams of red tape, this time delaying regulations indefinitely on the basis of cost criteria, in place of health and safety requirements.

In reality, OMB's capture of the regulatory process represented a victory for the President over the agencies. In the past, Presidents wielded substantial power over both executive branch and independent agencies. But this power was exercised through persuasion, budget, and appointments. Now there is a new twist: the White House, according itself new legitimacy through OMB, can control, discourage, or overturn agency actions that had previously served as a check on presidential power.

The question is not whether the President — or Congress, or the courts, for that matter — should control the regulatory process. No branch should have total authority; that is why we have a system of checks and balances. The question is whether any branch, or any elected or appointed official, should wield the power to weaken regulations that protect the public. In view of the demands of a complex, industrial society that now has the ability to destroy itself, the question is whether those regulations should be weakened by anyone. What this means is not that every regulation is final, or that costs should not be considered, but that society needs increasing protection from the ravages of those who can undermine its essential structure. So far, the experience of presidential "management" has led to decreased protection from the harmful effects of advancing technologies.

3

Dismantling America
The Policy Implications of Social Deregulation

I have seen moonscapes on mine sites. . . . There are no inspectors out in the field now. . . . This is now a captive agency, totally captive of the mining interests.
— An official of the Office of Surface Mining, Department of the Interior

Fewer regulators will necessarily result in fewer regulations and less harassment of the regulated.
— President Ronald Reagan

REAGAN SOON CONFRONTED his own cotton dust case, enabling him to demonstrate that this President would not capitulate, as Carter did, in the face of legal and political challenges. His personal clout, reinforced by cooperative regulators, proved an unbeatable combination when it came to achieving presidential hegemony over the regulatory process. The Office of Management and Budget (OMB) again proved a willing vehicle, showing the unlimited extent to which it could determine the final character of regulation with only the authority to "advise." Its secret, to exert power while maintaining a low profile, recalled carrots and big sticks. "OMB pretends it isn't there," said an official who works in the regulatory office. "We can recommend but we can't do anything. Technically, OMB has no authority, but uses bribery and blackmail instead. The executive order says we can consult, but the agency can't do anything while we consult. We can drop it into a black hole while the politicians decide what to do with it. It is just window-dressing to a power grab. We're not doing heavy analysis. The economic analysis is just window-dressing for the executive order."

Vanished into the dark recesses of OMB was a carefully wrought, fully documented, painstakingly deliberated set of regulations intended to prevent private industry from dumping toxic chemicals into municipal sewage treatment plants lacking the capability to handle them. Affecting sixty thousand industrial facilities, the "pretreatment" regulations, as they were known, sought to avoid the "pass through" effect: a process by which these chemicals worked their way through a sewage plant and passed without adequate treatment into rivers, lakes, and streams, where they posed the threat of impairing the quality of drinking water, or possibly entering the food chain.

"EPA's regs tend to be weak," explained Murray Weidenbaum, justifying OMB's role in monitoring environmental regulations. "They broadly define the mildest hazards along with the most serious."

In this case, the hazards involved chemicals targeted by the pretreatment regulations, including cadmium, which can cause kidney damage and chronic respiratory problems; lead, which damages the nervous system and is especially toxic to children; and mercury, which has been linked to brain damage and loss of hearing and vision.[1] In light of the potential dangers of these chemicals, it is hard to justify delaying their treatment.

Many of these toxic pollutants are collected into waste sludge and thus become even more difficult and expensive to dispose of — not to mention the dangers presented by keeping the sludge around, for the toxic chemicals in the sludge can contaminate the food crops, leach into the ground water and impair the drinking supply, or eventually evaporate into the air and contribute to air pollution. In some cases, the pollutants are sufficiently caustic to disrupt the functioning of the treatment plant itself. This occurred in Louisville, Kentucky, where the entire sewer system was shut down because of a discharge from a chemical known as HCP. In extreme instances, such chemicals have been known to corrode pipes, ignite, and cause explosions.

Despite all appearances to the contrary, EPA had not run amuck, but rather had developed the pretreatment regulations under a directive from Congress: the Clean Water Act of 1972. The act ordered EPA to develop regulations requiring industries dumping wastes in municipal plants to meet nationally established standards. In fact, EPA stalled as long as possible, to the dismay of congressional leaders, who planned what turned out to be an altogether too optimistic timetable: nine months for the EPA administrator to enact the standards; three years for industry to comply with them; and clean waterways for the nation by 1983.

When Congress reconsidered the Clean Water Act in 1977, the Senate expressed its disappointment at EPA's reluctance to begin developing the regulations, with senators leveling the blame at the EPA administrator. "This failure on the part of the administrator has resulted in the construction by communities of waste treatment facilities which have no capability to handle industrial wastes. . . . It is essential that the administrator establish pretreatment regulations for these kinds of pollutants."[2] The House also called the EPA's failure to promulgate pretreatment regulations "disappointing," and urged the agency to "make every effort" to move forward at "the earliest time" and give "major emphasis to this problem."[3]

Spurred by congressional discontent, as well as by an earlier lawsuit filed by the Natural Resources Defense Council (NRDC), the EPA initiated a full-fledged rule making.[4] Encouraging as much public participation as possible, EPA held four public hearings and sixteen public meetings in the development of the pretreatment rules. The agency received over four hundred comments from the public, which were filed in the record and incorporated in its final decision. After nearly four years, EPA issued final regulations in January 1981.

Suddenly, and without notifying anyone, EPA mysteriously

suspended the 1981 amendments to the regulations on April 5, 1981, three days after they became effective. The public, which included many of the groups involved in the development of the regulations, was never alerted that EPA was considering a suspension of the regulations, and some people wondered on what grounds EPA had acted. After all, EPA had published an analysis of the economic impact of the pretreatment regulations in accordance with President Carter's executive order, concluding that the pretreatment regulations lacked major economic consequences. Even without the prodding of the order, EPA had been doing economic analysis for a long time as a routine part of its regulatory activities.

The reasons emerged in the pages of the NRDC's 1981 lawsuit challenging the suspension of the regulations.[5] The data obtained during the course of the lawsuit illuminated the "black hole" at OMB, where regulations disappeared never to be seen again. The investigation also revealed the political pressures on the administration, and the ease with which OMB ushered regulations into oblivion. Immediately after the regulations were amended in January 1981, the suit charged, a number of industries and municipalities began a concerted campaign for their repeal. A total of twelve letters from industries and municipal sewage agencies urged the suspension of the regulations; only half of these communications were identified in the EPA record. Unclear themselves about who really wielded the power to suspend regulations, the industries' representatives contacted OMB, EPA, and the Vice President in their efforts to influence the process. Five of these letters alone came from the Chemical Manufacturers Association, several of them going to the acting administrator of EPA, to Boyden Gray, and to James Tozzi. Other letters came from the Association of Metropolitan Sewerage Agencies, the American Paper Institute/National Forests Products Association, the Ford Motor Company, and the Chicago Association of Commerce and Industry.[6] Several letters urged EPA to suspend the regulations; others urged OMB and the task force to intervene and order EPA to withdraw the regulations. Nine of the letters were sent in the critical two-week period before the suspension of the regulations. "This matter is so important to the chemical industry and the regulatory reform program in general that we would like an opportunity to discuss with you the general pretreatment regulations and their impact before any Task Force decision is made,'' said the Chemical Manufacturers Association in a letter to Boyden Gray. ''We strongly recommend that the Task Force on Regulatory Relief categorically reject EPA's recommendation.''[7]

The campaign was successful. EPA suspended the 1981 regulations ''until further notice,'' later notifying the court that its analysis would not be completed until April 1982, one year and three months from the time it had stopped the regulations. Just what the agency and its own masters were looking for in this extended analysis was unclear, but no such fuzziness stood in the way of their subsequent assurances to the business community. EPA advised one segment of the electroplating industry, for example, that it could now postpone efforts to comply with pretreatment standards limiting the industry's discharge of eight toxic pollutants — cyanide, lead, cadmium, copper, nickel, chromium, zinc, and silver — assuring the involved companies that they could relax until further notice. The agency also told the remaining electroplaters that they could take an additional nine months to meet the standards, and suspended regulations requiring local municipalities to develop a pretreatment program and obtain federal approval before receiving federal grants to construct sewerage plants.

The impact of EPA's capitulation to the executive order affects thousands of industries and sewerage treatment plants. After years of public consultation and review, the agency, under direction from OMB, proceeded to unravel a policy of national importance without consultation with anyone but the business community. James Miller and James Tozzi had both argued that the doors of OMB stood open, welcoming any group wishing to consult with them, and that meetings under this system also would be open. In the light of subsequent events, however, their guarantees reveal some glaring discrepancies. ''The open door is meaningless unless you know a decision is being made,'' said Frances Dubrowski, a senior attorney with NRDC. OMB has no mechanism for telling the public that meetings are being held; their meetings are not announced in the *Federal Register;* and OMB keeps no formal records of such meetings. Most important, OMB and the agency follow an unwritten policy of working primarily with industry groups, to the dismay of others interested in having an impact on environmental policy. In the final analysis, EPA must operate under orders, from both OMB and the White House, and without looking too closely at traditional procedures.

Judging from OMB's past behavior, any industry group finding the back door to OMB open can expect regulatory relief from decisions that have been developed over the course of many years. In accordance with EPA's rule-making process, industry had four years to present its case to EPA and to file its comments on the public record; yet it made its final appeal after the official comment period had closed. The extraordinary circumstances in which the law would allow EPA to suspend regulations were not present in the case of the pretreatment rules; nor did EPA ever feel the need to offer any such excuses to justify its actions. EPA referred only to the executive order, leading to the assumption that the regulations were just too controversial, which would still be insufficient justification under the Clean Water Act for suspending a regulation. Even so, EPA would probably be too embarrassed to offer economic impact as the excuse for delaying the pretreatment rules, since according to its own calculations the regulations lacked major economic consequences. Its findings were based on actual operating experiences of pretreatment programs already in existence on the state level.

Ultimately, if it takes a lawsuit to produce even the sketchiest information about buried regulations, does this not jeopardize the entire body of law governing the regulatory process? The implications of this case grow beyond the boundaries of environmental regulation as these questions continue to surface. If the EPA and OMB actions were to become standard practice, the public could expect small, private rule makings to occur every time a controversial regulation came up for White House review, revising one of the most basic principles of the regulatory process: openly conducted rule making. The framers of the Administrative Procedure Act recognized that agencies cannot listen only to those in sympathy with the administration, and by their actions ignore others with an opposing point of view. Open rule making becomes a crucial component, not only for basic fairness, but also in terms of ensuring an "informed" decision-making process; an open record reveals whether the decision was based on information gathered from a variety of reliable sources, or whether it was limited to data supporting a narrower focus.[8]

In the case of the pretreatment regulations, there was a happy ending. The court ordered EPA to reinstate all of the amendments to the regulations that had been indefinitely postponed, and sharply criticized the agency, and, by implication, its OMB mentor. The court concluded that EPA had "without notice and the opportunity for comment, abrogated rules which had been proposed, which had undergone years of notice and comment procedures, and which had been promulgated, with an effective date, in final form."[9]

By postponing the rules indefinitely, EPA had reversed its own course of action, without adequate explanation. "That reversal itself," the decision continued, "constitutes a danger signal."[10] The only reason offered by the agency for the postponement of the amendments, Executive Order 12291, did "not constitute good cause for EPA's failure to comply with the APA [Administrative Procedure Act]," ruled the court.[11] What most concerned the court was the agency's attempt to circumvent the procedural requirements of the act through its own procedural sleight of hand. "We cannot countenance such a result," said the court.[12] Although the court here only intervened on questions of process, this proved not to be as narrow a focus as it may seem, given the close link between procedures and the substance of regulations.

In general, however, litigation as a method of recourse, or as a means of uncovering more data, is an expensive and sporadic remedy, and depends on financially hard-pressed groups, like the NRDC, willing to expend time and resources to follow up regulatory issues on behalf of their constituents.

Deregulating for Whom?

Evidence continues to emerge that indicates a pattern of White House intervention in other agencies as well as in EPA. The policy directions were clear, reversed only under public pressure of the most intense kind. Under the banner of "reforming" the process, a version of the "imperial presidency" has reappeared, which has been highly successful in achieving policy objectives through the regulatory route. The results are also becoming clear in the aggregate, as set after set of gutted regulations produce a picture of the losers — children, minorities, the poor, the aged, teen-agers, workers, miners, women, consumers, and those who breathe the air and drink tap water.

Women's groups, for example, voiced their dismay at the suspension of regulations ensuring that government contracts would not be awarded to companies that discriminate. Like the pretreatment regulations, these regulations took years to develop before they were finally published by the Department of Labor's Office of Federal Contract Compliance Programs (OFCCP) in December 1980. Based on consultations with industry representatives as well as civil rights groups, the regulations were generally regarded as strong, with most loopholes closed. Then, suddenly, the day before the regulations were to go into effect, the effective date was postponed indefinitely, without any notice or comment accompanying the surprise move. A sense of mystery enveloped the postponement, this time focusing on accountability.

"Who is the policy maker?" asked Donna Lenhoff of the Women's Legal Defense Fund, a group involved with this issue from its inception. "Who is making the decision? OMB? The Department of Labor? This administration has a complete disregard for and lack of public input. They've left the perception that affirmative action is dead, and bring into question the manner in which regulatory relief is being taken."

The "black hole" has also swallowed up other rules and occasionally entire agencies, who regulate to the letter of the executive order even when they are not certain a specific regulation is involved. As part of its deliberations over the permissible levels of lead in infant formula and other baby foods, the Bureau of Foods at the Food and Drug Administration (FDA) has embarked on a lengthy cost-benefit analysis to determine the economic impact on baby food manufacturers before it recommends "action levels" — the point at which the FDA can act to seize a product — to the FDA commissioner. Studies have shown lead to be an extremely potent toxin that affects neurological functioning. The FDA had not set lead levels for baby foods, or revised its lead levels for evaporated milk for over ten years. By October 1981, the FDA staff had already worked for six months on the economic impact study with still more work to do. Meanwhile, what happens to all of those children who risk exposure to toxic substances? "If such delay can occur for an action with respect to which the executive order may not even apply," explained two members of the Alliance for Justice, a national association of public interest law firms, "it is not difficult to see how much delay can occur where OMB directly insists on rigorous and detailed analysis."[13]

Untold numbers of infants also had to wait, this time for eighteen months, while the FDA — under White House pressure — dragged its feet over issuing regulations on nutrient deficiencies in infant formula. The statute involved, the Infant Formula Act, was passed in 1980, following the discovery that some manufacturers were producing formula lacking essential ingredients for growth and development. The absence of vitamin B_6, for example — discovered in a formula that was later recalled — can lead to convulsions and, in some cases, to brain damage. Although legally the rules could have been issued within the year, nothing happened until 1982, when the agency finally issued rules requiring companies to run frequent tests on the nutritional quality of their products. FDA commissioner Arthur Hull Hayes, testifying on Capitol Hill, explained that President Reagan's requirements for cost-benefit analysis were the major reason behind the delay.[14]

According to a staff report prepared for the Oversight Subcommittee of the House Energy and Commerce Committee, the new rules "adopted virtually in every respect the suggestions of the infant formula industry to relax the proposed rules and add 'flexibility.' " "The regulations disappeared into a black hole of Reaganomics," said Rep. Albert Gore, Jr., Democrat of Tennessee, who wrote the legislation. "They absolutely refused to enforce the law." But Jim Greene, an FDA spokesman, argued, "It's not as detailed as some people want it, but we think it meets all the requirements needed to protect the consumer." According to Mr. Gore, an additional three million cans of formula were marketed without vitamin B_6, during the eighteen months' delay.

The aged as well as infants are also affected by the Reagan effort to unravel the fabric of social regulations. Under another deregulatory initiative, the Reagan reformers have suggested the elimination of many of the regulations governing nursing homes, such as rules on hiring attendants with no communicable diseases, fire safety, and maintaining a safe, clean environment. Eliminating such rules would undoubtedly cut costs for the nursing home industry, but what risks would "reforms" of such dubious merit bring to the 1.3 million senior citizens now living in these establishments? Under a storm of protest from highly respected national organizations, including the American Public Health Association, the Reagan administration announced, on March 20, 1982, that it would back off from its efforts to unravel the rules governing eighteen thousand of the nation's nursing homes. "I will not turn back the clock," said Health and Human Services Secretary Richard S. Schweiker, in an apparent about-face.[15]

Teen-agers also would do well to keep an eye on the Reagan deregulators, and then look for someone else to protect their interests. Toward the end of Reagan's first year in office, the Department of Labor announced it was considering the revision of rules affecting child labor. Although agency spokespeople did not specify the direction these revisions would take, those who watched Reagan's performance in every other area of social deregulation did not ponder long before predicting a trend toward relaxation.

Without a Political Action Committee (PAC) to protect their interests, mothers and young children (up to age five) too poor to receive adequate nutrition will also suffer from the effects of regulatory "reform." Following a plot line right out of a Dickens novel, this time the administration decided to undo rules governing a special $900 million a year food program for women, infants, and children, known as WIC. Written in response to pressure from cereal manufacturers, the new rules would allow the use of sugared cereals in the program; other changes permitted the inclusion of flavored milk. Nutritionists argued that the proposals would add unnecessary sugar to the diets of the poor and would reduce the cost effectiveness of the program by adding to its total cost.[16] These rules were delayed, presumably because of the upcoming 1982 elections.

While they may offer industry temporary relief, Reagan's deregulatory policies have left the administration wide open to charges of bias, specifically, that regulatory relief is directed solely to the business community, with the public left to make the necessary sacrifices while the economy straightens itself out. The approach, to jettison as much social regulation as possible, is unselective, paralleling the administration's early budget initiatives — to cut as much out of social programs as possible before tackling other budget items. On both levels there are victims; on both levels there are groups making sacrifices disproportionate to the rest of society.

Unlike social programs, however, regulatory reform potentially affects a much wider public: everyone drinks the same water, breathes the same air, and relies on government to maintain the high standards Americans have come to expect in terms of their health and safety. As deregulation becomes equated with the dismantling of these protections, public confidence in government will erode, with critics fearful that the new laissez faire will leave the country increasingly susceptible to major hazards like the tragedy in Love Canal, New York, that will take years to correct. And years to bankroll. In 1983, the EPA administrator announced that the government would buy the houses on dioxin-contaminated soil in the town of Times Beach, Missouri. No one can even estimate how many more towns, houses, or farms are affected by the 255 to 275 metric tons of hazardous waste accumulated in the United States each year.

Meanwhile, the future of regulation lies in the hands of OMB, whose domination of the regulatory process as the President's agent completed Jimmy Carter's original plan for achieving presidential hegemony over the regulatory process. Since OMB keeps limited records, it is impossible to determine the magnitude of its activities, or the real extent of presidential intervention. No one knows what additional regulations are yet to be suspended, or what regulations never saw the light of day, held back by agencies fearful of OMB intervention.

Working with agency heads on regulatory matters from its new position has given OMB such an inordinate amount of political clout that the delicate balance developed over the years has tilted heavily over to the presidential side. To some extent, that balance was guaranteed by procedures spelled out by the Administrative Procedure Act, which made provision for some degree of input from outside groups as well as from technical experts. Moreover, that balance protected the public's interests by insulating the agencies against the most blatant kind of political interference, in the hope that this would help them arrive at fair and equitable policies. Under this new presidential system, the Administrative Procedure Act seems to have fallen into disuse without being officially repealed.

The new system also has upset the balance between Congress and the executive branch, effectively eliminating another form of public protection. Congress has long relied on the agencies to implement the laws according to the intent of those laws and within the timetables often specified by statute. The time limits included in the Clean Water Act were exceeded, for example, by the suspension of the pretreatment amendments. Confronted with this capture of the administrative process, Congress came up empty-handed, angry, bereft of ideas and remedies. Members of Congress regularly hold oversight hearings that produce reams of publicity embarrassing to the President, to OMB, and to the agency heads; but after the dust settles, Congress has little to show for its efforts. The decade of the 1980s, of budget crunches and program cutbacks, has robbed Congress of its only potent oversight tool: the budget. The new agency appointees no longer quake at the threat of a budget cut. To them, less money means less regulation — as well as diminished responsibility for the consequences.

Now in the firm grip of OMB and the President, the agencies have entered a new period of captivity, one quite different from the past, when regulatory agencies labeled "captive" were presumed to have capitulated to the industries they were supposed to regulate, instead of serving the public and its broader interests. The Interstate Commerce Commission, for example, was widely regarded, first, as a captive of the railroad industry, then of the trucking industry; the Federal Communications Commission was a captive of the newspapers and the networks. The newer social agencies were never subjected seriously to this accusation; they regulated a range of industries and not one particular industry, which left them without much opportunity to develop the cozy relationships typical of their predecessors. When industries objected, for example, to environmental regulation, they lobbied as single companies or under the umbrella of their trade associations. From these vantage points, it was far more difficult to develop the long-term, "captive" relationships that were possible with single-focus agencies. President Reagan solved this problem by becoming the representative of the business community and capturing the errant agencies under the much more efficient jurisdiction of the presidency.

The Agency Heads and Regulatory "Relief"

In informal speeches to the staff at OMB, Vice President Bush reiterated a theme common to the Reagan "reform" effort, namely, that Reagan's appointees were far more crucial to the success of their program than either OMB or the executive order. While the public interest organizations had been a major talent bank for the Carter administration, which gave these consumer-oriented, anti-business activists considerable latitude in decision making, it was the antiregulatory, business-oriented groups that provided key personnel for the Reagan administration, which kept them on a shorter leash.

Ronald Reagan set out to be a tough, single-minded President who brooked no interference in pursuing his stated goal of maximum deregulation. His choice of top regulators followed a consistent pattern. While President Carter selected those who believed in regulation and looked for ways to expand the impact of regulations, President Reagan appointed critics of the regulatory process who had been fighting government regulations long before they arrived in Washington. The Reagan appointees echoed their boss's view that most regulation was burdensome, inflationary, and unneeded.

Carter had difficulty managing regulation, according to James C. Miller III, because he gave his ideologically committed administrators relative independence in making final decisions — a pattern corrected by Reagan, who turned this authority over to OMB. But how can OMB oversee the entire regulatory process, with its dozens of agencies and thousands of regulations, with a staff of several hundred? "I'd need ten thousand people at OMB if I had the Carter people," responded Miller. "There are always problems getting people off the reservation" — a bureaucratic expression for the White House's perennial problem of keeping political appointees from switching their loyalties from the President to the agencies and constituencies. "We have a team."

Miller's comments were corroborated by many of Carter's appointees, who recalled the President's policy as one allowing substantial independence, even in controversial cases. The policy sometimes backfired, particularly when an agency head was as reluctant as the President to make an unpopular decision, and both looked for ways to escape the political fallout. It was generally believed, for example, that EPA administrator Douglas Costle stalled the issuance of coal emission standards in the hope that President Carter would personally intervene and counteract the intense congressional pressure orchestrated by Robert C. Byrd, then Senate majority leader.

Under Reagan's leadership, appointees have the latitude only to deregulate, a task that many of them tackle with the enthusiasm of the true believer, as Miller indicated when he described the appointees as having "religion." "There are a lot of Watts out there whom Reagan has appointed," said an OMB official, referring to the controversial secretary of the interior, James Watt. "It is through them, and through the agencies, that regulatory reform is really being done. This is the biggest success of the program —what the agencies have done in terms of self-evaluation and restraint, directed by the high level people."

A stroke of Secretary Richard Schweiker's pen, for example, changed regulations issued by the Department of Health and Human Services (HHS) so radically that almost one out of five families receiving benefits was affected.[17] Some of the cuts involved barring states from making payments to pregnant women before their sixth month of pregnancy; forbidding the states from paying welfare to strikers; and tightening up considerably on eligibility requirements in general. Opposed by welfare groups, labor unions, and some state and local officials, the regulations would eliminate about 408,000 of the 3.9 million families covered by the Aid to Families with Dependent Children (AFDC) program. They would also save the federal government approximately $5 billion.

Regulatory intervention does not necessarily have to mean unraveling regulations; it can be proactive as well, and involve adding new regulations reflecting the ideology of the regulator or of his or her White House mentors. The best example of this was the "squeal rule," so named because of its requirement that parents be notified within ten days when their children received contraceptives from a clinic receiving federal funds. The rule was issued in February 1983 by HHS Secretary Richard Schweiker.[18]

Another regulatory stroke of the pen attempted to alter school-children's luncheon menus across the country, and gave the Democrats in Congress a field day. In keeping with the cost-cutting mood of Reagan's regulators, the U.S. Department of Agriculture, under the leadership of Secretary John R. Block, proposed regulations lowering the minimum nutritional requirements of school lunches by allowing the substitution of pickle relish and ketchup for a vegetable, decreasing the size of portions of meat, bread, fruit, and milk, and allowing substances like soybeans to be used as substitutes for meat. The forty-six Senate Democrats invited reporters to watch them eat what later became known as the Stockman lunch, which consisted of a meat and soybean patty, a slice of bread, a few french fries, and a partly filled glass of milk. In essence, the new regulations would have saved local school districts $300 million, but were eventually withdrawn for "further study." Even Republicans were embarrassed. Republican Senator John Heinz, whose family owns H. J. Heinz, a maker of ketchup, called ketchup a condiment and the proposed rule "one of the most ridiculous regulations I ever heard of."[19] In an attempt to separate himself from this policy and shift the blame to the agency head, Stockman blamed Block, stating that the department not only had "egg on its face, but ketchup, too," and announced that he was withdrawing the proposed regulations. Angered by Stockman's comments that the regulations were a result of a "bureaucratic goof," Block went straight to the President, then announced that *he* and the President — not Stockman — had made the decision to reconsider the guidelines.

Another administrator, Raymond Peck, Jr., head of the National Highway Traffic Safety Administration (NHTSA), overruled the senior staff at his agency and ended the twelve-year effort to require either air bags or automatically closing seat belts in automobiles. Peck claimed total responsibility for the decision, brushing aside accusations that he was influenced by his superiors in the

87

administration.[20] The decision, he said, represented "my best professional judgment." He could not have been unaware, however, of White House efforts to aid the ailing auto industry, which included a thirty-four-point regulatory relief package issued the previous spring. The decision was praised by the three top auto companies, and condemned by consumer groups and auto insurance industry representatives. "It condemns to utterly needless deaths tens of thousands of Americans who will be killed in car crashes just in the coming decade," said the Insurance Institute for Highway Safety. The Reagan administration held that increased public education to persuade more Americans to use safety belts (only 12 percent of all motorists currently use seat belts, according to a NHTSA study) was the preferred approach, leaving the choice up to the individual and keeping one more coercive government regulation off the books. The Supreme Court later upheld the air bag rule.[21]

In another blow to consumer interests, the Treasury Department killed a proposed regulation that would have required labels on wine and other alcoholic beverage bottles listing the ingredients, or providing an address where consumers could write for information. Advocates of the regulation argued that the labeling requirement would allow consumers to protect themselves against harmful additives or substances causing allergic reactions. In line with the executive order, Assistant Secretary of the Treasury John M. Walker, Jr., announced that the costs of such labels would far exceed the benefits, and those costs would be passed on to the consumer. Estimates of the cost of labeling, offered by the regulation's opponents — members of the California congressional delegation, vintners, bottlers, and other groups representing the alcoholic beverage industry — ranged from $90 to $140 million a year. This figure was challenged by consumer groups, who argued that the costs were negligible, since the rule was not scheduled to take effect until 1983, when new labels would have to be printed anyway. The real reason, they argued, was that the California vintners, who had a special relationship with the President and Congress, feared that if people knew what chemicals were added to the beverages they drank, they might be inclined to buy less or switch their allegiance to unadulterated products. (Both California senators and forty of its representatives wrote, in June 1981, to Walker urging that ingredient labeling for wine be revoked immediately.) Now the consumer cannot make an informed choice between, for example, wines made with pure grapes and those mixed with ingredients such as urea, ox blood, dyes, sugar, and an assortment of chemical preservatives. The incident showed also that Congress is not always a check on the President; in this instance, members of Congress were using their influence to encourage the administration to dismantle rules that had already worked their way up through the regulatory process.

The Department of Agriculture also moved to change some of its meat-labeling rules, easing up on the extent to which manufacturers must list the ingredients in processed meats. In keeping with Reagan appointee John Block's promise to reduce the department's emphasis on consumer issues, the department has embarked on a regulatory review intended to dismantle many of its health-related rules. "The best thing for consumers is a good healthy agriculture," said Block.[22] Economic health, however, appears to have little relationship to physical health, as indicated by the department's plans to relax cooking requirements for tuberculosis-infected hogs, to strike labeling rules so that manufacturers would no longer have to list bone particles ground up in processed meats, and to change the rules governing meat inspection from having inspectors on every site to a "quality-control system" with only random inspections.[23] A general downgrading of the USDA's enforcement function has led to other significant changes, such as a halt to the agency's relatively new policy of listing meat and poultry processing plants that have consistently failed to meet inspection standards, as well as a general decrease in its food safety compliance program.

Eventually the Agriculture Department rescinded a regulation that required labeling to reflect that pulverized tissue, bone, and bone marrow were used in processed meats such as frankfurters and salami. "A little bit of bone, or whatever you're going to get, isn't going to hurt you in the least," said John McClung, of the agency's Food Safety and Inspection Service. "The industry argued that the label previously required was so frightening to consumers that they wouldn't buy the product."

Rescinding regulations is not without political risk, however. An outbreak of disease traceable to tuberculosis-infected hogs or diseased poultry, for example, could create a ground swell of public reaction that could eventually cost the Republicans votes for years to come. Even critics generally supportive of deregulation have warned that the Reagan administration's efforts to reform regulation may backfire politically if the public eventually sees the program for what it is: totally geared to business. "If President Reagan's efforts to reform regulation are seen simply as a set of favors for corporations, a new wave of antibusiness populist sentiment may develop in the 1980's," wrote Robert Crandall, in *Regulation*.[24] Consumers participate in this process only incidentally, mentioned in the administration's public relations statements as an afterthought. "Again and again," Crandall continued, the Reagan administration "has announced regulatory proposals as 'regulatory relief' — relief principally for industry, not consumers," although such proposals may be accompanied by a statement — "as a sidelight — that prices to consumers will be lowered."[25]

Consumers are also in for a rough period with James Miller, who moved from OMB in the fall of 1981 to head the Federal Trade Commission (FTC). In his first press conference after taking office, Miller announced that he intended to do something about truth-in-advertising rules arguing that not only did they add to the cost of the product but that consumers were intelligent enough to differentiate without the help of the FTC. This proposal was opposed by many in the advertising industry, however, who feared that unscrupulous, fly-by-night manufacturers could make fictitious claims that could drive responsible manufacturers out of business. This was tacit acknowledgment of the principle that regulation often aided business.

Miller also promised that the commission would no longer seek to protect consumers from "imperfect" products, on similar grounds. In effect, Miller was advocating the right, especially of the poor, to buy imperfect products in ignorance, without government interfering with that right. The policy was attacked by a wide spectrum of groups and media, including the *Christian Science Monitor,* which assailed Miller in an editorial entitled "FTC's Green Light to Shoddiness." The *Monitor* questioned Miller's reasoning behind this significant policy shift, adding that this would convey to businessmen the message that "they can, in effect, get away with the marketing of imperfect products and even questionable advertising, so long as the product is not blatantly imperfect and the advertising message outrageously false.''[26] Many others, including the *Monitor,* argued that not only was the new policy orientation not in the best interests of consumers, but in the long run it would hurt the business community as a whole, by allowing the hucksters to taint their more legitimate counterparts in the corporate world. Similar policy directions have already placed American industry at a disadvantage with Japanese and European industrialists, who have already stressed quality control to attract international buyers.

Miller later demonstrated more concern for consumers of medical care, fighting the medical profession's efforts to be exempted by congressional action from the FTC's antitrust jurisdiction. Miller's adversary was formidable: the American Medical Association, whose PAC had outspent all others in the 1982 elections, managed to find many grateful supporters in Congress. Under the glare of intense media attention, Congress eventually refused to accede to the AMA's demands.

Those who breathe as well as those who buy are affected by the actions of the Reagan regulators in charge of the environment, whose mission is clearer than the air and water will be when they leave office. Their strategy, which has been to use all managerial resources available to them, has proved initially successful in unraveling environmental regulations that took years to develop, and in reducing a staff of experts that could take years to reassemble. EPA administrator Anne M. Gorsuch provided a case in point. Moving swiftly, Gorsuch put her imprint on environmental regulation not only by influencing specific rules but also through management policies guaranteed to sharply reduce EPA's activities. In her initial budget request to OMB, for example, Gorsuch recommended cutting her agency's budget by 50 percent, to be spread over a two-year period. This would have meant a reduction in EPA spending from $1.36 billion a year to $950 million by fiscal 1983. The net effect of this cut would be the dismissal of thirty-two hundred of the agency's ten thousand employees, with the reductions in force (RIFs) aimed specifically at executive levels. Under pressure from Congress, the actual reductions were not as severe as Gorsuch originally intended, but were still serious. Hardest hit along with the personnel budget was the research office, which lost more than half of its budget for 1981–83, after factoring in inflation. Reducing the research needed to produce and monitor regulation is an effective way of cutting down environmental regulation.

To weaken any remaining regulatory activity, Gorsuch eliminated the Office of Enforcement, dividing its functions among other bureaus in the agency. She argued that each program could enforce the laws more effectively at the divisional level. The results of this action over the next six months bore out initial fears that the reverse would be the case, that enforcement would be sharply reduced without the personnel to enforce the laws. The number of cases referred to the Department of Justice by EPA for enforcement provided the evidence substantiating this view. In the first nine months of 1981, the agency referred fewer than fifty cases involving violations of the environmental laws; only twelve of these cases progressed after Gorsuch took office. By comparison, the department had referred 230 cases in the first nine months of 1980, and 200 cases over a similar period in 1979. Through her spokesperson Byron Nelson, Gorsuch justified these cutbacks by stating that she planned to have polluters clean up voluntarily, instead of hauling them into court every time the agency identified an offense. She did not intend, she said, to follow the policies of her predecessors and "count beans," but would seek other ways to produce results.[27] By 1983, EPA enforcement actions had fallen considerably, marked by an 84 percent reduction in the number of cases referred by the agency to the Justice Department, and by a 78 percent reduction in the number of cases brought to court by that department.

It is too early to determine the long-term effects of these cuts, but even industry critics of EPA are fearful that without a strong federal presence in the environmental area, they will be left to the mercies of state and local officials, and to an even more uncertain political fate. Indeed, if EPA is not staffed to cope with future Love Canal and Kepone-type crises, state officials will surely fill the vacuum; and after a few years of dealing with outraged local officials, perhaps even federal regulators will sound like the voice of reason to the business community. No doubt the absence of an EPA presence will result in untold confusion, as a mosaic of state environmental laws develops and corporate lawyers watch their earlier

92

problems with EPA multiply by fifty. While the business community struggles with local politicians and with state legislatures, air and water pollution will continue to grow unabated and unchecked by a meaningful government presence. Like many other national problems, pollution ignores state and local — even national — boundaries, as indicated by the dramatic example of acid rain. Soon the emasculated EPA may be forced to recall to a larger public the original purpose of federal environmental regulation — to eliminate exactly this type of confusion, inequity, and inconsistency.

The Gorsuch tactic of allowing budget and management to drive policy conflicted not only with national needs but also with the laws of the land. Congress made the EPA responsible for enforcing and implementing the Clean Air and Clean Water acts, as well as the law governing the disposal of hazardous waste. How can the agency possibly review seriously the ten thousand effluent permits required by the Clean Water Act without sufficient personnel and resources? How can the agency function at all in fulfilling its responsibilities under the law with such crippling constraints, especially as those responsibilities continue to increase? Gorsuch was not the only Reagan regulator to ignore the congressional mandate, but Congress, deprived of its budget-cutting influence, has been unable to do much to stop the Reagan steamroller.[28] Ironically, Reagan has robbed Congress of its most potent club over the regulators — the threat of cutting their budgets. Reagan's regulators were the first in recent memory to applaud budget cuts, not fight them, in keeping with the prevailing philosophy that less government means less regulation.

At the Occupational Safety and Health Administration (OSHA), similar cutbacks in enforcement were reported. Total inspections supposedly declined by 15 percent compared with 1980, while findings of willful violations of the Occupational Safety and Health Act declined by more than 40 percent. OSHA attorneys claimed to be swamped by the requirements of the regulatory review process, which kept them too busy to regulate. They also have sought extensions in court proceedings involving the regulations dealing with lead and medical records in the hope of altering those standards, both issued in the final days of the Carter administration.[29]

A sharp drop in the enforcement of FDA regulations has also

been reported. Enforcement actions fell by 50 percent during 1981, compared with the average rate per year for the preceding four years, although a pattern of decreased enforcement could be seen in the last year of the Carter presidency.[30] These actions include prosecutions against companies, seizures of defective foods and drugs, and injunctions to prevent companies from manufacturing defective products. Related to the overall policy of reducing enforcement is the plan to speed up the drug approval process. The agency proudly announced that it had approved twenty-seven new chemical entities in 1981, the most since 1962, when Congress amended the drug laws to require proof of a drug's effectiveness as well as its safety.[31] The first to benefit from this policy was the antiarthritic drug Oraflex, which was approved by the FDA in April 1982, even though the agency had rejected it two years earlier because of its links to deaths from liver and kidney failure. Banned in Great Britain for these reasons, the drug was voluntarily recalled by its manufacturer, Eli Lilly and Co. Speedy drug approval and decreased enforcement may produce short-term gains for the drug companies, but long-term problems for the public and the industry. At best, it makes for high-risk public policy.

Mine safety has taken a similar downturn under the Reagan administration, indicating the swift and devastating effects of social deregulation. Two tragic disasters, on December 3 and 15, 1981, claimed the lives of 24 miners, bringing the 1981 death toll to 155 fatalities, a 17 percent increase over the previous year. Under President Reagan, for the first time since 1972, three years after passage of the Federal Coal Mine Safety and Health Act in 1969, the number of mining disasters rose; before that time they had steadily declined. By all predictions, mine disasters in 1981 should have decreased, not increased, since the number of overall work hours dropped as a result of a ten-week coal strike in the spring of that year.

One of the reasons given for the increase in mine accidents was unrelated to politics, and involved geologically caused hazards, namely, recent changes in the earth's barometric pressure, which created unstable methane gases in the mines. But, at the same time, questions were being raised, most notably by *Business Week,* connecting Reagan's policy of deregulating mine safety with the current increase in mine disasters. The Reagan approach, consistent with his deregulatory policies, sought to decrease the adversarial relationship between mine operators and government officials at the Mine Safety and Health Administration (MSHA), located in the Department of Labor, by decreasing enforcement activities and relying more heavily on negotiation and consultation. In keeping with this policy, the new head of MSHA, Ford B. Ford, had instituted a new program giving district managers more latitude in negotiating settlements with mine owners. He also designed "compliance assistant" plans, by which inspectors give advice, instead of recommending punishment, for violators of safety regulations. Consciously, Ford tried to change the approach of his agency by instructing his enforcement staff in Beckley, West Virginia, to change its posture to a more cooperative and less confrontational one. "You should no longer be perceived in your minds . . . as MSHA's chief enforcement officers. Instead, you are to be MSHA's chief health and safety managers in the field." In well-run mines, like those managed by U.S. Steel, the cooperative approach might work. But how quickly will the other companies, when faced with "advice" instead of the threat of being cited for violations, correct safety hazards in their mines? Enforcement agencies that do not enforce will soon become obsolete, and laws like the Federal Mine Safety and Health Act will fall into disuse. In this sense, "compliance" reform should be recognized for what it is: a return to virtual self-regulation.

Budget cuts also have taken their toll on MSHA, a pattern begun under President Carter, who imposed a hiring freeze on the agency. In addition to a 10 percent reduction in inspectors due to attrition, the agency's budget has been reduced from $158 million in fiscal 1981 to $148 million in fiscal 1982. This will mean fewer inspectors on the payroll, and as a result, fewer inspections. The United Mine Workers (UMW) is already reporting a noticeable decrease in the number of mine inspections as the less responsible mine operators slacken their efforts in response to Reagan's antienforcement signals. "Safety committees are reporting to me they're not getting the same inspections they were a year ago," reported Bernard B. Shrewsberry, a UMW safety inspector in southern West Virginia.[32]

A reduction in the number of mine inspectors from 1,940 in 1978 to 1,684 in 1981 coincided with a 50 percent increase in mine deaths. Richard L. Trumka, president of the United Mine Workers, did not believe that the relationship was purely coincidental. He called the reduction in inspectors a "transparent effort to coerce Congress to accept deregulation through the budget process." Under union pressure, the agency added 205 inspectors in 1982, and the number of fatalities declined somewhat. "We don't think there's any proof of a correlation [between the number of inspectors and fatalities]," said Noel Milan, a public information officer for the Mine Health and Safety Administration.

Recruiting the Regulators

An examination of the backgrounds of the regulators appointed by the Reagan administrators, especially in comparison with those who served under President Carter, clearly indicates their policy preferences: almost all have business backgrounds. The importance of this linkage was emphasized early in the Reagan administration by Murray Weidenbaum, who applauded this development in an article in *Nation's Business*. "There will be new faces at the agencies," he wrote. "People do matter and, given the tremendous amount of discretionary power vested in the regulatory bureaus, the people who run them can exert great influence." In discussing the differences between Reagan and Carter regulators, he went on to say that "a reform-minded head of the Occupational Safety and Health Administration would not have resisted a federal court's admonition to establish a 'reasonable relationship' between benefits and costs in its proposed benzene standard."[33]

The benzene issue highlights the essential differences between Carter and Reagan regulators. The head of OSHA under Carter, a public health professor from the University of Cincinnati, Eula Bingham, initiated the benzene issue originally by issuing an emergency order temporarily cutting back workers' exposure to the chemical, believed by some medical experts to cause leukemia. Like the Reagan administrators, Bingham also had wanted to eliminate the petty regulations for which OSHA had become notorious, such as those that placed smaller businesses at a disadvantage. Instead, she wanted to concentrate on major health hazards — particularly those involving toxic chemicals — in the work place that had long concerned the labor unions. Her appointment was greeted enthusiastically by the unions and by Dr. Sidney Wolfe, director of Ralph Nader's Health Research Group, who had "pushed hard for her to get this OSHA job . . . for her strong worker viewpoint."[34]

Like Bingham, many other agency heads came from the network of Nader organizations or similar kinds of public interest groups. They were activists who had fought for tougher enforcement of the laws through regulation, and many of them had been involved in lawsuits reflecting that point of view against the agencies they rose to administer. Peter Petkas, who headed the Regulatory Council, had served as legal consultant to Ralph Nader from 1970 to 1973; he also worked for the Southern Regional Council, a civil rights advocacy organization. Another Nader lobbyist, Joan Claybrook, came from a directorship at Congress Watch, an organization that lobbied Congress on a variety of public interest measures. "Organizations founded by Ralph Nader contributed half a dozen people to the Carter administration," estimated the *National Journal,* adding that key regulatory posts were also filled by leaders of the Natural Resources Defense Council, the Environmental Defense Fund, and the Consumer Federation of America.[35]

Bingham's successor at OSHA, Thorne Auchter, reflected a diametrically opposed view of government regulation. A thirty-five-year-old Florida businessman when appointed, Auchter viewed OSHA as a symbol of government overregulation, and pledged immediately to deal with the agency's "regulations and procedures of nitpicking and whimsy."[36] Auchter, the choice of Labor Secretary Raymond Donovan, who also came from a construction industry background, was the vice president of the Auchter Company, a family-owned business. According to the Labor Department, the Auchter Company was cited forty-eight times for OSHA violations since 1972; in one 1979 citation, inspectors fined the company for failing to take adequate safety precautions when using divers to inspect wharf pilings. In another instance, often used by Auchter to illustrate the "nitpicking" orientation of OSHA, the agency fined the company for "unsanitary conditions" based on its finding that construction workers threw drinking cups on the ground.

Many of the Reagan regulators, like Auchter, came from backgrounds in which they had either fought excessive regulation or been victimized by it, making them perfect candidates to carry out Reagan's policy of social deregulation. Still others made their preferences on regulatory policy clear through speeches and the media. The new assistant secretary of agriculture in charge of the national forests, John B. Crowell, Jr., used to advocate allowing timber companies to cut down more trees on public lands, in his former job as general counsel of the Louisiana-Pacific Corporation.[37]

For those in charge of protecting the environment, the pattern remained consistent. Secretary James Watt came to the Department of the Interior directly from a post at the Mountain States Legal Foundation, where his primary job was to initiate legal challenges to government-inspired environmental protection. In one of those lawsuits, he was joined by twenty-seven Colorado state legislators, who contested EPA's authority to apply sanctions against states in order to force them to institute an auto inspection program. Other lawsuits challenged federal and state land use policies, many of which Watt began to dismantle during his tenure at Interior. Immediately after his arrival, Watt also imposed a hold on regulations from the Office of Surface Mining, to the delight of mining interests, particularly in the Appalachian states, where state regulation is less vigorous than it is in the western states. According to officials from the Office of Surface Mining, Watt's policy was felt within six months.

"I have seen moonscapes on mine sites," said an official with the Office of Surface Mining, after returning from a trip to Tennessee. "This is now a captive agency, totally captive of the mining interests. There are no inspectors out in the field now; they only inspect in response to citizen complaints. I found tons of overburden on one slope, and couldn't find the mine operator ["overburden" is the rock and coal left after the mining company has taken out the coal it can sell]. At the second site there was eighty feet of overburden.

"Overburden is highly toxic," he explained. "At each mine, it could amount to thousands of tons. It destroys the topsoil, leaving virtually no topsoil to reclaim. This is only happening in the

Appalachian states — Tennessee, Kentucky, and Alabama. It doesn't occur in the western states, where good mining practices are written into the state laws. In Montana, cows graze on recently mined land." After finally locating one inspector, the official attempted to find out why the regulations were not being implemented. "It will cost me my job to cite these guys," the inspector reportedly said.

Like Gorsuch at the EPA, Watt also has scaled down his department's regulatory efforts by reducing its enforcement function, which was easily accomplished by the dismissal of fifty-one employees in the solicitor's office (including twenty-eight lawyers) and the transfer of others to where they could do no harm. Harold Baer, an attorney in the Denver office who specializes in minerals, oil, and gas, was transferred to Washington, where he will work on wilderness, grazing, and right-of-way law. "They told me they needed my expertise," he reported, adding he was not familiar with his new field.[38]

Watt's top appointees reflect his and the President's views favoring deregulation through decreased enforcement, and, again like them, identify with groups hostile to the regulatory process. In fact, the top appointee in charge of enforcing federal strip-mining laws, James R. Harris, director of the Office of Surface Mining, was so closely tied to two coal companies that the question of conflict of interest arose during his Senate confirmation hearings.

What emerged from the hearings were allegations that while serving in the Indiana legislature, Harris had engaged in private business transactions with Peabody Coal Co. and Amax, Inc., at the same time that he chaired two legislative committees responsible for drafting and overseeing strip-mining laws. Harris and a partner had purchased twenty-five hundred acres of land from reclaimed strip-mined land in southern Indiana, which was then subdivided and sold at a huge profit.[39] Although Harris defended the transaction in terms of his shrewd business acumen, questions were raised concerning the propriety of a lawmaker doing business with companies under his jurisdiction. The question never answered was what the companies received in return for their favors to Harris. One possible answer is the resolution he helped push through the state legislature that led to Indiana's decision to join a case challenging the federal strip-mining law, a law Harris has now sworn to uphold.

Other top appointees at the Office of Surface Mining shared the same type of background of fighting the very regulations they must now administer. Under their supervision, state plans have an easier time winning department approval; in fact, one employee in the Office of Surface Mining put up a sign that read: "State Permits Approved While You Wait." Meanwhile, strip mining has proceeded rapidly as the federal presence recedes.[40]

Watt's counterpart at EPA, Anne M. Gorsuch, also entered office with a background of support for deregulation and the accelerated application of cost-benefit analysis to environmental rules. Recommended by Watt, who knew her in Colorado, Gorsuch had worked for the Mountain Bell Telephone Company as an attorney specializing in land problems, and had also served in the state legislature. Although she described herself as an environmentalist, her background in the state legislature indicated otherwise. One issue of special concern to the state's leading environmental group, the Colorado Open Space Council, involved her opposition to proposed legislation to establish a state program of hazardous waste management. As chairman of a legislative committee charged with reviewing programs in the hazardous waste area, she opposed strong environmental action and successfully led the battle that resulted in blocking Colorado's participation in EPA's waste program under the federal Resource Conservation and Recovery Act. Instead, she proposed a bill restricting the state health department's authority to determine the location of dump sites.[41] During the same period, she supported the Mountain States Legal Foundation, a group then headed by James Watt, in its effort to restrict auto emissions inspections.

Gorsuch's initial choices for her top staff positions reflected her ties to the business community, and raised a chorus of outcries from environmental groups, who particularly objected to the selection of people whose professional backgrounds linked them with industries accused of polluting the environment. Frank Shepherd, the associate administrator in charge of legal counsel and enforcement, was a partner in a Miami law firm that represented General Motors, an opponent of the auto emissions section of the Clean Air

Act. The chief of staff, John E. Daniel, was a lobbyist for the Johns-Manville Corporation, which manufactures asbestos, and, before that, was with the American Paper Institute, the major lobbying group for the paper industry, where he directed the legislative affairs office. His predecessor at the American Paper Institute, Kathleen M. Bennett, also joined EPA as its assistant administrator in charge of air, noise, and radiation. The department's general counsel, Robert M. Perry, came from Houston, where he represented Exxon in cases involving coal leasing, offshore oil and gas leasing, and other environmental impact issues. The preponderance of attorneys at EPA also included: Nolan Clark, from the Washington law firm of Kirkland and Ellis, which represented the Dow Chemical Company in its fight to prevent the pesticide 2,4,5–T from being banned by the EPA, in charge of policy and resource management; Thornton W. Field, an attorney with the Adolph Coors brewing company, in charge of hazardous wastes; and William Sullivan, Jr., whose consulting firm advised cities with steel mills. Only one scientist, John A. Todhunter, was appointed to the top level of the agency.

Most of these early appointments to EPA went virtually unnoticed at the time, unlike the outcry one year later over the nomination of Rita M. Lavelle, former director of communications for the Aerojet-General Corporation, to head the agency's program to clean up hazardous waste dump sites. Lavelle had two strikes against her. The first involved her background in public relations, troublesome to those who preferred a candidate with some scientific or technical expertise. Second, the question of potential conflict of interest was raised: Aerojet's liquid fuel plant in Rancho Cordova, California, was one of the worst offenders in the area of hazardous waste pollution, prominently featured on EPA's priority list of the 115 worst toxic waste sites among thousands of such dumps across the country. In California, the Aerojet plant is regarded as one of the three worst polluters, charged by the state in 1979 with dumping twenty thousand gallons a day of toxic chemical wastes. Appointed despite intense opposition from environmental groups, Lavelle ran the $1.6 billion superfund program, in her position as assistant administrator for solid waste and emergency response. Initially, she pledged to avoid any appearance of conflict of interest by not dealing with any action involving her former employer, Aerojet, but this later appeared to be an empty promise.[42]

The EPA team worked in tandem with OMB in its effort to reevaluate expensive environmental regulations affecting the former employers and clients of these appointees.[43] At least a dozen of the regulations dealing with emissions standards under the Clean Air Act affect the auto industry, in addition to the utilities and chemical and petroleum industries. Estimates of costs to the auto industry to reduce nitrogen dioxide emissions from trucks alone hover around the $4 billion mark. Effluent guidelines for utilities, paper, and steel are also targeted for review by the very people who were fighting them from the other side; here, too, savings from nonregulating climb into the billions. The chemical industry, among others, is similarly affected by Reagan administration appointees dealing with targeted regulations affecting hazardous waste (chemical and nuclear), as well as toxic substances and pesticides.

The Reagan administration's efforts to dismantle EPA collapsed in March 1983, when Anne Burford (Gorsuch) and her top aides were forced to resign in the wake of deepening scandals affecting the agency. (Just before her resignation, Gorsuch married, taking the name of her new husband, Robert Burford, an aide to James Watt and director of the Bureau of Land Management.) Congressional investigations throughout the winter of 1982–83 revealed widespread irregularities in the agency, which seemed more intent upon protecting corporate polluters than the public interest. As events pointed to White House involvement, headlines with the word "Sewergate" evoked comparisons to the Watergate era in the public mind; the agency's document shredding and lost records did nothing to dispel this association.

The hazardous waste program became the focal point of Congress's inquiry into EPA. Agreements between agency officials and industry representatives, Congress alleged, allowed companies to avoid billions of dollars in cleanup costs, with untold harm to those living in the affected areas. Instead of having to submit to ten-year reviews, some companies with the right political connections were given lifetime permits for hazardous waste sites. Added protection was given to those companies worried about public pressure when the agency issued policies reducing the public's right to inspect those sites.

When the appointment calendar of Rita Lavelle, head of the hazardous waste program, hit the front pages of the newspapers, the mechanics of these "negotiations" were displayed for public viewing. Lavelle's day-to-day professional life was filled with lunches and dinners at expensive Washington restaurants, as the guest of corporate officials doing business with the EPA. And despite her early promises to excuse herself from policy decisions involving her former employer, Aerojet, the calendar also revealed that she was present at a meeting at which the company's participation at the Stringfellow, California, dump site was discussed. The same calendar was instructive in showing who had access to EPA leadership; it was hard to find meetings with environmental groups or citizens' groups of any kind.

It took only a short time under the Reagan-Burford-Lavelle leadership to thoroughly politicize hazardous waste. Announcements of superfund grants were coordinated with the gubernatorial and congressional elections, with grants awarded to help Republican candidates. EPA was told to bend over backward to help Governor Richard Snelling, of Vermont, and Governor Thomas H. Kean, of New Jersey. Soon after a meeting between White House assistant Jim Medas and Lavelle, according to notes taken by an aide and released by the House Committee on Energy and Commerce, Subcommittee on Oversight and Investigations, New Jersey received sixteen cleanup grants, making it the second largest recipient in the nation. The same notes carried a section entitled "Seymour-Sweetheart," in reference to an agreement in Seymour, Indiana, announced a week before the 1982 election and allegedly urged by Republican Senator Richard G. Lugar, of Indiana. The $7.7 million settlement enabled the companies involved to avoid spending an additional several million dollars to clean up the site.

When Congress sought to obtain documents relating to malfeasance in the hazardous waste area, the agency refused to cooperate. Under prodding by Rep. Elliot Levitas (Democrat, Georgia), chairman of the House Public Works Committee's Subcommittee on Investigations, Anne Burford (Gorsuch) claimed executive privilege on orders, she said, from the White House. But Levitas, author of the legislative veto and an old foe of bureaucratic arrogance, proved tougher than the White House expected. When an agency refuses to turn over documents and national security is not involved, Levitas concluded, it can only mean that the agency's leaders have something to hide. Levitas persisted, and eventually, on December 16, 1982, the House cited Burford (Gorsuch) for contempt of Congress, the first time a top level federal official was cited by the full House. Joining the 259 Democrats in the contempt vote were 55 Republicans.

Other examples of the dismantling of environmental regulation included:

— A "hit list" of agency employees to be fired, hired, or promoted according to their political beliefs. The official who compiled the list, presumably at the direction of his bosses, was forced to resign in March 1983.

— The withdrawal of the nomination of James W. Sanderson, an aide to Burford (Gorsuch), after the Justice Department began looking into allegations that he had continued to represent a client of his law firm, the Denver Water Board, after joining the EPA as a consultant.

— Evidence suggesting that the Dow Chemical Company had been allowed to influence the writing of an EPA report in such a way as to minimize the company's culpability in the dioxin contamination of two Missouri rivers. Dioxin is one of the most toxic chemical substances known.

— Allegations that the same official involved in the Dow report, John Hernandez, had vetoed an EPA supervised cleanup of lead contamination in a low-income neighborhood of Dallas, where school playgrounds revealed lead concentrations ten times higher than the danger threshold. Rep. Levitas said he had information that Hernandez had stopped three smelting companies from voluntarily cleaning up the contaminated areas.

Hernandez denied all the charges, although he testified to Congress that he had urged that Dow's comments be "heard" before the agency issued its final report.

President Reagan finally capitulated to congressional pressures and fired the top management of EPA, including Anne Burford (Gorsuch). He also agreed to release some of the requested documents to Congress. By this time, perhaps the President was chastened by an ABC-*Washington Post* poll showing that the public was nearly as critical of Reagan for the EPA crisis as it was of Burford.

The poll, released March 5, 1983, almost three months after the contempt citation, found that a majority of Americans believed the President would rather protect polluters than clean up the environment. If not, then why did he appoint environmental managers whose backgrounds revealed their dedication to unraveling these protections?

Virtually no category of social protection was left untouched by regulatory "reform." In the area of affirmative action, the Reagan administration's strategy appeared to be to appoint the most inexperienced person it could find, then sit back and wait while the appointee embarked on the most expensive on-the-job training program in Washington. In the meantime, while the appointee learned the field, regulations could be held in abeyance indefinitely, the ultimate in regulatory relief. After what was called a national talent search, the name of William M. Bell was submitted to head the Equal Employment Opportunity Commission. EEOC is an independent regulatory commission whose mission, to enforce laws against employment discrimination, represented another target on the regulatory hit list. As the appointment came under media and congressional scrutiny, it became glaringly apparent that Bell, a fifty-five-year-old Detroit businessman, lacked the qualifications to manage an agency of thirty-four hundred employees and an annual budget of $140 million. The president and sole employee of an executive recruiting firm in Detroit, Bold Concepts, Bell admitted to the Senate Labor and Human Resources Committee that the firm had placed no employees that year and was operating on total assets of $500. Disclosing that he also had never supervised more than four people at a time, Bell argued that he was qualified for the job, largely because he had been a victim of discrimination. A storm of protest greeted the nomination from civil rights organizations representing women, blacks, and Hispanics, all of whom attacked Bell's qualifications for the job, arguing that under his leadership the EEOC would cease to be effective. It was the first time in history that black groups opposed the nomination of a black to a major appointment. Promises that Bell would appoint a strong director failed to appease the opposition; even Republican senators on the committee, such as Lowell Weicker of Connecticut and Dan Quayle of Indiana, indicated they would join their Democratic colleagues and vote against Bell's appointment. Many wondered why the Reagan administration did not do the obvious and appoint the acting head of the EEOC, a black Republican, J. Clay Smith, Jr., an attorney with a long and distinguished record, to the chairmanship. Perhaps it was Smith's open support of affirmative action that spoiled his chances with an administration pledged to unravel regulations in that area. It was difficult to discover why the administration stood by Bell's appointment. Did it demonstrate the administration's contempt for affirmative action, or was it part of a larger plan to downgrade this particular agency and its regulatory activities? Ultimately, the White House acceded to the protests, and the nomination was withdrawn.

The Reagan regulators also could be expected to go along with the administration's use of budget and personnel cuts as a management tool. In the President's initial budget proposal for sixteen of the independent regulatory agencies, it was apparent that the regulatory agencies would bear a disproportionate share of the budget and personnel reductions ordered for the entire government. Although these agencies employ only 2 percent of the federal civilian employees, they took an 8 percent reduction in personnel, as well as budget reductions twice as large as those for all government offices.[44] Some agencies, like the Consumer Product Safety Commission (CPSC) hung on by a thread, somehow surviving administration efforts to bury it in the Commerce Department. The CPSC suffered a 30 percent cut in its tiny $45 million budget, including a cut of 145 employees from its 728 member staff. It will not need those extra staff members if the agency follows the philosophy of its chairman, Nancy Steorts, who advocates voluntary industry compliance in place of mandatory regulation. In all, the cuts followed the strategy outlined in Reagan's economic recovery message of February 18, 1981: "fewer regulators will necessarily result in fewer regulations and less harassment of the regulated."[45]

Believers in presidential power applauded the victory of the White House over the agencies, a goal of every President in recent history. To control his bureaucracy, President Roosevelt added to it, creating many of the "alphabet agencies" that became famous as instruments of presidential policy. Harry S Truman complained about dealing with the executive branch, as did Dwight D. Eisenhower. As he was cleaning out his desk, Truman was supposed to have said: "Poor Ike. He's used to the military. He's going to come in here and say, 'do this' and 'do that,' and nothing's going to happen."

A few years later, John F. Kennedy continued the trend. "I can do it, but I don't know if the government can," he answered in response to a request. Presidents and their supporters in the academic community all worked from a commonly held assumption: the President ought to have more centralized control over the agencies — executive and independent.

Through the years, the complaints continued to mount, building up a compelling case for increased presidential authority over the regulatory process. The presidential power advocates receded from view for a few years during the Watergate crisis, when Richard Nixon's performance made the idea of increasing the President's power over anything less appealing, but they surfaced again during the Carter administration, when the regulatory "reform" movement began in earnest.

"What about the abuse of presidential power?" asked those with an institutional memory. "Recourse at the polls," was the conventional response. "If you don't like what the President has done, you can elect someone else in four years." Even if you disagree with his policies, the argument continues, society is better off with increased presidential control than with the continuous jockeying of regulatory problems among the courts, the White House, and Congress.

Or is it? Even without the sea change brought about by the Carter and Reagan administrations, the balance always tipped in favor of the President. This was true, despite often-cited laments, even regarding the President's power over the independent agencies. "When the President stares, the Fed blinks" is an old axiom, referring to the most recalcitrant of the independent agencies, the Federal Reserve Board. If the President always wielded this kind of power, why did he need more?

Part of the answer is found in the short experience of the social regulatory agencies, an easy target for the President because there were no traditions governing their relationship with him. They were also easy to dominate because they lacked the kind of allies acquired by their fellow agencies, who made friends with the specific industries they regulated, and were protected by them — often with help from Capitol Hill — from serious incursions by the White House. By contrast, agencies like EPA, OSHA, or the mine safety bureau could not offer the kinds of rewards that make friends for government; rather, these agencies found themselves in the position of taking away resources, and thereby developing formidable adversaries.

Who, then, is left to protect the public if these agencies are left without the political resources to protect themselves? Congress at times has come to the rescue, but Congress lacks the kind of positive power necessary to check regulatory abuses on a consistent basis. The courts also lack the resources to monitor the process on a regular basis; they can enter a case only on narrow procedural grounds.

Won't the process be self-correcting as countervailing pressures take over? asks another defense of presidential power. To some extent, this has occurred, as witnessed by the effect of the "green vote," observed in the 1982 congressional elections, in which many candidates supported by environmentalists were victorious at the polls. But what about all the other regulatory issues, many so sweeping that countervailing pressures would take years to develop, perhaps too late to reverse the effects of present policies? In that sense, the electoral cycle can be limiting as well as liberating. Presidents look toward the next election, responding to pressures that will maximize victory for themselves or their party. Issues like hazardous waste extend well beyond that time frame — indeed, nuclear waste takes thirty thousand years to decompose — and require a certain consistency of policy that does not jibe with these political constraints.

The politicization of enforcement is perhaps the most potent argument for the preservation of the process, in order to provide at least minimal insulation against the current dismantling of regulations governing strip mining, worker safety, the environment, food purity and drug safety, mine safety, and a rash of others. Accomplished with such precision by the Reagan administration, the politicization of enforcement happened too fast and on too many fronts for the normal procedural checks to fight back effectively; it also showed how easily presidential power can dominate the field of regulation. Maintaining the sanctity of the process could have protected the public against the Reagan regulators, who changed regulations as a substitute for their inability to change the laws that governed those regulations.

The Reagan experience showed the need for an even-handed approach. By subverting the regulatory process through executive order, the President made government the handmaiden of one set of groups, who got what they believed was "relief" from government intervention — at least for a while. But once the process is permanently skewed, any group could potentially dominate and exclude its opponents, depending on the sympathies of future White House occupants.

How would the business community react if some of its public interest adversaries held sway over OMB, conducting regulatory affairs through secret meetings, followed by suspended regulations? And who would benefit from a set of appointees as hostile to business as the Reagan administrators were toward many of the regulations and laws they had sworn to uphold?

The object of the regulatory process is balance and equity, the guarantee that all groups have equal access to government. As indicated by the Reagan experience, the President has more than adequate outlets for his policy preferences through his power over appointments and budget. He does not need to change the process, too.

4

Particles of Truth
Cotton Dust and Cost-Benefit Analysis

*Those who hackle in the flax and hemp to prepare it
for being spun and wove, afford frequent instances of
the unwholesomeness of their trade; for there flies out
of this matter a foul mischievous powder, that entering
the lungs by the mouth and throat, causes continual
coughs and gradually makes way for an asthma . . .
for 'tis a sordid profit that's accompanied with the
destruction of health.*[1]
— From an eighteenth-century text on the "diseases of
tradesmen"

"I AM ONLY FIFTY-SEVEN YEARS OLD and I am retired and I can't
even get to go to church because of my breathing. I get short of
breath just walking around the house or dressing [or] sometimes
just watching TV. I cough all the time," said a woman cotton mill
worker testifying in 1978 about the symptoms of her lung disease.
"I suppose I had a breathing problem since 1973. I just kept on
getting sick and began losing time at the mill. Every time that I go
into the mill, I get deathly sick, choking and vomiting, losing my
breath. It would blow all that lint and cotton and I have clothes

right here where I have wore and they have been washed several times and I would like for you all to see them. That will not come out in washing."[2] Other descriptions are just as harrowing.

"When they started speeding the looms up the dust got finer and more and more people started leaving the mill with breathing problems. My mother had to leave the mill in the early fifties. Before she left, her breathing got so short she just couldn't hold out to work. My stepfather left the mill on account of breathing problems. He had coughing spells till he couldn't breathe, like a child's whooping cough. Both my sisters who work in the mill have breathing problems. My husband had to give up his job when he was only fifty-four years old because of the breathing problem."

"I had to quit because I couldn't lay down and rest without oxygen in the night and my doctor told me I would have to get out of there. . . . I couldn't even breathe, I had to get out of the door so I could breathe and he told me not to go back in [the mill] under any circumstances."[3]

Exposure to cotton dust, minute particles of fabric that are the by-product of textile manufacturing, has become one of the most serious occupational hazards of working in the cotton mills. Inhaled over a prolonged period of time, cotton dust can precipitate a disease called byssinosis — popularly known as brown lung — which, at its worst, leads to a loss of pulmonary functions and, eventually, to death from heart failure. Debilitating in all of its stages, brown lung disease includes such symptoms as wheezing, coughing, chest tightness, and breathlessness — all of which result from irritations in the air passages, narrowed permanently by prolonged exposure to cotton dust.

Brown lung disease is common among textile workers, particularly in the South, and its most disabling forms have afflicted at least thirty-five thousand employed and retired cotton workers. A total of one hundred thousand more suffer from some form of the disease. According to recent studies, tens of thousands more risk exposure to the disease: one-quarter of the 864,000 people currently employed by the textile industry are involved in cotton production and, to some degree, are exposed to cotton dust.

Despite the fact that the disease had been well documented in legislative testimony and in medical journals, the battle over eliminating this hazard from the work place continued for over a decade. Industry representatives contended that the disease had been blown out of proportion: it was not irreversible, and could be cured if properly treated in its early stages. The dispute involved all three branches of government over a twelve-year period, and was finally resolved when the Supreme Court reaffirmed the right of the government to supersede the marketplace in protecting the health of the worker.

In dispute were regulations promulgated by the Occupational Safety and Health Administration (OSHA), which had set standards for reducing the amount of cotton dust from the work place by requiring the textile industry to install ventilation systems and impose sanitation practices sufficiently stringent to be effective. Installing complex engineering systems would be far too expensive, argued the textile industry, especially in view of what it considered limited returns on its investment. The industry contended that the disease was not that serious; that only 2 percent of the workers were affected by cotton dust; and those who were could be protected just as well — at far less cost — by respirators and other methods. In other words, the costs of cleaning up the work place far exceeded the benefits.

Raising the issue of cost-benefit analysis as its major legal challenge, the industry claimed that OSHA's standards were invalid because the agency had not shown that the costs of compliance ($656.5 million by OSHA's estimates) were justified by the health benefits. The Supreme Court in 1981 soundly rejected industry's challenge and upheld OSHA, saying that the agency was obligated by law to protect workers from exposure to toxic substances "to the greatest extent feasible," without being constrained to balance out the costs and the benefits.

"Congress itself defined the basic relationship between costs and benefits, by placing the 'benefit' of the worker's health above all other considerations save those making attainment of this 'benefit' unachievable," wrote Justice William Brennan for the majority. "Any standard based on a balancing of costs and benefits by the Secretary [of Labor] that strikes a different balance than that struck by the Congress would be inconsistent with the command set forth in the statute."[4]

The landmark "cotton dust decision" came as a shock to the regulatory "reform" movement, which by that time had become almost synonymous with the method of cost-benefit analysis. By refocusing attention on the requirements of the statute, the Supreme Court forced decision makers — mostly economists — back to legal basics. For even though the economists who rose to dominance in the Carter and Reagan administrations paid lip service to the phrase "unless specifically prohibited by law,"[5] they tended to pressure agencies to consider costs more carefully than benefits in writing regulations. When they found the benefits too difficult to factor into the equation, they ignored them. In the process, cost-benefit analysis, as it was applied to regulatory policy, became simple cost accounting. Although widely misapplied, cost-benefit analysis also dominated the field as virtually the sole criterion for regulation writing. Its enthusiastic proponents managed all too often in the face of economic pressures to disregard the clear intent of Congress as expressed in the enabling legislation that undergirds those regulations.

This occurred in the case of brown lung disease.[6] The ailment was not recognized as an occupational hazard of the textile industry until the early 1960s, although byssinosis had been described in the early nineteenth century in England and later in 1845 in a study of two thousand cotton workers in Belgium. A Senate report noted the time lag, wondering in print why the disease was ignored "despite repeated warnings over the years from other countries that their cotton workers suffered from lung disease."[7]

For many years, the disease was ignored by the government, until it reached alarming proportions. Finally, in 1968, the secretary of labor began to address the problem by limiting the exposure to cotton dust. Well before that time, it was apparent that the government would need a special agency with sufficient power and flexibility to deal with the changing needs of cotton workers, whose deteriorating health proved the need for stiffer standards.

President Richard Nixon proposed such an agency in a successful effort to gain the reelection support of George Meany, president of the AFL-CIO. Congress created OSHA in 1970, when it passed the Occupational Safety and Health Act. Located in the Department of Labor, OSHA's mission was to ensure "so far as possible every working man and woman in the nation safe and health-ful working conditions.''[8] Of all laws governing the social regulatory agencies, the law creating OSHA included one of the broadest man-dates. Laboring under the false assumption that breadth meant strength, OSHA's leaders moved quickly into the area of work place pollution, naming cotton dust one of five health hazards. (The oth-ers were carbon monoxide, lead, asbestos, and silica.) But in typi-cally ambivalent fashion, Congress had hedged its bets by making the statute purposefully vague. After all, what is the meaning of the phrase ''so far as possible''?

Political Obstacles

Scarcely a year after OSHA opened its doors, its efforts to carry out its congressional mandate met with powerful resistance. Inevi-tably, it soon became clear that the agency's path would always be restricted by political constraints, and cotton dust was no exception.

Almost as soon as the cotton dust standards came under dis-cussion, the White House moved in, a pattern that prevailed through the Nixon, Carter, and Reagan administrations. Presidential inter-ference led to a delay of almost a decade, and showed that the textile manufacturers wielded more influence than did consumptive cotton workers.

In one of the first and most blatant interventions, OSHA ad-ministrator George Guenther sent a memo urging his GOP bosses in the White House to use the threat of a ''Democratic-imposed cotton-dust standard'' as a means of raising contributions for Pres-ident Nixon's reelection campaign.[9] His efforts were rewarded by a $1 million contribution to Nixon's reelection campaign by the textile industry, one-third of which came from Roger Milliken, president of Deering-Milliken.[10] Thus, Nixon had it both ways. He created the agency to win the support of labor, and used the agency to gain the support of industry.

Several years later, a bitter battle was fought among officials in the Carter administration. It was not as crass this time, but just as political, with White House economists clashing with OSHA head Eula Bingham. Dr. Bingham's professional background in public health, coupled with close ties to the labor unions, set her on a collision course with the President and his key advisers, who regarded the cotton dust standards as inflationary. These advisers prevailed temporarily and were even able to enlist the direct participation of the President, who attempted to modify the final rules to favor the textile industry. Carter's intervention in the cotton dust standards was the first time a President had so directly and overtly involved himself in the details of regulation writing, and it was also the last. The White House failed to predict the political reaction, which was unexpectedly intense and came primarily from the labor unions and the Nader-backed public interest groups. From that moment on, Carter was careful to cover his tracks when he intervened in a regulatory decision.[11]

Carter retreated from the cotton dust issue because much of his support came from the unions and the public interest groups. Galvanized earlier by the Guenther memo, these groups had coalesced around the cotton dust issue and, in fact, were using the controversy to help organize the southern textile industry.[12] Yet Carter also relied on the South for political support, and could not afford to alienate the cotton growers and textile manufacturers. This explained his initial tendency to side with his economic advisers at the Council on Wage and Price Stability (COWPS) and the Council of Economic Advisers (CEA), who argued that the engineering standards were too costly and the health benefits too low to justify the OSHA regulations. The economists preferred giving the textile industry more flexibility in reducing their workers' exposure to cotton dust. They favored regulations that proposed broad "performance standards" — such as curbing pollution — and letting industry decide how to address the problem rather than defining the specific actions to be taken.

The results would be the same, and the costs would be considerably less, they argued. Instead of forcing industry to install expensive engineering systems — the "command and control" variety of regulations favored by OSHA — companies would be allowed to formulate their own methods. The textile industry favored techniques requiring workers to wear respirators, combined with improved medical surveillance techniques, to reduce the exposure to cotton dust in the work place.

OSHA rejected the respirator idea as an alternative to cleaning up the air in the factories through engineering systems. The agency argued that respirators caused severe physical discomfort, as well as safety problems of their own. At earlier OSHA hearings, uncontested testimony revealed that because of the difficulties of fit, respirators interfered with "vision, hearing, and mobility," while employees already affected by byssinosis or other breathing difficulties were unable to wear respirators at all.[13] Where respirators were already in use, forcing workers to put them on was almost impossible, and enforcement mechanisms were useless. OSHA concluded that it was also unfair to put the "burden of compliance" on the workers, who were not responsible for the poor quality of their work environment.

A compromise was finally struck between OSHA and the White House, and the regulations went forward in 1978. Although OSHA won its battle to clean up the work place through engineering controls rather than masks for the workers, it was evident that the economists gained some ground as well. The final decision revealed that cost control was a big factor, along with the adoption of "variable exposure levels" (an unusual policy for OSHA), which eventually reduced the price tag to $200 million a year, a large saving over the original OSHA estimate of $700 million.[14] By this time, Carter administration officials backed OSHA publicly; but with their eye on the textile interests, they defended the standards somewhat apologetically. Their hands were tied, they said, because the law prevented the secretary of labor from relying on cost-benefit analysis.

Nobody was happy with the compromise. The textile industry still considered the standards too onerous, while the unions objected that they were too weak. Both groups took their objections to court. One year later, the United States Court of Appeals for the District of Columbia upheld the regulations by a vote of 3 to 0, with Chief Judge David L. Bazelon writing the opinion. Citing medical journals, government studies, and legislative testimony, Judge Bazelon offered an assessment of byssinosis that contradicted the estimates of White House economists and industry spokesmen on the seriousness of the disease. Byssinosis, he wrote, is "the most serious health hazard for cotton workers. . . . When byssinosis reaches its advanced stage, the worker exhibits the symptoms of emphysema and chronic bronchitis. Ultimately, irreversible lung damage results."[15]

While the case was pending before the Supreme Court, the Reagan administration took office. In fact, the Court heard the arguments on January 21, 1981, one day after the President was inaugurated. Unlike Carter, President Reagan entered office without political obligations to those labor unions, OSHA officials, and public interest groups committed to the cotton dust standards, and without any commitment at all to the Justice Department's defense. The time was ripe for another presidential roadblock in the path of the cotton dust rules. It came two months later, when the Reagan administration asked the Supreme Court not to review the case, but to send it back to the Department of Labor for reconsideration in light of the President's regulatory reform policy. In effect, the executive branch was asking the Court to withdraw its exercise of judicial review in favor of a presidential policy — cost-benefit analysis. The Reagan administration was heartened by a similar decision handed down the year before — in which the Supreme Court struck down OSHA's standards regulating the chemical benzene — and expected to reap the benefits of that precedent. In the benzene decision, the Court held that OSHA had not justified the new standards by showing that there was a significant health risk, nor had it demonstrated that the standards were feasible technologically as well as economically.[16]

To the surprise of many observers, the Court rejected Reagan's request, and without diverging theoretically from the benzene decision, presented a decision that was substantively very different. In contrast to the benzene regulations, said the Court, the secretary of labor had correctly determined that cotton dust presented a sufficiently "significant health hazard to employees" that would be "significantly reduced" by the regulations.[17] The Court also agreed with OSHA's interpretation of its legislative mandate, which allowed the agency to protect the public against such health risks "restricted only by technological and economic feasibility."[18]

The Feasibility Standard

The key was "feasibility," not cost-benefit analysis. A more flexible theory, the feasibility guideline combined the health needs of the workers with the legitimate economic needs of the industry; in fact, certain agency decisions reflected an early adherence to feasibility, or the art of the possible, in the area of cotton dust. The agency rejected the union's proposal for more stringent standards, for example, on the grounds that the proposal was not within the "technological capabilities of the industry."[19] At another point, the agency found that "engineering dust controls in weaving may not be feasible even with massive expenditures by the industry," and proceeded to adopt less stringent standards for that particular industry.

The concept of feasibility enabled the Court to reject industry's claims that OSHA failed to consider the ratio of costs and benefits in determining the standards. OSHA was under no obligation to consider this ratio, said the Court, while it was still feasible to reduce health risks. "Feasible" meant "capable of being done, executed or effected," held the Court, referring to three standard dictionaries to justify its interpretation of the statute.[20] Perhaps it is of some significance that neither the Court nor Congress ever attempted an extensive refinement of the term "feasible," its vagueness an almost deliberate sign of the importance of maintaining flexibility in its application. Interestingly, the industry never really argued that reducing the risks from cotton dust was not feasible, only that it was expensive. Indeed, in arguing for the cost-benefit test, the textile manufacturers expressed the fear that without such a criterion, there could result a "serious misallocation of the finite resources that are available for the protection of worker safety and health."[21]

How finite? To some extent, Congress and the courts agreed with the textile industry. The workers would not be protected if their employers were put out of business — a distinct possibility if the agency had demonstrated inflexibility in its regulatory practices. Where Congress and the courts both diverged from the White House in their interpretation of the feasibility standard was in their interpretation of degree; some businesses would suffer economically from the imposition of cotton dust standards, but that was to be the price of reducing risk. "Standards do not become infeasible simply because they may impose substantial costs on an industry . . . or even force some employers out of business," wrote Judge Bazelon. "Otherwise the act's commitment to protect workers might be forever frustrated."[22]

Industry shifted its own emphasis from arguing in terms of economic damage to debating the health and safety criteria that preoccupied OSHA and the courts. Minimizing the extent of the health risks, the industry claimed that fewer than 2 percent of its workers were victims of brown lung disease — a direct challenge to nonindustry studies that had shown that 25 percent of all workers involved in cotton textile production were affected. The Textile Institute argued that the industry already had spent an enormous amount of money — $130 million of its total $1.6 billion capital outlay — on safety and health, including measures to combat cotton dust.[23] Without balancing costs and benefits, there would be no end to this bottomless pit of expenditures, which could eventually threaten the existence of the industry without producing any visible benefit to the workers.

With each side offering contradictory data, the courts confronted an enormous scientific and legal challenge. The court of appeals took the position, later affirmed by the Supreme Court, that it was not its task to review and evaluate the data, but only to ensure that OSHA had followed its own procedures and had considered the best available evidence before issuing its own standards. But in reviewing the agency's record, the court, in effect, is evaluating the evidence itself before coming to the conclusion to reject industry's data challenging the consequences of exposure to cotton dust in favor of OSHA's judgment.

Ultimately, the feasibility standard resulted in a more humane calculus than the cost-benefit ratio, which often locks decision makers into the position of quantifying the impossible. The secretary of labor recognized this, said the Supreme Court, in "realizing that any meaningful balancing between costs and benefits involved placing a dollar value on human life and freedom from suffering."[24]

In the final analysis, the Court did not decide among competing theories of policy making, but among competing interpretations of the role of OSHA. To arrive at that determination, the Court took a closer look not only at the statute itself but also at its legislative history. The power of the Court is derivative, superseded by the intent and the laws of Congress. But because neither the intent nor the laws are crystal clear, the Court serves an important function in reconciling the actions of the executive branch with the policy directions set by Congress.

What was significant about the cotton dust decision in this light was not that the Court rejected cost-benefit analysis (it did not), but that it raised questions about the legitimacy of its application in all areas of regulation. "When Congress intended that an agency engage in cost-benefit analysis, it has clearly indicated such intent on the face of the statute," wrote Justice Brennan.[25] In the Flood Control Act of 1936, for example, Congress explicitly gave the federal government the power to improve the nation's waterways to prevent flooding on condition that "the benefits . . . are in excess of the estimated costs."[26] Later on, Congress specified the use of both the feasibility and cost-benefit tests in the Outer Continental Shelf Lands Act amendments of 1978, providing that offshore drilling operations utilize technologies that the secretary of the interior determines are "economically feasible" and cost efficient.

In both statutes, Congress accorded representatives of the federal government additional power, but power that was constrained by the ratio of costs and benefits. The implications of the Court's decision are both far-reaching and, to a certain extent, confusing. Does this mean that when Congress intended cost-benefit analysis to be used as a decision-making tool, it would have to be stated clearly in the statute or it would be prohibited?[27] Or would the prohibition also have to be clearly stated? What impact does this have on the executive orders of Presidents Carter and Reagan — neither of which has yet been put to a comprehensive judicial test — which superimposed cost-benefit analysis on agencies except where specifically prohibited?

In the case of OSHA, the answer was clear, at least to the Court. Tracing the legislative history of the act, the Court showed how far the new regulatory reformers had strayed from the original congressional mandate, as well as how important the decision was in putting them back on track. "The Congressional reports and debates certainly confirm that Congress meant 'feasible' and nothing else," said the decision, in unusually emphatic language. "Perhaps most telling is the absence of any indication whatsoever that Congress intended OSHA to conduct its own cost-benefit analysis before promulgating a toxic material or harmful physical agent standard."[28]

The legislative history also showed the commitment of the senators to weight the statute more heavily on the side of worker health and safety than on the side of the costs of improving the work environment. Senator Ralph Yarborough (Democrat, Texas), a cosponsor of the Occupational Safety and Health Act, dismissed the costs of cleaning up the work place as a cost of doing business, a political view more easily held in the less inflationary year of 1970.

"We know the costs would be put into consumer goods but that is the price we should pay for the eighty million workers in America," argued Yarborough, with a ringing denunciation of those who would place costs over other considerations.

One may well ask too expensive for whom? Is it too expensive for the company who, for lack of proper safety equipment, loses the services of its skilled employees? Is it too expensive for the employee who loses his hand or leg or eyesight? Is it too expensive for the widow trying to raise her children on meager allowance under workmen's compensation and social security? And what about the man — a good hardworking man — tied to a wheel chair or hospital bed for the rest of his life? That is what we are dealing with when we talk about industrial safety. . . . We are talking about people's lives, not the indifference of some cost accountants.[29]

Senator Thomas Eagleton (Democrat, Missouri) supported his colleague, adding his own version of the set of choices confronting the legislature: "Whether we, as individuals, are motivated by simple humanity or by simple economics, we can no longer permit profits to be dependent upon an unsafe or unhealthy work site."[30]

The Court also pointed out that when attempts were made to weaken the legislation by inserting language that would raise the value of the cost factor, those efforts failed. Fearing that the act could, "if literally applied, close every business in this nation,"

Senator Peter Dominick (Republican, Colorado) fought hard to amend the language to eliminate what he considered OSHA's impossible mandate. In the floor debate on the bill, Senator Dominick argued that it was "unrealistic to attempt . . . to establish a utopia free from any hazards. Absolute safety is an impossibility." The senator offered the example of a streetcar conductor who is exposed to air pollution throughout the course of his working life. "How in the world . . . can we set standards that will make sure he will not have any risk to his life for the rest of his life? It is totally impossible for this to be put in a bill."[31]

Senator Dominick's concerns were eventually addressed through the introduction of the feasibility test as a compromise. To some extent, this satisfied the senator, who worried that otherwise the statute would be misapplied to address "frivolous harms that exist in every work place."[32]

What is left unanswered by both the Court decision and the legislation is what would happen if the choices were harder, if they were presented in the form of their logical extremes? What if the cotton industry, for example, were so marginal that the imposition of the cotton dust standards would bring about its extinction? At what point, if any, is it worth sacrificing the health of a discrete percentage of the workers to preserve the economy of an industry? What if it were not "feasible" to protect the health of the worker and the health of the textile companies? What then? Who sacrifices: the worker or the industry?

Neither the feasibility nor the cost-benefit guidelines provide an answer to those questions, and the Court enjoyed the luxury of deciding the case with the comfortable assurance that "although some marginal employers may shut down rather than comply, the industry as a whole [would] not be threatened by the capital requirements of the regulation."[33] In that sense, perhaps even cost-benefit analysis — with the benefits properly quantified — would have led to a decision to uphold the cotton dust standards, especially when the health costs of not regulating became sufficiently apparent to establish their correct weight in the equation.

How Theory Drives Policy:
The Political Domination of Cost Factors

Cotton dust represented only one of many health and safety issues subject to the spurious standards of cost-benefit analysis, a theory whose flaws unfold as soon as they are held up to public scrutiny. For the vast majority of these issues, sadly, there is little likelihood of public debate; after all, cotton dust traveled all the way up to the Supreme Court before the attention of decision makers finally focused on the fallacies and biases of cost-benefit analysis as a dominant policy tool.[34]

Even so, the Supreme Court decision seems to have had little impact on the ongoing regulatory policy making of the legislative and executive branches, both of which continue to rely heavily on the cost-benefit calculus to deregulate the social environment. Congress, for example, has changed considerably from the heady days of the early 1970s when a favorable social and economic climate made it possible for progressive social goals to be written into law. Today, Congress's commitment to cost-benefit analysis is expressed in drafts of regulatory reform legislation, cosponsored by liberals and conservatives alike. By mandating a series of complicated steps that each agency must take before issuing any regulations — steps that require detailed and intensive cost-benefit analyses — the act's intended effect will be to discourage agencies from regulating.[35] Agency procedures are already sufficiently complicated; adding new procedural obstacles — all versions of cost-benefit requirements — will virtually guarantee a dignified burial for new regulatory policies. At this point, it is not merely analytical tasks that are responsible for delaying the regulations, but rather policy makers hiding behind a wall of unnecessary procedures.

Add to the congressional legitimization of cost-benefit analysis the clout of two Presidents — Carter and Reagan — and the theory's hegemony over the policy process becomes almost complete. The presence of cost-benefit analysis dominated the language of both Presidents' executive orders on regulatory reform, and the agencies quickly got the message.[36] To them, the orders signaled an era of minimal regulation, even when the law clearly stated oth-

124

erwise. And even when the courts ruled otherwise, executive power was felt. Within weeks after the Supreme Court handed down its decision on cotton dust, the Reagan administration's OSHA director, Thorne Auchter, ordered the withdrawal from circulation of two publications and a poster warning workers of the health hazards of cotton dust. His reason: they no longer represented agency policy.

The President and Congress reflected the political power of groups that brought cost-benefit analysis to the forefront of the policy process, once again affirming the axiom that those who dominate the formulation of an issue also dominate the end product. The groups that supported and promoted cost-benefit theory formed the critical mass, successfully compressing the issue of social regulation into an artificial set of restrictive guidelines. They were able to control a turbulent political environment, at least to the extent of constructing a scheme that looked neat, appeared to factor in all the options, and seemed neutral to the naked eye. Reducing policy to numbers made people feel comfortable; the process gave a sense of clarity to issues that had always defied easy definition.

By 1982, cost-benefit analysis was so much in vogue that hundreds of lawyers were paying $300 to $400 to attend workshops in the subject given by enterprising consulting firms, economics professors, and fellow attorneys with master's degrees in economics. In downtown Washington hotels and similar sites across the country, earnest devotees took careful notes, an investment in their own future of litigating within the confines of cost-benefit theory.

Despite rare challenges like the cotton dust case, current trends indicate the growing respectability of and public receptivity to cost-benefit analysis. This is largely due to the substantial political clout of its proponents, which far exceeds that of its critics, allowing its advantages to reach the public without anywhere near equal time for its disadvantages. Moreover, the sluggishness of the economy conveys an immediacy that renders short-term cost factors more acceptable and more urgent in the policy arena than long-term health and safety risks, and narrows the criteria for public intervention to the framework of cost-benefit analysis. In its application, the method has become even more circumscribed than when the public sector enjoyed the dividends of a buoyant economy.

Cost Analysis

Transposed to the public sector, cost-benefit analysis often turns out to be cost analysis, a simple accounting of the costs of doing business. This form of analysis goes back to the profit and loss ledgers of the private sector, where costs and profits are balanced out each year to determine the fiscal health — and sometimes survival — of a company. Products and services are easily added up in terms of production costs, and if a company cannot sustain a profit at the end of a given period, it quietly goes out of business. The benefit side of the equation, the firm's profits, are easily measurable, unlike the benefit side of public policy. In the private sector, a firm's obligations rest primarily with its own well-being, and only secondarily with society or the well-being of its employees.

That is the job of the public sector: to worry about what happens when the firm's efforts to maximize profits result in harm to society. It is clearly the government's responsibility, not the private sector's, to actively seek ways to put a stop to antisocial activities of that kind when they occur. The government is there to restrict the firm's freedom when the effects of doing business "spill over" into polluting the environment or creating hazards in the work place. In that context, the government quite legitimately puts its emphasis on the social costs of industrial practices in its efforts to regulate the private sector.

The problem is that on the government side, clear-cut profits (benefits) and losses (costs) are extremely difficult, if not impossible, to quantify. And so the calculations simply do not get done. Or they are done in a skewed fashion that justifies what the policy makers wanted to do in the first place, namely, deregulate social protections. At that point it becomes easier, as factors conducive to measurement become weighted more heavily than those that elude the calculator. Recent applications of cost-benefit analysis to the public sector reveal their private sector limitations: benefits are rarely factored fully or accurately into the equation, and costs are more often than not calculated for the short term, neglecting long-term productivity and health costs.

The best-known proponent of applying cost analysis to the

public sector is Murray Weidenbaum, former chairman of the Council of Economic Advisers (CEA), whose work on the costs of regulation formed the basis of President Reagan's reform program. While still a professor at Washington University in St. Louis, Weidenbaum and an associate published a widely quoted study citing the aggregate direct and indirect costs of government regulation.[37] According to Weidenbaum, the costs for the year 1979 alone totaled $103 billion, a projected calculation based on the data of previous years. Standing apart from other data and taken out of context, this calculation provided explosive ammunition for the opponents of regulation, who had been arguing all along that regulation was an expensive luxury. A closer look at Weidenbaum's tabulations revealed that his figures far exceeded the actual cost of regulation; more accurately, they reflected the aggregate costs of government. Weidenbaum arrived at his cost of regulation figures by adding up the budgets of certain regulatory agencies (both independent and executive branch); paperwork costs to business, which included filling out social security, IRS, and ERISA forms; the cost of import quotas; and the cost of regulation to the economy, using the rising Consumer Price Index as a key indicator. Weidenbaum also factored in productivity losses: time lost by employees who would otherwise be spending their time doing more "productive" work.

Weidenbaum's figures have been widely challenged, most substantively by Julius Allen, an economist with the Congressional Research Service. Allen questions whether agency budgets should be included in the category of regulatory costs, or should more accurately be labeled in the much broader context of the costs of government. He also notes the omission from the final figure of the *net* costs to society. In other words, what are the benefits to society produced by all this regulatory activity, and why are they not subtracted from the final figure?[38]

Even if the traditional health and safety benefits — so difficult to quantity — were dismissed from these calculations, there still remain significant benefits to the business community even from such onerous regulatory requirements as filling out government forms. In many areas, these forms help the statistics-gathering agencies of government to serve the business community with economic forecasts and other data that companies routinely utilize for their own future planning.[39]

Cost analysis eventually began to be passed off as cost-benefit analysis, creating the kind of near hysteria in the political arena most useful to those seeking to reduce regulatory burdens. Highly publicized and widely debated, cost analysis also convinced many that the excessive costs of regulation were illegitimate; and reducing them became the major objective. Whatever other factors appeared in the equation quickly became superfluous, and if they did not lend themselves to easy measurement on the cost side, they were eliminated.

Meanwhile, managers of some public agencies tried in vain to argue that profits and losses were inapplicable in their work; their "bottom line" is measured in terms of the effectiveness of the delivery of a service or the implementation of a program. All to no avail. Thus was a private sector methodology grafted onto public sector policy making. What was unmeasurable, or unprofitable, was accorded such low priority that its eventual disappearance was hardly noticed.

The Price of a Life: Measuring the Benefit Side

Pressed by the political forces that had welded regulatory tradeoffs to the cost-benefit abacus, government officials and scholars argued over how to quantify the benefit side of the equation. Their goals were also political: to shift the balance away from costs, and rivet public attention onto the benefits of regulation.

The method of choice also stretches credulity, namely, the claim that benefits can be quantified by placing a monetary value on human life. As applied to the regulatory process, putting a value on human life emphasizes both the monetary losses to society of not regulating, as well as the benefits of preserving life through a strong government presence. Taking their lead from negligence law, which decides rates of compensation for families of accident victims through this kind of calculation, theorists determined the value of a life by assessing the earning power of an individual, then adding up how much he would accrue in a lifetime. Known as discounted future earnings (DFE), this formula is useful in evaluating lost productivity, or the extent of economic loss to an individual's family in cases of accidental death.

On the level of the public policy, one of the more interesting government exercises in estimating the value of a life emerged in the wake of the Love Canal scandal, in a report quietly circulated by the New York State Health Department and innocuously titled "Organic Chemical Contamination of Drinking Water."[40] The study purported to formulate a regulatory strategy to deal with the problems of involuntary risk involved at Love Canal, where people were exposed to harmful chemicals against their will and without their full knowledge. The chemicals seeped into the ground water surrounding their homes, and over a period of time produced a high risk of cancer and birth defects. By selling the property around Love Canal to the local school board, the Hooker Chemical Company might have absolved itself of any responsibility to the victims of its pollution, passing the cost on to the state. If the state was going to spend money to make the area habitable (about $30 million at last count), it needed some idea of the economic value of reducing the probability of death. Most likely, the state also wanted to use these figures for political purposes, to justify the expenditures to a cost-conscious and skittish legislature.

Using the discounted future earnings computation, along with such factors as the cost of medical treatment, the study presented assorted figures for the price of a life that were very instructive. A middle-aged construction worker in Hempstead, Long Island, for example, was worth $550,000; a Buffalo schoolchild, $400,000; a Scarsdale stockbroker, $1 million; and a senior citizen from Brighton Beach, $60,000.[41]

Other government agencies on the federal level have also calculated the price of a life to convince Congress of the value of public programs. The Mine Safety and Health Administration has used a value of $165,000 per life, in measuring the benefits and costs of its Respirable Coal Dust in Mines regulation.[42] They reached this figure simply by computing the actual cost of compensating a victim of black lung disease; in other words, the money saved by preventing a case of black lung disease amounted to approximately $165,000.[43]

The Department of Transportation (DOT), the Federal Aviation Administration (FAA), and the National Highway Traffic Safety Administration (NHTSA) have all used this approach in evaluating the costs and benefits of accident prevention programs; since 1973, the FAA has used figures based on airline settlements of wrongful death suits.[44] The Center for Disease Control also utilizes this approach, but personalizes it less by relying on aggregate data. Looking at its program to eradicate measles, the center calculated that the benefits of federal intervention between 1966 and 1974 resulted in a savings of $1.2 billion, achieved at a cost of $108 million. The evaluation of benefits was arrived at by adding the figures for such factors as cases of measles avoided, premature deaths prevented, cases of mental retardation prevented, and physician days saved.[45]

Several of the problems of this artificial methodology are obvious. Putting a price tag on life, as Mark Green has pointed out, penalizes the poor, since their future earning capabilities are far lower than their counterparts in higher socioeconomic strata.[46] Similarly, older citizens find themselves at a distinct disadvantage, since the formula is based on their most economically productive years. The distributive consquences of applying this methodology to questions of public policy should also be evident: greater resources would be directed toward those from whom society could expect a greater return, at least as calculated in terms of their future contributions to the gross national product. Congress makes these choices every day in assigning implicit evaluations of this kind, noted the General Accounting Office, when the legislature "decides which programs to authorize and the level at which to fund them."[47]

The discounted future earnings method also discriminates on the basis of sex; with women still earning fifty-nine cents for every dollar earned by men, it stands to reason that young white males will remain the most highly valued members of society. Stephen Rhoads, who notes that figures based on this formula often "yield bizarre guideposts for policy," cites critics who ask if there "really are husbands and wives in their 30's who would want to pay twice as much to reduce the risk of death for the husband as for the wife, or if families would pay $60,000 to save a baby boy but only $35,000 to save a baby girl."[48]

The price-of-a-life methodology can occasionally be useful when regulators are clearly on a zero-risk mission, when it can be shown that the benefits of eliminating risk are so infinitesimal as to be meaningless. The steel industry, for example, estimated that it would cost $4,500,000 for every worker's life saved by installing controls on fumes exuded by coke ovens. OSHA's proposed regulations dealing with benzene were calculated at a potential cost of $300 million per death averted. "Spent this way, the total GNP would only save about 6,000 lives," noted sociologist Amitai Etzioni.[49]

Costs and Benefits as Competing Values

What the "price of a life" really fails to measure is the true value of human life, which cannot be calculated in quantitative terms. It eliminates all philosophical or normative discussions from the policy arena, dismissing them as rhetoric and becoming blind to such issues as human rights. "It's like the doctors in the movie *Coma,* who killed healthy people to use their organs to save other people, and defended themselves by saying, 'We saved two people for every one we killed,' " argued Stephen Kelman.[50]

In evaluating government exercises in this form of quantification, even the General Accounting Office concluded that "the true value of human life or the true psychic costs of injuries or illness cannot be calculated. In short, life-saving activities cannot be compared with the attainment of other goals such as reducing travel time or costs of production. . . . Clearly, any economic calculation of the value of a human life is incapable of correctly encompassing all the psychic costs of death, illness, and suffering."[51]

At a more subtle level of public policy, the debate moves from merely hard choices to making "tragic choices" when society asks how much of its limited resources it can expend to save lives or reduce risks.[52] Proponents of life-saving programs can make their case publicly; after all, who can argue rationally against their goals? But quietly, and less publicly, murmurings can be heard questioning the expenditure of keeping kidney patients, as one example, on dialysis at a cost of over $30,000 per year. Rhoads argues that debate ought not to occur on that level, because it individualizes the choices and distorts public policy. "It is demoralizing when society collectively and publicly places a value on life. It is especially so when a decision is made not to save an identifiable individual. Thus, we spend far more on rescue missions and kidney dialysis patients than on life-preserving preventive programs."[53]

The reduction of risk also leads to individual decision making, produced by the harsh choices of the regulatory environment. Several years ago, four women of childbearing age working at the American Cyanamid plant in Willow Island, West Virginia, "voluntarily" underwent sterilization in order to keep their jobs in the lead pigment department of the company. Company managers had led them to believe, the women alleged, that they would be forced to leave their jobs and take lower-paying jobs to avoid being exposed to toxic substances recently identified as harmful to embryos. With considerable justification, the company feared possible litigation at a future time from either the women themselves or from children who might have been born with birth defects directly attributable to hazardous chemicals. (OSHA had already identified twenty-four toxic substances as harmful to fetuses.) The company also regarded this form of protective exclusion — in this case the protection of the unconceived fetus, not the reproductive capacity of the women — as a legitimate exercise of personnel policy.

The incident uncovered a myriad of regulatory choices that increased the confusion surrounding the clash among values, science, and public policy. At this point, the government stepped in, acting on complaints from the employees' union. The agencies involved individually took up the cause, each reflecting its own mission. The Equal Employment Opportunity Commission (EEOC) and the Office of Federal Contract Compliance Programs (OFCCP) regarded protective exclusion as discriminatory and a violation of the civil rights of employees. Civil rights groups backed them up, arguing that the policy was paternalistic and yet another excuse to discriminate. "What are the risks to the reproductive capacities of the male workers?" they asked. OSHA, on the other hand, argued for the protection of the unborn and the workers from the hazards of toxic chemicals.[54] Neither the agencies nor the involved industries were able to accurately determine the extent of the risks, or their costs and benefits. OSHA estimated that twenty million jobs involved exposure to chemicals that could cause reproductive damage, but there were few data indicating the number of people removed from their jobs for this reason, or the precise location of these hazards.

Ultimately, the issue defied solution. The competing costs, risks, and benefits were reduced to competing values, namely, health, safety, productivity, and equal employment. These values all represent the views of different groups of people, each of whom argues that their benefits should take precedence in the regulatory scheme. The women's groups supporting the workers at Willow Island argued that industry should bear the burden of proving with reputable scientific evidence which jobs involve hazards and which do not, and then give employees the right to decide which risks to take. Industry argued that this open-ended freedom of choice left the company vulnerable to unfavorable public opinion, as well as to unlimited litigation.

In the competition among values in this case, an important group will invariably be excluded: the unborn. Who will protect unborn children from economic and physical damage if the workers choose higher-paying jobs over safety? Even if an employee waives her employer's liability, she cannot speak for her unborn children, who are being put in a position of inadvertent risk.[55] She cannot waive their future legal rights and guarantee that they will not bring damage suits against the company, nor can she answer to them for whatever deformities they must bear for a lifetime as a result of her early "freedom" of choice.

Cost-Benefit for Whom?

In the debate over regulatory choices, the political protagonists complained vociferously that since benefits could not be measured accurately, they should be downgraded in the policy equation. Since evidence of benefits is needed to justify costs, it is easy to see how the cost advocates quickly prevailed over fellow policy analysts in scaling down the regulatory process.

But before benefits can be measured, they must be identified — a task that has been shunted aside with the same alacrity as their measurement. The genuine identification of benefits moves closer to the crux of the political problem: the struggle over what funds are expended and for whom.

The most common pattern, when benefits cannot be easily measured, is to discard or to trivalize them. "How do you put a value on the view over the Grand Canyon?" asked vice presidential aide Boyden Gray when queried about the methodology in which his administration had vested so much of its resources. Obviously, it cannot be done, but, at the same time, the answer masks the real issues. On the surface, it is easy to agree that it is not really worth the expenditure of billions of dollars to preserve the view over the Grand Canyon for the benefit of the tourists and their visual pleasure. Putting the question another way, however, lends a less frivolous cast to the issue. What is it worth to maintain air purity in the Southwest? After all, the air mass over the Grand Canyon does not stop at the boundaries of that giant crevice; it moves with the wind currents, and affects vast numbers of people, most of whom are not out enjoying their holidays.

Benefits like the view over the Grand Canyon elude cost-benefit analysis even when they are not trivialized by decision makers like Boyden Gray. These benefits elude measurement because they are often indivisible: if one person benefits, all benefit. How can one measure benefits like clean air and water, good health, a minimum of pain, economic stability, preservation of the wilderness, police protection, and national defense? Known as "public goods," these benefits are also nonpurchasable, and since they cannot be bought, no single group can enjoy their special protection.[56] The question of providing these benefits brings the issue back to government, because no other body has the resources to protect the public, nor the mission. At the same time, the diffuseness of these benefits leaves them without powerful defenders, a political problem that recurs continually in the regulatory arena.

Recognizing the political importance of presenting benefits in quantitative form, several researchers have pursued this line of inquiry. According to a study prepared by Nicholas A. Ashford of the Massachusetts Institute of Technology for the Senate Governmental Affairs Committee, "the American people save billions of dollars each year as a direct result of federal regulation in the areas of health, safety and environment."[57] Ashford remains one of the few economists in the country known for his research in the area of quantifying benefits. Some of his examples included:

- Crib safety standards, which have reduced infant injuries by 44 percent since 1974.

- Flammable sleepwear standards, which reduced by 20 percent the frequency of serious burns and burn deaths to children.

- Automobile safety controls, which have saved over twenty-eight thousand lives over an eight-year period, and seat belts, which have reduced injuries by 34 percent and deaths by 20 percent.

- OSHA rules on work place safety, which have prevented sixty thousand lost workdays due to accidents and 350 deaths over a two-year period, and reduced the cost to society ($15 billion per year) of industrial accidents.

- Air pollution standards, whose benefits were tallied at from $5 to $58 billion per year.

- Water pollution rules, which resulted in a $9 billion gain due to increased recreational use.

The tendency to downgrade benefits also leads to the question of cost-benefit for whom? Who are the true beneficiaries of public policy in the unbalanced cost-benefit equation? The polluters are the definite victors in the battle to dismantle EPA: they have increased their short-term profits and decreased their capital expenditures for antipollution equipment. The strip miners in Appalachia have emerged the winners in the recent "reorganization" of the Office of Surface Mining, a bureau now less inclined to enforce federal legislation preventing the gutting of the land. And if the courts had not stepped in, the textile industry would have been counted among the victors in the battle over their notion of benefits, namely, profits versus the health of their employees.

For the same reasons, namely the lack of protectors, there are many pieces of legislation that would never have seen the light of day if put to the cost-benefit test, simply because the debate would have assumed the shape of balancing apples and oranges. An appropriately slanted cost-benefit analysis of the Endangered Species Act, for example, could jettison regulatory activity under that act, especially in view of the act's potential for balancing people against species of animals. Enforcing the act less vigorously in order to permit the construction of oil pipelines, for example, might ensure considerable benefits to energy consumers, a goal that might outweigh the costs of eliminating an endangered species. Can quantitative costs be assigned to preserving polar bears, then balanced against the value of oil exploration on the North Slope of Alaska? Are the polar bears equal to the potential benefits of cheaper energy and the reduction of United States dependence on foreign oil? The task is impossible. It is also useless and unproductive, because the choices are value choices and ought to be recognized for what they are — well outside the realm of any balance between costs and benefits.

The difficulties in debating these values in the political arena paved the way for the dominance of the cost side: costs were easier to comprehend and easier to justify. "The fact that they are simple and quantitative gives them the appearance of objectivity," said the *American Journal of Public Health.* "Cost-benefit analysis is an evaluation tool that may bias political decisions."[58]

In skewing the balance, the real issue, as well as the real beneficiaries, is masked. The textile manufacturers knew that if OSHA were forced to justify its expenditures on a cost-benefit ratio, the scales would tip in their favor. They could quantify the costs of cleaning up the factories, but they could bank on the fact that the difficulty in measuring lung damage would guarantee that it would not be done. In this case, the beneficiaries — albeit short-term — would be the textile manufacturers, whose executives' offices were far removed from the lethal sectors of the work place.

In one of its more enlightened periods, Congress recognized this political conundrum, along with the fallacies of cost-benefit analysis as a policy tool. With specific recognition of its inadequacies in providing equal weight to benefits, Congress prohibited the calculation of costs in certain pieces of legislation. In addition to the act creating OSHA, Congress also required "unbalanced" decisions in the Clean Air and Clean Water acts, as well as in the Delaney amendment, which forces the Food and Drug Administration to eliminate from the marketplace all additives in food that cause cancer in laboratory animals, regardless of their effect on humans. In that way, Congress also protected the agencies from succumbing to the familiar pattern of the "captive agencies," those too closely tied to the industries they were responsible for regulating. Implicitly, Congress was also recognizing the different time horizons distinguishing the public and private sectors, with government more willing to build in protections for future generations, in contrast to the short-term planning more characteristic of the private sector. Applauding the cotton dust decision, AFL-CIO representative Sheldon Samuels noted: "This decision means OSHA can't decide how many people can get sick or die in order to save a particular business or plant."[59]

Rebuilding the Equation

In lieu of costs and benefits, there are other questions that are rarely asked by the current practitioners of regulatory policy. Judge David Bazelon, whose decisions have consistently stood well ahead of his time, addressed some of them. "The efficiency label," he wrote, "may frequently mask special benefits for special interests. The real questions should be more qualitative ones. Who will be affected? In what ways? On what bases are these predictions made?"[60]

Invariably, those who ask the questions get first crack at making the choices. With cost-benefit analysis the marketplace essentially makes the regulatory choices, since it is their needs that are addressed and given priority, and their data that form the basis for decisions. Time after time, the marketplace has exaggerated the costs and minimized the risks, even though both categories often fall in the realm of the unknown. In the cotton dust case, industry argued that brown lung disease was reversible, that it affected an infinitesimal percentage of the workers, and that controlling it would place an unfair burden upon their companies. It took two outside consulting firms, employed by OSHA, as well as the separate evaluation of that evidence by two levels of federal courts to reject industry's contention.

Not every regulatory decision gets the benefit of that kind of scrutiny; more often, industry data are the only game in town, and heavy reliance is placed upon their findings. Even when the data are essentially correct, the interpretation of them can distort the conclusions. Chrysler makes a good case against the burdens of regulation, for example, that is shared by the other major auto companies, namely, that energy regulation, safety rules, and environmental standards have made them less competitive than Japanese auto makers.[61] Omitted from that argument is the fact that the Japanese companies are subject to the same regulations if their cars are to be sold on the American market; they must install the same catalytic converters, safety belts, and other devices mandated by the government as the American companies. Also omitted are other key factors — such as management and investment strategies — that enabled the Japanese to pull ahead of their American competitors while adhering to similar regulatory ground rules.

Not only are there gaps in the available data, but there are vast realms in which the data needed for intelligent regulatory decisions simply do not exist. Cutting the EPA research budget in half, as President Reagan has done, will merely exacerbate the problem of the data gap, although it will ensure less regulation, because the agency cannot regulate without research. Meanwhile, over sixty thousand chemicals have now been identified, with an additional one thousand discovered each year. Few of these have been adequately researched — their effects often unknown until years later. Yet the public risks their release into the environment with uneven protection from the public sector. The effects of the synthetic hormone DES (diethylstilbestrol), given to pregnant women to prevent miscarriage, were not known until twenty years after their prescription; the drug failed to prevent miscarriages, but has since been related to cancer in the offspring of those who unwittingly took the drug. In this case, the drug companies did not know the effects, since no benefit or risk data were available.

The tendency to ignore the unknown in the cost-benefit calculus shifts many of these regulatory decisions to the courts, where the limits of the law parallel those of science. "The role of the court," said Judge Bazelon in an interview, "is to ensure that proper procedures have been followed and that the agencies utilize the best available data before issuing regulations.

"Agencies should announce in words of one syllable what they've done, and why they're doing it," he continued. "The problem is that there are deep uncertainties. In Vermont Yankee [a case involving nuclear waste], the Nuclear Regulatory Commission gave us only in-house experts. They said in one hundred years we'll have the answer. I said their procedures were inadequate. There was no cross-examination, for example. I was reversed. There weren't enough smart people around in 1973 to know disposal would be a problem. The record was inadequate because there were inadequate opinions."[62]

Facing the unknown also leads the more extreme among the free market advocates to argue for less regulation on the grounds that liability laws will protect the public from irresponsible corporate behavior. Given the condition of uncertainty surrounding this body of law, their assessment is unfair from the public's point of view as well as the private sector's. "Such uncertainty makes a finding of negligence liability unlikely, inappropriate, and therefore ineffective in protecting society from these dangers," argued Judge Bazelon.[63]

For liability laws to have some effect, blame must be attached to an individual or to a company. Very often, it is impossible to trace a pollutant to its source; more often, its effects may not be felt for years. Even if the source can be determined and blame properly affixed, the company may long since have gone out of business and be unable to pay damages. In addition, a company may also have fully protected itself from subsequent legal damages, as did the Hooker Chemical Company when it turned over the Love Canal property to the local school board, which was duly warned of the health hazards. Witness also the decision by the Johns-Manville Corporation, the nation's largest asbestos producer, to file for bankruptcy protection to avoid fifty-two thousand asbestos-related damage suits.

Who pays for the consequences of these acts? In the case of Love Canal, the government of New York State, aided by the federal coffers, paid the damages for the private sector. In the case of the asbestos manufacturers, the jury is still out, but discussions among members of Congress involving the creation of worker compensation funds indicate that the government once again will probably step in to pick up the tab.

To be fair, companies may innocently produce products whose toxicity may be uncovered at a much later date. If they remove these products from the market immediately after their hazards are revealed, as Proctor and Gamble did following reports linking the Rely tampon to toxic shock syndrome, should the company then be liable for damages in the thousands of legal suits that now plague them? No one really knows the answer, but recent evidence shows that juries are more sympathetic to the plaintiffs, spelling potential financial disaster for many manufacturers.

What of the less responsible companies — the fly-by-night operations polluting the air and water — who are as elusive to prosecutors as the chemicals they leave for society to clean up? The midnight dumpers, who leave toxic wastes in dump sites of their own choosing, are as difficult to apprehend as they are to identify. How do liability laws protect the public against them? Once again, the government ends up paying for the cleanup, but should this be included as a cost of regulation? Any cost analysis would show that careful regulation and enforcement at an early stage are much cheaper than cleanup costs later on. Not to mention the health costs, which are rarely factored into the equation.

In the final analysis, the dominance of cost-benefit analysis over regulatory policy shunts aside the management of risk and negates the government's role in managing risk. Although we cannot achieve a risk-free society, government is the only agent with the capacity to protect the public against untoward risk, and it remains the only agent whose purpose is to protect the public. Industry cannot be trusted to make these determinations, and should not be accorded the legitimacy to make those decisions. The task of a firm is to make profits, not public policy, and there is no justification to fault its social consciousness if it neglects to weigh considerations other than self-promotion. It is up to the regulatory system, with guidance from Congress, to make policy decisions and to provide the constraints necessary to preserve the public's interests.

Moreover, the political system, unlike the private sector, makes its policy in the open; its deliberations are guaranteed by law to be open to public debate and to public view. Though often flawed, its policies are also open to change, when change is warranted.

Although cost-benefit analysis can be useful in determining the most cost-effective alternative among competing regulatory devices, it should be laid to rest as a dominant policy tool — as inadequate, inequitable, and subject to excessive political distortion in its application. In the private sector, it has led to discussions and decisions of chilling proportions, such as the decision to market the Pinto, which weighed profits against safety in designing an automobile.

Regarded as irresponsible in the private sector, this kind of decision making has no place in the public sector; indeed, it is surprising that it has achieved the level of respectability it enjoys today. Ultimately, it omits the human factor, with unfortunate results for those who count on government protection. After all, testified a victim of industrial lung disease, "Dying is a tough way to make a living."

5

High Noon at the FTC
Mixed Mandates from the U.S. Congress

If you think the women's libbers are a problem, wait until you get the mothers of America on your back. This is where we are getting the static. . . . We are rather literally besieged . . .
The committee always receives inquiries in the form of flak. Almost universally, it is in reference to television advertising and its impact on children. What has the commission been doing in this area?
— Former Senator Gale McGee (Democrat, Wyoming), berating the FTC chairman in 1974

The FTC is a king-sized cancer on our economy.
— Rep. Bill Frenzel (Republican, Minnesota), six years later

ON A WARM, SUNNY MORNING in May 1980, Michael Pertschuk stepped out of his Cleveland Park home in suburban Washington and into his chauffeur-driven car for the twenty-minute ride to his office, just off Capitol Hill, where he served as chairman of the Federal Trade Commission (FTC). When he arrived, the agency was closed. It had been shut down by Congress for the first time in its sixty-six-year history.

Congress had used the power of the purse to withhold funds from an agency whose prickly personality and combative stance had led to its virtual political isolation. The attorney general had ruled that in the absence of a congressional appropriation, the agency could work only to shut itself down. Employees packed up their offices, court appearances, hearings, and meetings were canceled, and agency officials returned from trips.

"The administrative and clerical people were scared to death," Pertschuk recalled, "but we knew it was just a charade. To the outside world this appeared to be a low point for the commission, but President Carter had assured us that we would survive." For the agency's top echelon, "there was a kind of subdued hilarity about it, which was not at all what we conveyed to the outside world."

Pertschuk was wrong. Despite his whistling-past-the-graveyard approach, the temporary closing of the agency indicated that, at the very least, it enjoyed less than robust health. The shutdown was hardly a surprise. Many of the agency's seventeen hundred employees had started revising their résumés two months earlier, when a deadlock in the House-Senate conference committee indicated that Congress planned to vent its hostility toward the agency's consumer protection activities. By the time Congress finally granted the FTC a new three-year authorization, it had added a legislative veto to ensure continuing surveillance over the wayward agency. Congress reserved the right to countermand all FTC regulations. "We are seeing an end to government by bureaucratic fiat," asserted Rep. Elliot Levitas, Democrat of Georgia, sponsor of the congressional veto.

But Rep. Bob Eckhardt, Democrat of Texas, warned, "What we are doing in this legislation today is commencing a plucking of the powers of the only agency that we can call a consumer agency in the entire U.S. government."

Thus was the issue framed. Was the FTC a case of bureaucracy run wild? Or was it a government agency trying to come to grips with the excesses of increasingly powerful corporate interests? Only six years earlier, Congress had vested broad powers in the FTC. Was resistance to those powers an indication that they had been abused? Or was it an indication of a new political climate, in which jurisdictional skirmishes reflect underlying changes in political clout?

High Noon at the FTC

One man's arrogance is another man's unswerving devotion to duty. The FTC derived its powers from Congress, granted at a time of mounting public concern over rampant corporatism. Now those powers were being scaled back. The two-day closing of the FTC followed a six-month battle in Congress, spurred by a campaign orchestrated by the corporate lobbies. When the dust settled and the FTC reopened, the agency had been effectively restrained. It had been pulled off major investigations, and was too frightened to initiate others. The coup de grâce was delivered in the form of a two-house legislative veto, which was a provision of the 1980 appropriations bill and made the FTC a virtual hostage of Congress. In effect, Congress had repealed more than half a century of its own legislation, laws that clearly spelled out the agency's mandate. Without changing those laws, Congress was able to dismantle the agency — a feat of legislative strategy that fooled only the public.

Ironically, Pertschuk got into trouble for taking the FTC's mandate too literally, and for the openness with which he campaigned on the agency's behalf. The FTC's original legislative mandate was first articulated when President Woodrow Wilson convinced Congress in 1914 to create a federal agency to safeguard the free enterprise system as well as to ensure fair treatment for the public.[1] Initially intended as the government's trustbuster, the FTC's authority was expanded with the passage that same year of the Clayton Act, which prohibited any business activities that led to decreased competition or the creation of monopolies. During that early period, the agency's consumer function was subordinate to its antitrust activities, a pattern that continued until the early 1970s. Despite this apparent duality of function, in the minds of many industrialists the two were inextricably entwined into an agency potentially hostile to business interests, a factor that only served to increase the FTC's political problems. During the attacks over the FTC's role in children's television advertising, for example, many wondered about the extent to which the cereal companies' involvement was connected to a pending antitrust action against them.

Congress strengthened the FTC's consumer role in 1938 with the passage of the Wheeler-Lea amendment to the original FTC act. By prohibiting "unfair or deceptive" business acts and practices, the amendment allowed the FTC to act against businesses without first having to prove the existence of anticompetitive behavior. Successive legislation upheld by the courts expanded the agency's investigative and enforcement powers in a variety of consumer areas, among them:

- protecting the public from false and deceptive advertising, particularly in the areas of drugs, food, cosmetics, and therapeutic devices;

- requiring that labels on fur and textile products be accurate; and

- regulating the packaging and labeling of consumer products to prevent deception.[2]

Despite its arsenal of legislative weapons, the FTC did not begin to take its consumer function seriously until 1964, when the agency launched a campaign to regulate cigarette advertising on an industrywide basis. Pre-empted by the tobacco lobby from rule making on its own, the FTC's activities nonetheless generated legislation banning cigarette advertising on electronic media, and started the agency on its long-overdue awakening in the area of meaningful consumer protection. Previously, the FTC had relied on case-by-case investigations, as well as on voluntary compliance from the business community. This obviously was not working, and under the chairmanship of Caspar Weinberger the agency started to revise its image and began to adopt an activist consumer role. Although staff members had argued for years that the agency had industrywide rule-making powers, it became clear from their experience with the cigarette manufacturers that added legislation was needed to legitimize these powers if they were to be effective.

The Magnuson-Moss Act of 1974 addressed this need, giving the FTC its first major rule-making power.[3] Instead of singling out businesses on a case-by-case basis, the FTC now had the power to make rules for an entire industry, in order to correct what it determined were unfair and deceptive trade practices. Ironically, the act was passed after considerable pressure from some segments of the business community, which felt that the FTC's actions against individual businesses were anticompetitive. Looking forward to regulatory relief, these advocates neglected to consider the consequences of another provision of the Magnuson-Moss Act: the "unfairness doctrine." This sweeping new mandate allowed the agency to issue rules industrywide to correct unfair and deceptive practices, rules that carried the force of law. Prior to the promulgation of any new rule, affected parties were entitled to due process hearings and cross-examination.

The Magnuson-Moss Act gave the FTC an arsenal of new legal resources, hailed at the time as a great victory for the consumer movement. But in the aftermath, its proponents in Congress contributed little else, putting the agency in a politically untenable position, which became abundantly clear less than three years later.

Getting "Pertschuked"

"You can always depend on Congress to overreact," advised Senator Dale Bumpers, Democrat of Arkansas and a former governor who has taken an active role in the area of regulatory reform. A sea change in the public's attitude toward regulation — from the idea that regulation was a necessary public tool in a complex industrial society to the view that regulation imposes unnecessarily costly and inflationary burdens upon businesses and consumers — explains in part why "deregulation" has become the war cry both in the White House and on Capitol Hill. Another factor was the increase in the number of interest groups and Political Action Committees (PACs), whose power expanded dramatically during this period.

The FTC was a target of both choice and opportunity. It was visible, aggressive, and increasingly isolated. But one must wonder how Pertschuk, a fifteen-year veteran of Capitol Hill, was so effectively outgunned and outmaneuvered. How did it all happen so quickly?

"We exceeded our implicit mandate not to challenge power," said Pertschuk, a witty and unassuming man of fifty-one, with a shock of unruly hair and a shy smile. His rumpled look and Mr. Chips manner belie his tremendous drive and commitment, which led him to take a small, sleepy agency known as the "Little Old

147

Lady of Pennsylvania Avenue'' and turn it, at least temporarily, into a vigorous protector of consumer interests. Under Pertschuk, the FTC attacked on many fronts — the broadcasters, insurance industry, morticians, citrus growers — which then united in a nearly successful attempt to destroy the agency itself.

"Wendell Ford [Democrat, Kentucky] told us," continued Pertschuk, that "if you had wanted to alienate every prominent citizen in every major town, you couldn't have done a better job — insurance salesmen, funeral directors, doctors, dentists, used car dealers — if the commission had chosen to get everybody up in arms, it did exactly the right thing.''

Although many of the FTC's most controversial initiatives preceded his 1977 appointment, Pertschuk adopted them so enthusiastically that he was soon identified with all of them. This perception was not entirely inaccurate: as staff director and chief counsel for the Senate Commerce Committee for twelve years prior to his chairmanship, Pertschuk had nurtured and drafted virtually all of the major consumer legislation, including the Magnuson-Moss Act. His power as a Senate staff member was so extensive that he was sometimes called the 101st senator.

As a key Commerce Committee aide in the heyday of the consumer movement, Pertschuk quickly developed a reputation for being antibusiness, which he later took considerable pains to erase by maintaining that "proconsumer" did not have to mean "antibusiness.'' Yet his relationship with business had deep adversarial roots, which he found difficult to overcome. Pertschuk recalled a telephone call in 1970 from a former senator and majority whip, Earl Clements (then a lobbyist for the Tobacco Institute), rebuking him for a press release attacking the tobacco industry. The release went out under Senator Frank Moss's name, but the cognoscenti recognized Pertschuk's imprint. "You know, Pertschuk, when you're on the side of the angels," said Clements, "it's easier to stretch the truth.''[4]

Clements's phone call meant a lot of things to Pertschuk. It was both a tribute to his power and a rebuke for his self-righteous rhetoric portraying the tobacco industry as "the forces of greed to be bridled.'' It was also a reminder of the days when the tobacco industry, like many industries, found itself holding the line against public interest advocates.

148

Clements's phone call also highlighted the tension within Pertschuk, an inner conflict that separates him from his more plastic counterparts in Washington political life. The humanistic side of him enjoyed the teasing friendship with Clements, which he described as the "comfort of a relationship with a courtly and still powerful figure." That Pertschuk could maintain such a friendship is a tribute to his wit and sense of humor. At the same time, the social activist in him recognized the dangers of that kind of Washington friendship, which is part of a "fabric of artful ingratiation . . . which . . . gradually displaced my early outrage at the marketing of a product which kills three hundred thousand people prematurely each year."[5] Thus does Washington's social life homogenize ideologues, and blunt the cutting edge of indignation.

Ever a bellwether, Clements called Pertschuk four years later on behalf of the new senator from Kentucky, Wendell Ford, who had just defeated an outspoken advocate of the tobacco industry, Marlow Cook. "You will like Wendell Ford," said Clements. "He led the fight for consumer protection in Kentucky, and he'd like to be a member of the Commerce Committee."[6]

Skeptical of Clements's bona fides on behalf of consumer activism, Pertschuk quietly shelved the idea and told Clements there was no vacancy on the committee. Considering the possibility of the committee membership remote, he never even raised the issue with his boss, Senator Warren Magnuson, chairman of the committee. Pertschuk's power was such that he felt free to veto a key lobbyist's recommendation without even consulting his senator. A week later, Pertschuk was jolted to find the Senate Steering Committee had assigned Wendell Ford to the Senate Commerce Committee. In a twist of fate, Ford eventually rose to chair the Consumer Subcommittee of the Commerce Committee and negotiate the undoing of the FTC. The 101st senator had gone into an eclipse.

Another prophetic incident occurred during a speech Pertschuk gave a few years later to an audience of chief executive officers, convened in Washington to discuss the policy implications of corporate conglomeration. With his usual self-effacing style, Pertschuk ruefully conceded he had the "poor tact and lapsed tactical sense to deliver a warmed-over lecture prepared earlier for an academic audience at Berkeley." The speech challenged in "bellicose rhetoric" the excessive concentrations of political power engendered by the increase in corporate acquisitions, and was less than a rousing success before this group of hard-nosed CEOs.

"Power," cried one of the participants. "We don't have any power. Jane Fonda has power. Why don't you go after Jane Fonda?" As Pertschuk thought about his answer, he heard a member of the audience murmur, in a stage whisper, the prophetic words: "We're going to get you next year."[7]

Although hailed by consumer groups and endorsed by an enthusiastic President Carter, Pertschuk's appointment in 1977 was not universally applauded. One trade magazine reported that "early marketing reaction to Pertschuk's appointment was that he was the best of two unpleasant choices — the other was rumored to have been former New York Congresswoman Bella Abzug." Their reason? "Pertschuk, after all, had worked closely with Ralph Nader since taking the congressional job in 1966."[8]

Aware of these mixed reactions, Pertschuk nevertheless set out to make the FTC into what critics and friends alike have called the "best public interest law firm in Washington." With a characteristic zeal, he traveled the country, talking openly about his views of the FTC as a "cop on the beat of competition — the silver bullet of deregulation." At an FTC hearing in 1977, Pertschuk told his audience: "We've got to police virtually the whole economy."[9]

Sending chills down the spines of those he was empowered to regulate, Pertschuk used language highly reminiscent of the 1960s to warn the public of the abuses of power by the corporate sector. "In our economy, companies possess great power that can be expressed in many ways," he told the *Philadelphia Inquirer*. "Sometimes they express it through monopoly, but also, more recently, through the abuse of the media. Our role, as I see it, is to redistribute power to the people."[10] This was a revolutionary-sounding goal for a public man appointed by a politically moderate Democratic President. Indeed, an official of Formica called him a "complete socialist" and "one of the most dangerous men in America."[11]

Unlike the lobbyists who work behind closed doors, Pertschuk played his hand openly, with daring and style. To the media, he was David fighting Goliath; to the Goliaths of the Business Roundtable and their allies in hundreds of groups and trade associations, Pertschuk was eventually turned to good advantage — becoming a

vivid symbol against which they could easily unite. Pertschuk rel-
ished his role, at times surprising himself that he could create so
much trouble on such a small budget. He reminded audiences that
the FTC's paltry $73 million budget could run the mammoth De-
partment of Health and Human Services or the Pentagon for only
fifteen minutes.

Pertschuk's demeanor was said to have exacerbated the problem. He was accused of arrogance, and even his allies admitted the
dangers of his style. Senator Bob Packwood (Republican, Oregon),
who more than once rescued the FTC from its congressional attack-
ers, regretted Pertschuk's approach and the effect it had on setting
the tone for his subordinates. "You can do more damage to your
cause by lack of manners than lack of substance," warned Packwood. "Apparently, Mike early on . . . then others from the commission, were very, very obnoxious in their testimony. Insulting.
The arrogance of the FTC was what bothered Congress." Pertschuk's defenders argued that Pertschuk was not really arrogant,
that he was knowledgeable, occasionally flip, and always superbly
well prepared, which people seemed to resent the most. One
congressional staff member described Pertschuk as "thoughtful,
thinking about more than the amendment of the moment, . . .
[thinking] about what's down the road in terms of impact.

"People are intimidated by his knowledgeability; they feel as
if he's putting them down. . . . He was always well informed.
And if he wasn't, he didn't say anything. And he nailed everybody
that came near him.

"I know that when the funeral rule, the mobile home rule, and
a couple of other things came up . . . people pursued their boss's
interests and those particular rules with vigor just because Pertschuk was there. No other reason."

Under Pertschuk, the once obscure job of FTC chairman became a national dart board, with Senator Hollings warning Pertschuk that "it was a good thing they passed the antilynching laws
before Pertschuk." Hollings had recently returned from a trip back
home to South Carolina, where informal polls taken among his constituents revealed that after inflation, the FTC was next on the list
of the most serious national problems. Like Hollings, no other
member of Congress was immune to complaints about the FTC,

which gave a new lease on life to congressional advocates of the legislative veto.

Getting "Pertschuked" became a new Washington verb, which encompassed a variety of FTC activities. Of Pertschuk's numerous investigations and uneven successes, Hollings concluded: "Pertschuk, you're like a cross-eyed javelin thrower. You never hit anything, but you keep everybody on the edge of his seat."

Ironically, Pertschuk's appointment did not precede but followed the initiation of many of the most controversial rule makings, and the agency was, in fact, starting to operate in reverse, according to Robert Reich, who headed the FTC's Office of Policy Planning. "The FTC was most active in terms of new initiatives during the early 1970s, during the Nixon administration," recalled Reich. "A lot of the major controversial cases, like the cereals case [Kellogg] and the oils case [Exxon] were in the 1972–73 period, and then the major rule makings all began in 1975–76. . . . By the time we got here, all of this stuff was in the hopper. I have spent most of the last four years trying to pare down the initiatives that we started in the early 1970s, as have Mike and the rest of the commissioners; so there's been an irony in the reaction that's been setting in."

But the rhetoric against the FTC took on a reality all its own. Under Pertschuk's direction the FTC was being led for the first time in its history toward a stricter adherence to its original legislative mandate — ensuring fair treatment for the public. Armed with an even stronger mandate from the Magnuson-Moss Act, along with clear signals from members of Congress to reinvigorate the consumer protection functions of the FTC, Pertschuk believed himself secure and moved quickly. What he failed to see were the political dangers that caused the agency to quickly lose its early momentum. Like the other agencies attempting to fulfill a vaguely written public interest mandate, even with more than adequate laws to back them up, it was clear that a too literal interpretation of those mandates could lead to trouble. Inexorably, trouble came in the form of an unexpectedly intense reaction and effective challenge from those whose livelihoods were threatened by the impact of the FTC rules. Stack those vested interests against an agency without a clear and well-organized constituency, and there is no contest. Indeed, the issue, Pertschuk's personality, recedes if viewed in a larger context: the question of whether the FTC could ever fulfill its mandate in a political environment so increasingly unfavorable to regulation.

Kid-Vid and Big Business: A Question of Fairness

Pertschuk made an easy target for groups that had been lying in wait since the passage of the Magnuson-Moss Act. "The business community was scared to death," recalled lobbyist Jeff Josephs of the Chamber of Commerce. "After all, 'unfair' is a highly subjective definition. . . . We held a briefing on the Magnuson-Moss Act in 1975, and five hundred people showed up in our Hall of Flags," he added. From that point on, the chamber became the focal point for anti-FTC activity. It organized and coordinated all the groups fighting the FTC, each of whom then made congressional contacts on its own.

Josephs works in a large sunny office whose walls are papered with charts ranking members of Congress with different colors and codes. Seated behind a twelve-foot desk piled high with papers, he waved at the charts, referring to the members who opposed President Reagan's budget cuts as "our hit list."

"The chamber's worst fears regarding the built-in dangers of the unfairness doctrine were fulfilled by the FTC," said Josephs, who accused the agency of a kind of malevolent serendipity in the way it selected the targets of its rule making.[12]

"There wasn't a member of Congress that hadn't been bitched to about the FTC," continued Josephs, describing how easy it was to mobilize the business community against the FTC. "It was small industries that were hurt the most. . . . We organized all the groups . . . funeral, insurance, food, toy, used cars. They made their own congressional contacts. We guided the train."

With the best of intentions, the FTC embarked on a crusade, armed with a doctrine of unfairness that segments of the business community felt was never clearly defined but, rather, described in "I know it when I see it" language. While this carries a certain

153

validity in areas where there is broad societal consensus, the potential for trouble increases when this kind of discretionary power is used where agreement is lacking.

Officials at the FTC never clearly defined "unfair," which created the impression in Congress and other quarters that it was pursuing a scattershot approach to decision making. Conflicting signals from Congress and the courts only added to the confusion, and ultimately expanded the agency's opportunities for discretion. What this meant to the business community was that no business was safe from FTC intervention; even the agency's pre-rule-making investigations held the potential for economic damage. Statements by FTC officials only reinforced suspicions about the highly selective way in which the FTC went about choosing its targets. In a revealing interview, Pertschuk admitted the absence of rational process in the highly controversial investigation of children's television, popularly known as "kid-vid."

"I decided to go after kid-vid. We didn't go through any process. The consumer constituency was my constituency. Carter had called consumer groups and Ralph Nader before appointing me, and I was their candidate. I had an obligation to them. At the time (1977) there were no new cases coming up. I needed something to convince them [the consumer groups] that we were going to do something serious. This was a significant social and economic issue. If I was going to be there four years, I wanted to do something worthwhile.

"I felt strongly about this issue," he continued. "Congress had been pushing the FTC for ten years to take on this issue. The day after I took office, the Appropriations Committee demanded that we tackle this issue. The commission had farted around for years, had promised but not delivered."

True enough, but insufficient justification for upsetting an apple cart full of major industries and their political allies. In fact, Ralph Nader said he had warned Pertschuk not to tackle children's television advertising, fearing the excessive backlash.

The FTC opponents had long complained about the confusion surrounding the definition of "unfair and deceptive" advertising; the interpretations were based on a combination of government pressure, legal decisions, and self-regulation. Now they felt justi-

fied in charging that "unfair" was also being defined on an issue-
by-issue basis, by what was viewed as the whims of FTC lawyers,
commissioners, and a few members of Congress. Pertschuk needed
an ironclad case to tackle this issue, not his personal feelings, political loyalties, and altogether honest instincts.

Not that there wasn't an ironclad case to be made. Anyone
who watches television commercials sponsoring programs geared to
young children cannot help but be struck by the prevalence of advertisements promoting sugared cereals. All kinds of attractive cartoon characters — elves, Easter bunnies, and the like — sing the
praises of products of doubtful nutritional value, which may be potentially harmful as well. Large quantities of sugar can cause tooth
decay, heart disease, high blood pressure, and diabetes, according
to many experts, including FDA commissioner Donald Kennedy,
who testified at FTC hearings that sugared snacks posed a dental
health hazard to children. His testimony was bolstered by the surgeon general, Julius Richmond, who argued that very young children were too vulnerable to make an informed choice among a variety of commercial messages.

These ads are not deceptive, argued their defenders. None of
them pretends to cure tooth decay. But are they really unfair? Is it
unfair merely to influence the buying habits of children and their
parents? If their products are really harmful to children's health,
they argued, they would not be on the market at all; they would be
under the jurisdiction of the Food and Drug Administration, which
could remove them from the marketplace.

Consumer advocates emphasize the disparity in resources to
document the nature of unfairness. Arrayed on one side are the
giant cereal companies, the sugar interests, the candy companies,
and their multimillion-dollar advertising agencies; on the other side
are the young children whose health may be permanently impaired
by excess sugar in their diet, along with their parents, who purchase these products out of sheer ignorance, a laissez-faire attitude,
or because they, too, are convinced by the ads.

Senator Packwood, the only member of the Senate Commerce
Committee who voted against the final compromise that thwarted
the FTC's efforts to curb the children's television advertising industry, was quoted in *Newsday* arguing in favor of maintaining the

unfairness standard: "If you say, 'Buy sugared goodies, you'll like the way they taste,' there's nothing untruthful about that. I'm sure kids will love them. But it is still unfair. The unfairness is that the sugared goodies aren't good for you, but the kid doesn't know any better."[13]

Two years later in an interview, Packwood made a further distinction in support of the unfairness standard. "It is not the business of government to prevent capitalistic acts between consenting adults," he said, "which often the FTC and other federal bureaucracies feel that they need to do. . . . But there is a legitimate role for government as the protector of consumers where a rational consumer cannot know . . . where one side has so much power that you cannot have a fair contract, as in the case of antitrust."

The FTC argued that television advertisements geared particularly to young children were inherently unfair because children could not grasp the nature and purpose of the advertising — presumably to sell products — and thereby wrongfully interpreted the ads as beneficial. For older children, the FTC focused on the harmful effects of sugar consumption, hoping that reduced advertising in this area would prevent the formation of destructive eating habits.

Buoyed by several congressional supporters and Pertschuk's commitment, the FTC pursued the issue, hoping to carve out new legal ground for its initiatives.[14] Commerce Committee staff member William Diefenderfer argued that ample legal precedent already existed for protecting children from harmful societal activities under the child labor laws, laws preventing children under certain ages from entering into legally binding contracts, and laws governing statutory rape. He argued, "In the 1700s and 1800s, we had no laws on child labor, and parents sent their children down into the coal mines to work. It was hazardous, dangerous, tough work that children were particularly good for because they were tiny and because they did not know any better. So Congress got together and said, 'Hey, that's not right. Somebody's got to protect these kids.' And so we decided we'd protect the children's bodies, and prohibited child labor."

Laws were also enacted to protect children in contract negotiations, presumably because they lacked the mental capabilities to evaluate complex legal documents. Preventing them from signing away their lives and their capital protected them from individuals who did not have their best interests at heart.

In keeping with this line of reasoning, the FTC turned its attention to children's television advertising. Many of the FTC's defenders still feel that the unfairness doctrine should be left deliberately vague. "Unfairness" was never intended to be rigidly defined — similar to the way in which the due process clause remains subject to constant interpretation and refinement by the courts. When a theory is left deliberately flexible, the agency retains its capacity to deal with the unknown. This is what it was trying to do in attempting to regulate television — a relatively new technology — and the impact of its advertising policies.

George Kopp, a former FTC official who now works for the House Committee on Science and Technology, defended FTC flexibility, comparing it to prosecutorial discretion: "Go over to the U.S. attorney's office and ask them how they decide what to prosecute, or the Justice Department and ask which labor union they decide to go after. I used to do a lot of criminal work there and a recurring theme in a number of cases was, 'Why me?' That is not a defense. The real question is, are you moving against someone who is acting against the public interest, and is there damage there? I was an attorney and a supervisor at the FTC and one of the things that used to drive me nuts was the review process before you could get anything off the ground. It could sometimes take months to make sure the complaint was exactly right. It was a very thorough process."

But regulatory agencies still lack the legitimacy enjoyed by the judicial system — at least in terms of using their discretionary power. To outsiders who did not read the FTC's five-hundred-page studies, the agency gave the impression of being highly idiosyncratic in its rule-making initiatives, which eventually led to accusations that the FTC was unfairly singling out entire industries for persecution. Before the Magnuson-Moss Act expanded the FTC's authority to issue industrywide regulations, the agency tended to proceed on a case-by-case basis, an approach that was more cautious and rarely evoked the kind of virulent political attack that became typical following the passage of the act.

Dismantling America

In retrospect, prosecuting one company was infinitely easier for a variety of reasons. Not only was it simpler to document the unfair trade practices of one company than those of an entire industry, it also avoided the inevitable complaints that the industry was being penalized for the excesses of a few. But the most important advantage of the case-by-case approach was political: industries tended to stay out of the political arena when only one company was in trouble. In fact, other companies often secretly welcomed watching a competitor fall on hard times. Further, if only one company was tackled at a time, conceivably only one congressman would come to its aid, which did not pose much of a threat to the agency. With wholesale rule making, however, the picture changed considerably, with the FTC now facing down entire industries located in hundreds of congressional districts. From this vantage point, the FTC's adversaries mobilized formidable coalitions, attracting not only representatives from their own economic groups but a constellation of allies whose connection to the issue was tenuous at best.

The Magnuson-Moss Act also positioned the FTC as an agency almost totally without a constituency, setting it apart politically from the other independent regulatory agencies, almost all of which have rewards to allocate — licenses to operate on the airwaves, monopoly-creating franchises, lucrative truck and air routes. But the FTC appeared only to take existing privileges and profits away — an extremely unstable position in the long run.

The investigation into kid-vid brought home this truth to the FTC, giving the agency a painful lesson in the political pitfalls of the Magnuson-Moss Act. Kid-vid was Pertschuk's first awakening, and came right before the first congressional oversight hearing in 1978 on rules affecting children's television advertising. Pertschuk made a halfhearted attempt to see members of the House Appropriations Committee, warned by one of his cronies on Capitol Hill that he was going to run into trouble. "There are thirty-two groups meeting this afternoon, just to consider what to do to you," he was told.

Before this time, Pertschuk admitted his own lapse in political savvy in neglecting to cultivate members of the House: "When I got to the FTC, I forgot the basic lesson of the Senate, which is: to know the Senate is to know nothing of the House." Relying on his strong relationships in the Senate, he made the mistake of thinking those friendships would carry him through his legislative travails. To make matters worse, he admitted, "I was cocky, arrogant, and set the wrong tone."

(Indeed, because of his advocacy role, Pertschuk was disqualified by federal judge Gerhard Gesell from participating in the kidvid case after a group of advertising representatives sued on those grounds. He was eventually reinstated, but the question remained unsolved as to the extent to which a regulatory agency commissioner could expand his role beyond neutral judge to single-minded advocate.)

A week before the FTC appropriations bill was drafted, in early 1978, Pertschuk got another signal that he was in trouble. He telephoned a key member of the Appropriations Committee only to hear that "Tommy Boggs was already sitting in his office." Boggs, his leading adversary and head of the kid-vid coalition, had by that time lined up eight votes on the committee. The son of Rep. Lindy Boggs, Democrat of Louisiana, and the late majority leader Hale Boggs, Boggs represented the Mars Candy Company, which paid him an annual retainer of $300,000.

Although they were adversaries, Pertschuk respected Boggs and claimed they worked well together, at least in terms of sharing information. Unlike many of the other lobbyists, who wanted to destroy the agency, said Pertschuk, Boggs recognized the value of the FTC. "We traded information; our interests coincided in a narrow way. Boggs only wanted to kill the kid-vid rule, not the FTC. Others wanted to kill the commission."

But the two men came from different worlds that were bound to collide. Pertschuk mistrusted business, and surrounded himself with young lawyers who shared his views. Boggs, whose tracks appear all over Washington in the regulatory world, personified a different perspective. At a dinner at the home of Senator William Proxmire, Democrat of Wisconsin, Boggs berated the senator for being too tough at a confirmation hearing of the chairman of the Home Loan Bank Board. "That's why you can't get decent people to work for the government," Boggs chided. Proxmire exploded: "For Pete's sake, if people can't stand up to my questioning, how can they stand up to industry pressures?"

Dismantling America

The FTC did not stand a chance against the kid-vid coalition. Estimates of how much the combined industries spent to defeat the rule range from $15 to $30 million, an estimate challenged by Boggs. "There was no grassroots campaign. It was all sophisticated lobbying at very little cost. We had an ad hoc group of companies that met here once or twice a week — broadcasters, ourselves, and manufacturers of children's products." What amazed Boggs was the ease with which they won their battle. "We were really astounded," he recalled. "We went to the House Appropriations Subcommittee. The only opposition we ran into was Yvonne Burke. She had given a commitment to proconsumer types. The attitude was just there. We never could have created it. It became symbolic of deregulation."

But the money and the power expended on the kid-vid rule meant nothing compared with the quality of influence exerted on the Congress. The first surprise was the response of the media. Until the FTC's troubles with the appropriations process began, the FTC enjoyed a fairly laudatory press. Pertschuk was always accessible to the press; moreover, he was so consistently articulate that he always made good copy. But the electronic media was another story. Alerted by the kid-vid activists and fearing a loss of advertising business, the major networks began to mobilize their local affiliates in a concerted effort to influence members of Congress to curb the FTC. Indeed, the broadcasters derive their strength from the fact that they are located in every congressional district.

"If you want to take a force that scares the wits out of Congress, the broadcasters are it," recalled Pertschuk. "Kid-vid was a motherhood issue. It didn't matter that a Harris poll had just revealed that 78 percent of the public favored no advertising for children at all. Congressmen are scared to death of local broadcasters."

For the broadcasters as well as many others, it was easy to turn the kid-vid issue into a question involving the abridgment of the first amendment. If you censored children's television advertising, where else could the federal government encroach upon the rights of its citizens? There was a lot of resistance in Congress, according to Rep. Elliot Levitas, specifically on the first amendment issue, which he felt should have made the FTC more delicate in its approach. "In the case of children's television advertising proceedings," said Levitas, "you were dealing with a very sensitive — and I don't mean politically sensitive — area, a first amendment area, where there was a lot of strong feeling. Leaving aside the networks, my feeling was that the FTC, in approaching the whole thing, had a preconception as to where they were headed, and were not really going to be deterred by policy counseling — the kind that says, 'You know, you are treading on some very sensitive grounds, you really ought to take it easy, you ought to make sure you touch bases.' When you're dealing with a first amendment type of case, you've got to be a little bit more sensitive to the public than when you are dealing with a deceptive advertising type of thing.

"I never got that feeling [with the FTC]," Levitas added. "They knew what was right, by God, and they were going to go forward with it. They felt accountable to no one other than themselves or whatever activist constituency they had out in the country."

The worst blow from the media came in the form of an editorial in the *Washington Post,* the first sign of unfavorable press coverage from the print media. The *Post* editorial ridiculed the FTC for playing the "national nanny," usurping the parental role of controlling what their children watched on television. When the FTC staff recommended dropping their investigation three years later, the newspaper, in an editorial headlined "Farewell to the National Nanny," reminded its readers that they were "among those who, from the beginning, found the children's television proceedings misguided. The federal government has better things to do than to play national nanny, monitoring what children see and hear on TV. . . . The people to deal with that problem are the parents of those children, acting individually and collectively against the products that are so advertised."[15] The newspaper's ownership of radio and television stations raised questions at the time in the minds of many pro-kid-vid activists as to whether their editorializing constituted a conflict of interest.

In strategic terms, the FTC's opponents won their most important victory of all with the *Washington Post* editorial. They succeeded in dominating the formulation of the issue, winning the support of a seemingly neutral but highly influential source. This, along with the weapon of ridicule, was ultimately more harmful than the most expensive lobbyists the sugar and cereal companies could provide, mainly because it succeeded in making kid-vid look frivolous.

Another nuance in the kid-vid episode involved the tobacco industry, whose long history with the FTC made it a natural enemy.[16] Initially it was unclear just why the tobacco companies, who were not permitted to advertise on radio or television, bothered with the issue at all. Then the real reason emerged: the tobacco companies, upset over the vagaries of the unfairness standard, were fearful that it would be applied to their billboard, magazine, and newspaper advertising in an entirely separate rule making. If the FTC were successful in the kid-vid debate, they reasoned, it would only be a matter of time before the agency returned to harass an old and favorite target, the tobacco companies. Rumors were also floated at that time of a rule making designed to force the tobacco industry to produce counterads: advertisements that would require the cigarette companies to remind consumers that their products were dangerous to their health — a warning that now appears on all cigarette packages, as well as on all print advertisements. The industry saw a golden opportunity in the kid-vid issue to strike a blow at the unfairness doctrine and thus prevent further incursions into their business.

As their swift response to the rumors indicated, the tobacco companies viewed rule making at the FTC as a "sneak, Pearl Harbor attack on the industry," in the words of a young FTC lawyer, rather than what the Magnuson-Moss Act intended — a process that would enable the agency to develop a record on which to base an informed decision on whether or not to promulgate a rule, as well as what kind of rule would be best for industry and consumer alike. The tobacco companies were not alone, given similar responses from other industries. In fact, by 1981, FTC staff members wondered whether lobbyists, lawyers, and trade associations invented rumors of rule making as a device to rally support against threatened federal intervention.[17]

Until 1979, the FTC could count on a crucial ally. He was Senator Wendell Ford, chairman of the Consumer Subcommittee of the Commerce Committee and a man who not only prided himself on being a consumer advocate but could also boast of having saved the agency from congressional attacks. Ford had urged Senator

Howell Heflin, Democrat of Alabama, for example, to delay an amendment in November 1979 that would have forced the FTC to stop four to five major antimonopoly inquiries and would have blocked similar attempts by the House to curb additional agency investigations. But there were signs that his loyalty was being tested.

When it became apparent that Ford was changing his position on the FTC, the agency and its supporters tried to counter the tobacco companies' considerable grassroots influence with their own heavy artillery. Ralph Nader made trips to Kentucky and Missouri to attack Senator Ford as well as Senator John Danforth, who was also lining up with the anti-FTC forces.

"If you were a senator from Kentucky and the FTC did that to one of your constituents, wouldn't you be a little upset?" Ford asked at one of his hearings.[18]

While that strategy may have worked five years earlier, it initially seemed counterproductive in 1979. Angered by the attacks on him, Ford told President Carter there would be no FTC until Nader was called off. Carter countered by saying he did not control Ralph Nader. Further evidence of the limited success of Nader's campaign emerged in his treatment of Senator Hollings, whom he called the most disappointing member of the Senate — not the worst, which would have been preferable, but the most disappointing. When the next FTC bill came up, Hollings called Pertschuk to say, "I'm voting against your bill because I want to send a message to Ralph." But in the end, Nader's impact was proven effective when Ford backed off from his initial position, in favor of a compromise acceptable to the consumer groups.

The kid-vid rule making was plagued from beginning to end by charges of poor political planning, even within FTC ranks. One high level FTC official, who supported the kid-vid rule but did not want to be quoted for attribution, admitted that the kid-vid battle personified the "kind of overkill that was the problem with many of the FTC's major initiatives." Isolating the problem at the staff level, he continued: "In trying to win, they were too thorough. [The staff assigned to the kid-vid proceedings] presented a proposed rule with a report that was three or four inches thick. This would frighten off everyone, because it was one of the first indicators of government intervention, and in that form it looked very formidable and frightening." After this experience, commissioners and bureau chiefs agreed informally on simplified packaging and that, in the future, they would be better off being less threatening in appearance, in the hope of preventing similar mobilizations against them.

The kid-vid rule was soundly defeated by Congress in a subsequent three-year funding bill, known officially as the Federal Trade Commission Improvements Act of 1980, and unofficially dubbed "the Christmas tree" because of all the gifts under its branches for selected trade groups. Along with other agency-crippling provisions, the act allowed the FTC to save face on children's advertising while effectively killing any substantive activity in that area. This was accomplished by allowing the FTC to continue its rule-making proceedings with the constraint that any rule be based on whether the advertising is "deceptive," not "unfair," and by extending this prohibition to all trade regulation rules affecting entire industries. Since "unfairness" was the centerpiece of the FTC's campaign against children's advertising, Congress's prohibition accomplished its intended objective: one year later, the FTC withdrew its investigation.[19]

The aftershocks of the kid-vid fight were felt far beyond the rule itself, as Pertschuk's friend, Washington attorney Bernard Koteen, later explained to him. What Pertschuk had done in tackling such a formidable array of opponents was to "awake the sleeping giant." After that, "it was so easy for Tommy Boggs, an open invitation for everyone to go to the Hill when they had a complaint about the FTC," or any other regulatory agency, for that matter.

As for Pertschuk, he admitted he had learned his lesson, and was not surprised again. "I've spent the last two years undoing the damage," he said. "From November 1978 on, I started making love to every congressman I could."

The American Way of Regulating: The FTC and the Morticians

Another catalyst to Congress's dismantling of the FTC was the agency's attempt to protect consumers from what it regarded as unscrupulous practices common to the funeral industry. The regulations were minimal; they merely required funeral directors to itemize their prices, give those prices over the phone, and be truthful. Yet the prospect of these regulations created such an enormous stir that a little-known congressman from Chicago, Marty Russo, was able to persuade the House into voting to prohibit the FTC from regulating the nation's $6.4 billion funeral business. Only the later intervention of the Senate in conference saved the FTC's efforts, and the FTC was given permission to issue a funeral rule. The 1981 rule, however, was much weaker than its predecessor, issued in March 1979, which had fomented the controversy. But by 1981, the staff had gotten the message, and for the first time in recent memory, bureau chiefs in a complete turnabout were heard to criticize the cautiousness of the staff, complaining that "they gave everything away."

To everyone's surprise, the morticians proved politically potent, with much more clout at the grassroots level than their numbers might suggest. There are at least twenty-two thousand funeral directors throughout the country, with an average of forty or fifty in each congressional district. More to the point, they are businessmen with a considerable amount of time on their hands: the average funeral director conducts an average of only two funerals per week. This affords them the opportunity to join a large number of civic organizations — Kiwanis, Lion's Club, Catholic War Veterans, Jewish War Veterans — accumulating power disproportionate to the size of their group.

"They join and join and join," said Rep. James Scheuer, a New York Democrat chairing the House subcommittee with FTC oversight responsibility who soon became known as one of the FTC's most ardent defenders. "They have the time to do the 'scut work' that no one else has time to do, and they get elected president. They rise to the top of all the local organizations and they have a lot of clout.

"Congressmen are terrified of them," he added, a theme that emerged clearly in the House floor fight on the funeral rule. Pertschuk related that one senator told him he supported the FTC's efforts because he had been "ripped off" on his mother's funeral arrangements, but could do nothing because of the power of the black funeral directors in his state. The FTC's legislative liaison, a former consumer activist, Kathleen Sheekey, was also taken by surprise by the power of the funeral lobby; she had predicted that of the two amendments to reach the House floor on the FTC appropriations bill, the funeral rule would be the easier to win.[20] She soon found out why funeral directors could mount such a persuasive lobbying campaign:

"There are funeral directors in every congressional district, and they are very important to elected representatives. In the South, they traditionally lend their offices to aspiring or elected politicians; they lend their bank of phones during a campaign. The funeral director in a district can sometimes either make or break you politically. One congressman told me he goes to thirty or forty funerals a year, and it is a very important means by which he meets constituents in his district. If the funeral director looks kindly upon you and seats you next to the widow, you are in a very good position vis-à-vis the people at that funeral. He is the man who will take you around and put you in contact with a lot of people; he will actually invite you to the funerals."

The funeral directors, she continued, formed a network "vital to politicians, and one they were not about to reject easily." They counted among their powerful friends Speaker of the House Thomas P. "Tip" O'Neill, Jr. (Democrat, Massachusetts), who, in supporting the Russo amendment, sentimentally recalled for reporters how his local Cambridge funeral home had buried O'Neills all the way back to their Irish antecedents. The year before the Russo amendment arrived on the House floor, O'Neill had advised a convention of funeral directors to take their case to Washington.[21]

The funeral directors took O'Neill's advice and, to their delight, found a highly receptive antiregulatory environment just beginning to develop. "In an antigovernment environment, this is not the time to tell people what color to put in their caskets," said Rep. Scheuer, referring to a questionable practice of some funeral directors, who order gaudy fabrics for their cheap line of coffins in order to direct people to more expensive ones. As in other FTC skirmishes, the merits of the case quickly fell victim to political variables. The FTC allegedly neglected to communicate to industry representatives at the outset, setting an adversarial tone that became hard to reverse, and the congressional solution reflected the "baby out with the bath water'' syndrome now common to recent FTC oversight battles.

The funeral rule resembled the kid-vid controversy in that it represented a well-intentioned effort by the FTC to protect consumers from what were alleged to have been widespread abuses in the funeral industry, amply documented by Jessica Mitford in her book *The American Way of Death*.[22] Unlike the kid-vid controversy, however, no one seriously questioned the legitimacy of the FTC's inquiry into the funeral industry under its Magnuson-Moss authority after an injunction brought by the National Funeral Directors Association (NFDA) on these grounds was denied in U.S. district court.

The FTC based its case on the undisputed impact of the funeral industry on consumers. The two million funerals conducted each year represent the third most expensive purchase — after a home and a car — ever made by a consumer, with at least half of the population involved in arranging a funeral at least once in a lifetime. The nub of the agency's argument was that since funerals can be very expensive (the typical traditional funeral with ground burial costs between $2,200 and $2,400), the FTC was obligated to protect consumers from being cheated by questionable industry practices that were alleged to have become standard operating procedure.[23]

Anecdotal evidence of these practices surfaced constantly on the floor of the House during the debate on the Russo amendment. "I even heard of one case where the funeral director persuaded the family to let him put springs in the bottom of the casket because surely they didn't want their loved one to lie on the bare floor,'' said an outraged Claude Pepper, the feisty octogenarian from Florida who is the House's most outspoken defender of the rights of the senior citizen, arguing against the Russo amendment on the grounds that the funeral industry was "vulnerable to abuse" and required regulation.

"About two-thirds of the people who die are elderly people, and generally the people who are the ones left behind to make the funeral arrangements are elderly people also," he added.[24] Other abuses illustrated how unscrupulous funeral directors take advantage of people at their most vulnerable: pressuring grieving survivors into buying more expensive funerals than they can afford; embalming without the family's permission; refusing to give price information over the telephone; and convincing consumers they needed caskets even when the body was scheduled to be cremated.

A six-hundred-page FTC staff report concluded that these practices were not "isolated occurrences confined to an unethical few," but were "widely used and even condoned by a large percentage of the nation's twenty thousand plus funeral homes." The report is quick to point out that the more "egregious and attention-grabbing abuses addressed . . . such as body snatching or refusing to release remains" are rare, and condemned by a majority of morticians. On the other hand, the more subtle practices considerably raised the price of funerals to the consumer. One example cited by the report was the reluctance of the undertaking trade, anxious to elevate itself to the status of a profession, to advertise its prices, to provide price information over the phone, and to encourage the preplanning of funerals. "As a consequence," said the report, "price information has been difficult to obtain, and price competition, which could reward efficiency and exert downward pressure on prices, has been notably absent." [25] To the FTC, the consumer stood at a real disadvantage in a funeral transaction because of a serious disparity in bargaining power between the funeral seller and the funeral buyer due to the consumer's ignorance of funeral practices and legal requirements, and the fact that the purchase "often took place under extreme time pressure and the effects of grief." [26]

Consumers at this unhappy time are also ripe for psychological pressures, according to Rep. Scheuer, who described how funeral directors used guilt and shame to goad the bereaved into spending more money than they had intended to spend. "This is the last time you can show your dad love, respect, and veneration," they would say. "All your mother's friends will be there." For those who held out, there was sarcasm: "You must have had a great relationship with your dad." Scheuer said when his own father died, the funeral director tried to sell his brothers and him a $25,000 coffin.

Some funeral directors are so convinced of the rightness of their position that they do not bother to restrict what are regarded as guilt tactics to the privacy of the funeral parlor. Responding to Michael Pertschuk, who argued against the expense of embalming during a March 1981 television broadcast of "The Phil Donahue Show," a funeral director in the audience stood up and compared

Pertschuk's alternative suggestions to the burial of a pet dog: "if you want to be buried like Rover, then you can be buried like Rover. Everybody doesn't want to be buried like Rover."[27]

In a heated confrontation on the House floor, Scheuer challenged Russo to defend his amendment penalizing "poor people, elderly people . . . at a time when they are least capable of understanding a very confusing and complicated decision about which they have very little prior knowledge."

Holding up a sheet of paper, he then read off a long list of supporters of the funeral rule, a list that included an impressive array of labor unions, public interest groups, and senior citizens groups, such as the AFL-CIO, American Federation of State, County, and Municipal Employees, Common Cause, National Retired Teachers Association, and Arizona State Board of Funeral Directors and Embalmers, to name a few.

"Now on the other side of this paper," he continued, "are the prestigious national organizations that support the Russo amendment. It's a blank page."

Then he turned to Russo and asked which "prestigious groups representing the general public, apart from the funeral directors of America, support this amendment."

Russo responded that it was not important "who supports or doesn't support my amendment . . . but whether the members of Congress vote on the facts." He then used his remaining few minutes of debating time to give the funeral industry's case against the FTC, accusing the agency of conducting a "biased proceeding, an invalid record," and a tendency to attack small business. None of the members, he added, had addressed the key issue: "whether or not the FTC has abused its rule-making authority, and whether or not the FTC has made its case."[28]

By a two-to-one margin, the House passed the Russo amendment, which ultimately proved to be a short-lived victory for the funeral industry, though it had spent an estimated $800,000 on its lobbying campaign. Ironically, the vote turned out to be a long-term loss for the FTC, for it signaled open season on the agency, a fact of life recognized by FTC lobbyist Kathleen Sheekey: "It was a vote against the FTC, a vote that took on all of the people who were angry at the FTC for other reasons, like the people who were angry about kid-vid."

Dismantling America

To the chagrin of many of those who supported the FTC's efforts to regulate the funeral industry, the issue became embroiled in a series of personality clashes. Echoes of the battle over kid-vid bounced off the walls of Congress during the funeral controversy — accusations of staff arrogance, an unwillingness to conduct a dialogue with business, and the familiar "I know it when I see it" presentation of evidence.

One illustration was the way funeral industry representatives were informed of the FTC's involvement, indicating the early establishment of harsh, adversarial, and counterproductive relationships, which only magnified the zeal with which the funeral lobby attacked the agency.

"We got a call in November 1972 seeking information on funerals from a professor at the University of Minnesota trying to become a consultant for the FTC," recalled Howard Raether, executive director of the National Funeral Directors Association (NFDA), a 13,500 member group based in Minneapolis and the largest group of organized funeral directors.[29] "It was our first tip-off that the FTC was interested. We later read about it in the following year in an article in the *Wall Street Journal*."

The funeral directors tried from the start to avoid a rule making, offering several alternatives instead. After meeting with Arthur Angel, FTC staff attorney, and Tom Nelson, a consultant in charge of the rule, the NFDA drew up a set of proposed voluntary guidelines, which they submitted to the FTC. The response, claimed Raether, was a one-page letter rejecting their proposal but promising to send another letter with fuller details explaining why they were turned down. The second letter never came, according to Raether.

The group then offered to show the FTC that the profession could police itself, by arranging to process any complaints sent by the FTC through their state affiliates. The FTC, agreeing to experiment with this arrangement, sent five complaints to the NFDA, which resolved three and rejected two as the responsibility of the cemetery management, not the funeral director. They claimed it never got another complaint before the FTC decided to proceed with a formal rule making.

The funeral industry's objections centered primarily on the potential cost of the proposed regulation, which it estimated at

$50,000,000 a year, but were soon expanded to include complaints of staff bias, improper administrative procedures, and staff misrepresentation of information. Pertschuk later admitted before a congressional oversight hearing that there was some basis for criticizing some junior staff in early rule-making proceedings for conducting "vendettas" against industries like the funeral industry, adding that these staff members were no longer with the commission.

To Raether, the real stumbling block was the FTC staff, particularly Arthur Angel, who he felt was conducting a "vendetta against the funeral industry." This signaled the beginning of a series of personality clashes that characterized the funeral fight and impeded constructive decision making throughout. Angel was later replaced, after admissions within the FTC that he had mishandled the case. "You could see the chip on Art Angel's shoulder," said Raether. "He would snap during [congressional] hearings. If he snaps to someone who voted on his salary, how do you think he treats people on the other side of the fence?"

Angel fared no better with people "on the other side of the fence" than he did with the NFDA. Called on the carpet in 1976 by members of the Subcommittee on Activities of Regulatory Agencies, Angel did not respond in the customary deferential manner expected of bureaucrats when appearing before congressional committees. The subcommittee voiced its concern that the FTC had launched a major rule making, as well as a $500,000 investigation, on the flimsy basis of "less than a dozen complaints." The following exchange between Arthur Angel and Rep. Millicent Fenwick (as director of New Jersey's Division of Consumer Affairs she had been responsible for her state's implementation of funeral regulations) signaled why the FTC ran into so much trouble with the Congress three years later.

MRS. FENWICK: Did you consult the various consumer divisions of the states to see what they had in the way of complaints?

MR. ANGEL: Number of consumer complaints? Only sporadically, only in a couple of states did we do that.

MRS. FENWICK: Well, now, gentlemen, seriously, your own kind hearts and six letters — they have consumer divisions in almost every State of the Union, and all you have to do is

171

write a letter. In many states it is the Division of Law and Public Safety it comes under, and in some the Department of Agriculture, which I don't understand.

But nevertheless, there are consumer divisions and they receive complaints. And this surely would be the first obligation, and it really constituted an inexpensive way of finding out what the situation is in the Nation. If you had written and found out they had 15 complaints in 8 years, wouldn't that have told you something?

MR. ANGEL: It would have told us something, but not everything, Congresswoman. The point, I think, that really needs to be emphasized here is that consumer complaints simply do not give you anywhere near the full picture of what kinds of abuses of problems exist.

MRS. FENWICK: What makes you think so, sir?

MR. ANGEL: Three and a half years of research, interviewing people.

MRS. FENWICK: I ran the division of consumer affairs.

MR. ANGEL: I understand that.

MRS. FENWICK: And I promulgated regulations. I just simply do not agree with you, there is no better way of knowing. If I were a Federal Trade Commissioner, I would have taken a bit more interest in the Pyramid case — now there is real abuse involving activities in one State very difficult to control on another State level. The Federal Trade Commission has certain things, in my opinion, that only it can do. Package deals that stranded poor schoolchildren in Paris, and I couldn't control it because it was organized in another state. I have dozens of things that I could hand you in the way of problems. To get triggered off by six letters and your kind hearts when you have thousands of consumers begging for help in other areas is to me absolutely an incredible way of operating an agency.

MR. ANGEL: Your characterization is unfair. It was not our kind hearts and six letters which triggered the investigation; I tried to make that clear before. I guess I failed at that.

MRS. FENWICK: Yes.

MR. ANGEL: We spent approximately six months reading magazine articles, dissertations, interviews with funeral directors.

MRS. FENWICK: That is pointless.

MR. ANGEL: It is not pointless.

MRS. FENWICK: Look, you took 6 months, and I don't know what that cost the taxpayers. But during those 6 months I could have given you several things, thousands of people that are hanging on the ropes. Surely, if we are going to choose — I don't mean to get so excited, and I'm

	sorry — but if you just knew what my consumers in New Jersey were up against, and that Mr. Givens of the FTC told me in all good faith, that he just didn't have the manpower to do anything about it. And you sit down here in Washington taking 6 months to read magazines about what is going on in the funeral industry. I could have told you, we were doing it. I was only there 15 months, and this is one of the many regulations promulgated during my time.
Mr. Angel:	We have regulations, too.[30]

No doubt the committee was prepared for Angel, forewarned by congressional staff members like Steven Lynch, who had already dealt with him. They first met by telephone, recalled Lynch. Angel called to ask Lynch why Congress was holding hearings before the FTC had concluded its hearing process. "He said, 'I just want to know who you think you are,' " Lynch reminisced. "I said this is the Congress, and these are the people who created your agency, and fund you, and they can do about anything they want to do up here. You've got to learn that."

"We never got along and hardly ever spoke after that," said Lynch, emphatically.

The uneasy relationship of the FTC staff with Capitol Hill set the tone for the following three years of rule-making activities, with charges on both sides alleging a variety of procedural and substantive improprieties. In the process, the issue became muddied by so much minutiae that it was virtually impossible to determine the extent to which each tempest was legitimate, or merely a clever diversionary tactic. In addition to accusations of staff arrogance of the kind documented in the Angel-Fenwick contretemps, congressional critics also accused the staff of bias, as well as perverting the administrative process (and the basis of that process, the Administrative Procedure Act) by resorting to questionable practices during the funeral proceedings. Allegations included (1) seeking out friendly consumer groups to receive public participation funds, without searching for groups on the opposing side that would also need public funding, most notably black funeral directors; (2) allowing cross-examination of certain witnesses; and (3) taking over a year to compile the final six-hundred-page report, yet initially only allowing thirty days for interested persons to comment on that report.[31] Congress also objected to the public campaign carried on by FTC officials on major national television shows before promulgation of the final rule — another questionable practice reminiscent of kid-vid. The FTC is, after all, a quasi-judicial agency, whose commissioners, like judges, are supposed to make unbiased judgments only after all the evidence is in. Before the funeral rule was promulgated, Pertschuk had appeared as an advocate of funeral industry regulation on two segments of "The Phil Donahue Show," and on "60 Minutes," while Albert Kramer, director of the Bureau of Consumer Protection, had appeared on the "Today Show."

The FTC's congressional defenders responded to these charges by asserting in a Dear Colleague letter that accusations of staff bias represented a smoke screen to "divert attention from the real issue." Rule opponents, they argued, were given every opportunity to respond, and in fact did respond, if the written comments by 853 individual funeral directors and testimony of 58 industry group representatives are any indication of the commission's outreach. "The postrecord comments by the NFDA alone exceeded five hundred pages," said the letter.[32]

To counter the criticism that the agency had only received six complaints before starting its proceedings, the FTC offered evidence of its own. "At the time they initiated their rule making," said Kramer, "the staff placed hundreds of documents on public record, including written comments totaling twenty thousand pages, which represented every viewpoint." The hearings that followed were similarly extensive: fifty-two days of hearings held in six cities across the country, ending in August 1976. From the testimony of over three hundred witnesses, a seventeen-thousand-page record was produced, along with four thousand pages of exhibits from a wide range of groups, including funeral directors' associations and trade groups. A year later, the presiding officer issued his report, followed ten months later by a staff report. After the staff report was released, another ninety-day public comment period brought an additional sixteen hundred comments. Another set of rule recommendations grew out of these comments, followed by an open meeting held by the FTC commissioners in February 1979. Not until 1981 was a rule finally issued, showing, according to Kramer, how "the Magnuson-Moss process sometimes results in lengthy proceedings.'' But, he added, ''the most striking feature is . . . that it works the way it was intended . . . to build an evidentiary record reflecting the knowledge, opinion, and experience of a broad range of interests.''[33]

A question that kept cropping up throughout the funeral controversy was why Russo became so involved with the cause of the funeral directors, his passion a surprise to friends and foes alike, especially in light of his early skepticism. ''I can't understand why you can't square things with that agency,'' Russo had told Howard Raether before the hearings. Ultimately, it was the hearings that galvanized Russo, a young, plain-spoken lawyer recently elected from the southwest corner of Chicago who became so totally identified with the issue that three years later people thought he had initiated the investigation of the FTC. ''It really aggravated me,'' he later recalled in an interview in his congressional office. ''I showed up one morning at a hearing and we had this guy named Arthur Angel. I asked him how many complaints do you have. A couple of thousand? He said not that many. It got down to six. They had read Jessica Mitford's book and that was the impetus, and based on that they made up their mind that they were going to move from there to some kind of rule. I said, based on six complaints you are going to continue an investigation of small business? I don't understand this.''

For its part, the FTC regarded the arguments over the number of complaints as a ''numerical red herring.'' The commission, a staff memorandum argued, ''never has initiated investigations based on an arithmetic function of complaints received.''[34] The FTC also argued that its former practice of relying exclusively on consumer complaints had been sharply criticized in the late 1960s and early 1970s. In response to those criticisms, the agency was moving toward identifying potential problems through policy planning instead of the complaint process.[35]

Privately, FTC staff members working on the funeral rule also argued that their initiatives represented a fundamental challenge to an industry accustomed to virtual self-regulation and to a marketplace unobstructed by government interference. Since packaging was a central element of the way funeral directors did business, any attempt to influence their system would be regarded as an assault on their professional freedom. All arguments about the FTC's lack of cooperation were spurious; there never was any basis for negotiation.

From then on, a number of events occurred that were perceived by Russo as personal affronts. After the subcommittee hearings, in 1976, Russo had relaxed, confident that the FTC had understood the signals from Congress to work out its problems with state and local authorities, and to ease up on its efforts to promulgate a federal rule. It turned out that Russo was lulled into a false sense of security, for the FTC proceeded to work on the funeral rule, apparently unconcerned with the signals of the subcommittee. But by 1979, the politics had changed, with Russo having taken over the chairmanship of the subcommittee from his predecessor, William Hungate (Democrat, Missouri), who had decided not to run for reelection. Not long after he became subcommittee chairman, Russo was told by his staff that the FTC had just contacted them to inform them of the agency's intention to pursue another funeral rule. Russo was caught off guard: "I thought everything was going along fine, and then boom, along comes a nine-page rule that would take another hundred pages to be implemented. Any rule that is that long will take ten times that much to implement, and that will increase the cost of funerals."

Russo then tried to negotiate informally with the FTC, which he claimed was more rigid than other agencies. "I've always believed in trying to work everything out. We had a problem with the FDA over labeling requirements with the independent bakers and we just sat both sides down and worked it out. We tried that with the FTC and it didn't work. They were really bent on coming out with a rule and you could see the biases in everything they said, and in the media hype. I tried to bend over backwards in meeting with them. I said try voluntary guidelines, and if they can't do it, knock them in the head. They couldn't even generate complaints when they actively tried to generate them, and that irritated me."

Russo also saw the FTC funeral campaign as discriminatory toward small business, an argument not without merit if the rules do in fact drive up the cost of funerals and further force the absorption of smaller funeral homes into the larger companies. The funeral industry is, in fact, "small business intensive."[36]

"The FTC lost its mission," continued Russo, building up his case. "It was not to penalize small business, it was to make them competitive. Here is something that is local in nature, strictly small business, and here is an agency that ought to be protecting small business. Instead of fighting antitrust violations and protecting these guys, they are knocking the heck out of them."

Russo never addressed the merits of the rule itself, defending his position on the grounds that the FTC never justified why it should be given the opportunity to regulate. "I believe it's not the people who should have to prove why they shouldn't be regulated but the reverse: the government has to prove why they ought to regulate. It's a state responsibility. In this case they fell short of it, even with their publicity campaign."

Russo's opponents disagreed. A study of state regulations conducted by the Consumer Federation of America, for example, estimated that less than 5 percent of the consumer protection provisions in the proposed funeral rule were included in present state laws. Some states even testified that the rule would be helpful to states; for example, the Arizona State Board of Funeral Directors and Embalmers endorsed further federal-state cooperation in the regulation of funeral industry practices.[37]

Russo's bitterness increased after efforts were mounted by defenders of the FTC to counter the Russo amendment. What others might have taken as the normal give and take of Washington politics, Russo regarded as an attack on his integrity.

"I wasn't upset until a press conference, where Esther Peterson [consumer adviser to President Carter], Scheuer, and Eckhardt were implying that I was being bought off by the industry," he later explained. "Esther Peterson gets up and says this is a special interest issue and anyone who votes for this amendment indicates where they're coming from. Who the hell is Esther Peterson to say that? Do I challenge her motives?"

"That was it," he continued, pulling a list from his drawer with the Russo amendment head count. "Then the crusade was on. I really got involved because I don't like anyone lying about me. I was ready to embarrass them like they'd never been embarrassed before."

(In a lighter vein, Russo told of an NBC reporter who came in after checking his contributions, and said, "Boy, Congressman, if you're being bought off by industry, you go cheap." Federal Election Commission records showed that Russo was not being "bought off" by the funeral industry. The NFDA didn't even have a Political Action Committee at that time.)

The FTC's supporters destroyed Russo's victory on the House floor with an interesting exercise in legislative maneuvering in conference, for which Russo never forgave them. Since he no longer served on the Commerce Committee, Russo sought appointment to the conference committee for the sole purpose of protecting his amendment. After his appointment, Russo claimed the committee was meeting secretly without telling him where and when they were meeting: "The rumors were always coming at me; you know you can't do anything around here and not have anybody find out about it."

In the middle of these curious activities, Russo was suddenly hospitalized at Bethesda Naval Hospital, with an inflammation in his stomach that caused him to lose four pints of blood. While recuperating, he found out that Harley Staggers, Democrat of West Virginia and chairman of the conference committee, had scheduled a meeting of the House conferees for the week he was hospitalized. From his hospital bed, Russo wrote to Staggers, pleading for an extension, "because there's no one who is on the conference from the House who's supporting my amendment."

"He didn't honor my request and they went ahead and compromised my amendment right out of the conference," recalled Russo.

Russo then asked the committee to let him present his amendment to the Senate, and by a vote of five to four was rebuffed again. Although Russo won a decisive victory on the House floor, his amendment was lost in the cracks of the legislative process, which shows what can still be done in the byzantine negotiating process of conferencing bills. Russo saw the whole exercise as yet another victory for big business. "To me, the funeral industry is small potatoes when you compare it to the agricultural co-ops — which affect the price of commodities — the insurance industry, Formica, and all the rest of the amendments that were in the bill. All of the amendments . . . dealt with big business. The funeral industry

178

didn't have any influence buying votes. He was a small guy who really couldn't muster anything. They had compromised for all the big people, so they had to hit somebody, and what they hit was the one with the most press. The funerals were a lightning rod. They got all the bad press. The rest were left alone.''

A look at the bill, the FTC Improvements Act of 1980, H.R. 3213, confirms Russo's point. One provision brought relief for the insurance industry, which was not even the subject of rule making, but the result of a hard-hitting FTC study showing not only the low rates of return on cash-value life insurance but also that buyers of life insurance paid ''$1.3 billion in excess premiums during the course of one year.''[38] The bill exempted the insurance industry from FTC investigation. Congress also made the Formica Corporation the beneficiary of yet another gift-bearing provision, one that effectively killed FTC action against the Formica trademark.

One year after the funeral rule, Pertschuk came in to see Russo, and the two principal actors finally sat down for a heart-to-heart talk. ''The problem was that we had never had a chance to chat directly before,'' said Russo regretfully.[39]

Where to Find a Congressional Mandate

It is an understatement to say that by 1980, Congress was hopping mad at the FTC. There was ample evidence of its fury. Rep. Bill Frenzel (Republican, Minnesota) called the FTC a ''king-sized cancer on our economy,'' and his fellow Republican, Senator John Danforth of Missouri, described the agency as ''out of control.''[40]

Never again, vowed many of the members, would they lose control over the agency. To prove their point, they attached a two-house legislative veto to the 1980 appropriations bill, giving Congress the power to kill any FTC rule if, within ninety days of the rule's effective date, both houses passed resolutions of disapproval.

But one cannot judge Congress by its rhetoric alone — or by a one-time, vindictive appropriations bill. To do that would lead to the false notion that the FTC was marching solely to the beat of its own drummer, insensitive to the wishes of Congress. The long view proves otherwise; indeed, the record shows quite definitely that the consumer protection initiatives that brought turmoil to the FTC originated with Congress, at the source of the congressional mandate: the appropriations process.

Looking back at appropriations hearings as recently as 1975 reveals the ironic picture of a timid FTC being badgered by senators urging its chairman to take a more vigorous role in protecting consumers. The greatest pressure seemed to come from the Senate, where a reluctant FTC chairman, Lewis Engman, responded to an angry Senator Gale McGee (Democrat, Wyoming), who wanted to know why the FTC had not pursued the question of children's television advertising. "If you think the women's libbers are a problem," said McGee, "wait until you get the mothers of America on your back. This is where we are getting the static, and I think, not without reason. . . . We are rather literally besieged."[41]

You have to understand, he explained, that "the committee always receives inquiries in the form of flak. Almost universally, it is in reference to television advertising and its impact on children. What has the commission been doing in this area?"

As if children's television advertising were not a broad enough canvas, especially in view of the commission's eventual abortive efforts, Senator Hiram Fong, Democrat of Hawaii, chimed in to ask why the FTC did not inquire into the excesses of all television advertising:

"While my wife watched the movie *Cleopatra* last night, every few minutes it was interrupted for several commercials. At one point, the commercial time exceeded the amount of time that they were showing the film. Is there some movement there to see that we get a little more of the public time rather than commercial time?"

Engman's response provides a sharp contrast to Pertschuk's stewardship of the FTC, highlighting the reversal of roles between the Hill and the agency that was soon to materialize. Gently explaining to Senator Fong that television advertising rested within the purview of the Federal Communications Commission (FCC), Engman tried to convince his congressional inquisitors that the FTC was addressing children's television advertising with just the kind of approach that would have delighted the advertisers and the networks. Needless to say, it was minimal. Engman talked about requesting a study from the National Science Foundation (NSF) on the effects of television advertising on children. Another approach focused on persuading industry to abide by voluntary guidelines. Engman displayed considerable faith in the voluntary approach, crediting the FTC's "catalytic ability" with the decision by representatives of the advertising industry to "set up a special effort to deal with the particular problems of children's advertising." "The commission's approach," explained Engman, "has been that if we can encourage the industry and the critics of the industry to sit down together and work out some of these problems, we will all be further ahead."

But the senators were not fooled. Senator McGee called the NSF study request "one of the biggest stalls in this town," and added that he hoped it would not be "used as an excuse for relegating this into limbo." He was equally acerbic on the virtues of the voluntary approach: "Our concern here is over the often poor track record of the voluntary approach. . . . The result is that it all comes tumbling down and here we will sit next year at this time, talking about the same thing again. They finally decide they can't do very much. We would not like to lose another year."

In language seldom heard in the antiregulatory environment a brief four years later — words that would have been music to Pertschuk's ears — McGee continued lecturing Engman that the FTC never would have originated but for the "failure of the private sector to discipline the conduct of an industry."

"That is almost the whole history of government," he continued. "If everybody were as good as you and I, we wouldn't need any government. But the trouble of it is there are a couple of guys around that don't quite live up to our standards. So you have to have the discipline, judgment, decision-making, and enforcement capabilities of government."

One could never have guessed from Engman's mild responses that following the passage of the Magnuson-Moss Act, he had launched eleven rule-making initiatives into vocational schools, mobile homes, food advertisers, hearing aid companies, and health spas, among others, demonstrating a style that some of those who followed envied. "Our key strategic mistake was that we should have kept our mouths shut, spoken softly, and carried a big stick,'' argued Robert Reich, chief of the FTC's Office of Policy Planning. "We should have continued very much in the Republican tradition, doing what we were doing fairly, working with the best segments of the business community. That is the only way a regulatory agency like this can survive. We did just the reverse. We pared back all the initiatives and we saber-rattled."

Three years later, the FTC was still getting formal encouragement from members of Congress, even, ironically, on the funeral rule. At an appropriations hearing in 1978, Pertschuk was queried by Senator Dale Bumpers, Democrat of Arkansas: "I was just curious how you are getting along with the funeral home industry?"

Pertschuk: "They have been quiet because we have been quiet. . . . I gather from a series of articles in the *New York Times* that many participants in the funeral home industry have begun to change their practices in anticipation of the kinds of requirements that were contained in the rule."

Bumpers: "Let me say that I certainly applaud your efforts. . . . I personally think you are doing a pretty good job."

Bumpers went on to further congratulate Pertschuk on the FTC's success in regulating the hearing aid industry, as a "classic case of a change that could be duplicated thousands of times."[42]

But the following year, the tables had turned, and Pertschuk's testimony before Congress began to sound more and more like Engman's, defending the FTC leadership's reluctance to protest Congress's growing intrusions into the agency's activities. Senator Lowell Weicker was particularly outraged by provisions in the authorization bill that terminated an antitrust case against Sunkist, as well as by the proceeding before the Trademark and Appeals Board on Formica that allowed the company to retain its monopoly over the name. Responding to Pertschuk's statement that at no time in the FTC's history had Congress ever halted an antitrust case, Weicker angrily asked if the FTC intended "to contest that type of congressional action legally."

Pertschuk's response that he did not know if the agency had the legal authority to challenge action by Congress drew an even angrier denunciation by Weicker: "I hope somebody jumps in there because I will tell you someday it is going to be my ox that is being gored, and I'll be damned if I want the President, the politicians, jumping into the act when I have got my case being determined. What we are all talking about is independence of procedure, judicial or administrative." He continued, "That is really what is of concern to me, and should be of concern to every member of Congress regardless of whether they have some constituent beating down on their head who feels they are being mistreated."[43]

Close scrutiny of appropriations hearings reveals that Congress had actually given the FTC a green light to pursue its consumer goals. The Magnuson-Moss Act and its legislative history, as well as key Supreme Court decisions, all pointed the way toward the development of a vigorous consumer-oriented agency. But, like *High Noon,* when the inevitable political pressures became too intense, Pertschuk stood alone in the dusty square, with virtually no one coming to his aid. Unlike *High Noon,* however, the shoot-out left the hero bloodied and bowed, and his challengers victorious.

At his last oversight hearing, Pertschuk talked about regulatory reform instead of the rights of the consumers, and about shifting funds from the development of new rules to the "implementation of rules on the books." The agency also functions, he said, with a new operating manual, directing "any staff opening an investigation that might lead to a rule making to begin in early stages to talk to the industry to find out what their reaction is to a proposed rule, to learn the consequences of any remedy, and basically to gain that education."[44]

Of his congressional supporters on the other side, like Weicker and, later, Senator Packwood, who expressed disappointment at Pertschuk's abandonment of kid-vid, Pertschuk replied: "They don't have to run an agency."

The Conflict Imperative

Without clear signals from Congress throughout the mid to late 1970s, the Federal Trade Commission found itself in a Catch–22 pattern of unabated conflict. Adversarial relationships normal to regulatory politics were refined to a new degree, as the drama unfolded to reveal all the rewards going to those who excelled at the practice of conflict, while those who advocated cooperation and negotiation were either reviled or ignored.

At the FTC, young staff lawyers were encouraged to enter the fray in an adversarial mode, following the leadership of their chairman, Michael Pertschuk. Their extreme youth (one out of every ten new FTC lawyers in 1977 was hired from that year's graduating class) and their short-term commitment to the agency (an average stay at that time was three years) only increased their determination to score quick and dramatic victories that would increase their value in the legal marketplace. The agency's incentive system, which rewarded these victories, worked inexorably against the avoidance of conflict, according to Robert Reich, who supervised many of these staff members in a frustrating attempt to work against the system's stronger imperatives:

"Many of the low level staff plan to go on into private practice, or into trade associations," he explained. "They want to sharpen their tools, they want to litigate, score some victories, gain some scalps. There's nothing in it for them in avoiding conflict, in anticipating conflict and developing solutions that will avoid conflict."

The business community predictably reacted very strongly to what they perceived as the antibusiness orientation of those on the front lines of the FTC. It was grist for the Chamber of Commerce, which experienced the greatest period of growth in its history during the first four years of Pertschuk's chairmanship. The chamber exploited the FTC issue, playing up business's legitimate fears of the unknowns inherent in the Magnuson-Moss Act. By the time the dust settled, the chamber's hegemony in the consumer field was secure, a solid wedge between the FTC and the business community.

To be fair, the FTC played a major role in setting the stage for this new political monopoly by consciously making itself more remote. In the middle 1970s, for example, the FTC sharply reduced its practice of giving advisory opinions to businesses requesting them prior to a proposed rule making or adjudication. "It was a management decision based on the fact that we wound up using a lot of resources, and getting very little mileage out of it," emphasized

Albert Kramer, head of the Consumer Protection Bureau, justifying the elimination of this particular service. From an organizational point of view, an agency with extremely limited resources made a sound management decision; from a public relations point of view, it was clearly a mistake. The FTC is an agency with few rewards — for individual businesses — and many sanctions. By withdrawing even this minor service, it lost numerous opportunities to relate positively to the business community.

Another policy was broader and more subtle, but its effects were similarly devastating, and by the time the FTC reversed itself, it was too late. The FTC had a policy, predating Pertschuk by at least seven years, of "not talking to industry." Reacting to charges that it was a captive of the business community, the FTC entered the mid-1970s in an adversarial mode, convinced it would never make gains in consumer protection, despite what Engman was telling the Senate. The agency's new posture was aided and abetted by a preponderance of lawyers, whose professional background only reinforced the continuing conflict. "No one was interested in dialoguing with industry," recalled Jeff Josephs, a lobbyist for the Chamber of Commerce, who said he tried each year to set up meetings between representatives of the business community and the FTC. "It wasn't in their job description to talk to business; it wasn't sexy to talk to business. Pertschuk in his first year said he wouldn't talk to us. After they were taken apart in the Congress, they thought it was a great idea."

The business community, emulating the confrontational posture of the public interest groups and the FTC, developed its own machinery to match its adversaries, and soon many segments of the business community abdicated to groups like the chamber, reluctant to approach the FTC on their own. This created yet another army of people with a vested interest in conflict, who knew they would be unemployed without an ongoing battle. "The intermediaries between business and government — the lawyers, the lobbyists, the trade associations — understand very well that their own vested interests depend on maintaining a monopoly of access and on heightening the polarity, the tension, the confrontation," said Robert Reich. "Issues that could be collaborative issues are turned into confrontational issues in which they can score clear victories because the more clear victories they can score, the more clients they'll have.''

Reich lamented the new legitimacy of the intermediaries, which made it increasingly difficult for him to deal directly with individual businesses, even in their interest. One striking example of the effects of this legitimacy surfaced in 1980, when Reich, in an attempt to avoid an antitrust proceeding, invited nine chief executive officers from the industry under investigation to meet with him and with the senior staff attorneys, "to try to find out why the problem existed; to warn them that if they didn't get their act together, we'd have to do something; but [to] give them an opportunity to come up with solutions." Reich talked to all of them individually, and each one said, "What a terrific idea, we're glad the FTC is getting involved before the fact, instead of being cowboys."

The meeting was planned, a date set, and then a week later every single executive independently called Reich with precisely the same reason for canceling his appearance. "Some were more candid than others," said Reich, "but essentially each of them said, 'Look, I've talked about this to my lawyer, my inside counsel, and my outside counsel, and my trade association adviser, and they all said it wasn't a good idea. We ought to wait till the issues get more crystallized. Why should we expose ourselves? We might become sitting targets.' ''

The advice the chief executives were getting was based on strategy, but the strategy represented an outside perspective, almost as if a general sitting on the battlefield was so limited in his discretion that he had to wait for clearance from headquarters before returning enemy fire. What disappointed Reich was that every one of the executives took the advice of intermediaries, and the meeting was never held. "The system is rigged to prevent any kind of constructive collaboration between business and government," concluded Reich, who emphasized the important distinction between the intermediaries, who were in the ascendancy, and the subordinate position of the business community. "It's the intermediaries who have an interest in conflict and winning. The business community is mature enough to know that they need the government; it's in their long-term interest to develop a very close relationship with the government. They're getting killed internationally because other governments — our competitors — are working very effectively with their industries.''

The conventional wisdom of political scientists going back to the founding fathers places enormous faith in the adversarial approach, which the experience of the FTC calls into question. The assumption, for example, that big business and big government will keep each other honest falls flat in today's world, with corporations whose budgets exceed the GNP of most countries lined up against an agency deputized to regulate them with an annual budget in the neighborhood of $70 million.

The increasing permeability of Congress to industry pressures tips the balance even farther away from the FTC. During the height of the kid-vid controversy, the cereal companies, the sugar interests, and the National Association of Broadcasters contributed a total of $265,898 in one year alone to key members of Congress.

It did not take long for other groups and their PACs to learn from the kid-vid experience, and they found the FTC easy pickings. In May 1982, the FTC experienced its first legislative veto over the used car rule, passed overwhelmingly by a Congress whose judgment paralleled its campaign contributions. The car dealers had contributed over $800,000 to congressional campaigns in the three and one-half years prior to the veto, an investment unmatched by their customers.[45] The rule would have required used car dealers to inform customers of a car's major known defects at the time of purchase.

The adversarial system can only work productively among equals. When the contest becomes as disproportionate as it did in the case of the FTC, it assumes the contours of a farce — or would do so if the public were not being disadvantaged in the process. The FTC is a ''cop on the beat of consumer enforcement, and they took his nightstick away,'' said Ralph Nader. The irony was that it was another branch of government, Congress, that dismantled the agency, in opposition to its own mandates and laws. Congress also found a willing ally by 1981 in the new FTC chairman, James C. Miller III, a Reagan appointee who shared the now dominant congressional view of minimizing the FTC's consumer protection functions.

In its present beleaguered state, the FTC also shows what happens to an agency with virtually no constituency; how quickly it is rendered ineffectual without political defenders. Unlike many of the other regulatory agencies with either independent or executive branch status, the FTC has nothing to give away: no licenses to operate, no scarce resources to allocate, no rate hikes, no tariff relief. With its combined antitrust and consumer functions under the same roof, the FTC just takes away: an industry's monopoly, its reputation, its profits. Even small business, its traditional defender, has backed away, angered by such industrywide rule makings as the funeral rule.

The FTC's political problems plague all of its sister agencies empowered to enforce the public good. Invariably this means removing power or resources from an entrenched group, rather than the more typical agency pattern of doling out rewards. Allocating rewards also enables an agency to attract and hold a constituency strong enough to ensure its survival. Not only does the FTC lack rewards, Congress has denied the agency the resources to offset its political vulnerability. Altogether, it is a recipe guaranteed to produce long-term ineffectiveness.

At this point, the FTC enjoys only the support of the consumer groups, whose power is limited, spread too thin over many agencies to sustain the political needs of any one agency against an angry business community and its allies in Congress. With mixed signals from Congress, and an increasingly uncertain mandate, the future of the FTC seems clear: the Little Old Lady of Pennsylvania Avenue, banished temporarily from the premises, has returned to settle in for the duration, or at least until a whopping consumer scandal once again dramatizes the need for a vigorous FTC. By that time, the agency may have learned its lesson of the seventies, and embark on a less adversarial strategy to ensure its long-term survival. The little old lady is putting on her gloves.

6

Political Meltdown
Reactors, Risks, and Regulation

We're still recovering from the mistakes of the 1960s. The agency still emphasizes reactor design, instead of the more important safety questions.
— Commissioner Victor Gilinsky, Nuclear Regulatory Commission

Nuclear power technology is low-risk energy whose risks are comparable to other technologies.
— Robert Szalay, vice president, Atomic Industrial Forum

ON A ROCKY BLUFF overlooking the Pacific Ocean, twelve miles west of San Luis Obispo, California, sits an idle, $2.3 billion nuclear power plant named Diablo Canyon. One of the best known, most expensive, and controversial of the nation's seventy-four nuclear power plants, it is a case study of Murphy's Law applied to the nuclear industry. The victim of incompetent management and virtual self-regulation, the huge nuclear complex collects problems as easily as it collects dust.

Diablo Canyon and its counterparts across the nation demonstrate why an industry on the cutting edge of technology (especially so dangerous a technology) needs vigorous oversight, if only for its own sake. Without it, the industry is left to its own devices, responding mostly to the dictates of the marketplace. Unfortunately, in such industries the merest laxity could wreak havoc and destruction far out of proportion to the negligence involved; that possibility alone provides sufficient justification for a powerful regulatory presence.

This presence never fully developed in the field of domestic nuclear energy, where the regulators still view themselves as a limited audit operation and the industry remains firmly entrenched in the position of senior partner. Taking full advantage of the situation, some segments of the industry cut corners, jeopardized public safety, and took inordinate financial risks. Their negligence affected the entire industry, resulting in a loss of public confidence that ultimately threatened the industry's very existence.

Nuclear power, which held the promise of cheap energy but also the threat of mass destruction, is at a standstill in this country. Some argue that its inherent dangers preclude peaceable uses, and that it should be forsaken. But the genie is out of the bottle, and there is no way to put him back. The technology is here to stay, and the question is whether we have the determination and the resources to master it.

In such a context, national efforts to conquer and control the technology have proven sadly inadequate. The fledgling nuclear industry needed strong regulation for its own development, as well as to ensure public safety and confidence. Instead, it worked too cozily with government regulators who all too often cast a blind eye to defects whose correction would have slowed nuclear progress but averted fiascoes and assured the industry's gradual growth. It was the very model of the nonadversarial partnership sought by business groups anxious to get government off their backs, but it proved once again the inability of the marketplace to regulate itself.

The nuclear industry had argued that it was based upon a complex, advanced science that was beyond the reach of the public at large. The regulators agreed. How could laymen contest the views of an elite corps of nuclear scientists, engineers, and technicians? But, incredibly, the ''ignorant'' layman proved wiser than the experts in the case of Diablo Canyon.

Political Meltdown

The misbegotten Diablo Canyon experience featured the construction of a nuclear power plant on an earthquake fault; a mix-up of blueprints that led to earthquake-proofing the wrong reactor; dozens of major errors in design; falsified records; intimidation of inspectors; senior operators who had failed their licensing examinations; and senior managers who continually assured the public that everything was fine. Through it all, the nuclear regulators insisted that Diablo Canyon was a safe facility.

The saga of Diablo Canyon began in January 1967, when the Pacific Gas and Electric Company (PG & E) initiated plans to build the Diablo facility, encouraged by the prevailing support and enthusiasm for nuclear energy as a cheap source of electricity. Scarcely a year after PG & E broke ground in 1969, geologists working for the Shell Oil Company discovered the Hosgri fault two and a half miles offshore from Diablo Canyon, but close enough to one of the two reactors to cause concern. By the time the geologists' findings wers published, reported to the utility, and passed on to the Atomic Energy Commission (AEC), three-quarters of the reactor was nearly completed. Only then did it become clear that the Hosgri fault was not just another in California's latticework of earthquake faults; it posed a potentially serious threat to public safety.[1]

The utility brushed aside fears with the assurance that the plant could be built to withstand earthquakes. It was just a question of "seismic design," explained the utility spokesmen. This meant the addition of structural supports around the piping, concrete reinforcements, and the addition of braces to ensure that "the plant could be shut down and its radioactive fuel cooled and protected should a strong earthquake occur."[2]

During the next few years, the utility managed to convince the regulators, if not the public, that it could overcome the threat of an earthquake with technological improvements, and that further delays would only impose unnecessary costs, which would be passed along to the consumers of electrical power. The Edison Electric Institute, representing PG & E, generated public pressure if not electricity. The institute estimated that consumers were paying $76 million for each month the Nuclear Regulatory Commission (NRC) stalled in granting a license to operate the plant, in addition to risking shortages of electrical power that could result in brownouts, particularly in the summer months.[3]

The NRC stood its ground as long as it could. But a nearby earthquake in California's Imperial Valley, measuring 6.5 to 6.9 on the Richter scale, must have given them pause, as it did local citizens' groups. The groups petitioned the NRC's licensing board to reexamine Diablo Canyon on the grounds that the quake was near enough to present a real threat to Diablo as well, PG & E's assurances notwithstanding.[4]

Their efforts failed, and in a highly detailed 180 page report issued in June 1981, the licensing and appeal board handed down its decision, which upheld PG & E's contention that Diablo Canyon was safe enough to operate and that the steps taken by PG & E to reinforce the plant were adequate to protect the public health and safety.[5] Although the board agreed the reactor was safe, it hedged its bets with the warning that "seismology is an evolving science," perhaps implying that the safety issue was not totally resolved by even the best available data.[6]

Acting on the advice and with the full confidence of its own licensing and appeal board, the NRC finally granted PG & E a license to load fuel and begin conducting low-power tests of the reactor. The decision was unanimous, with all five commissioners voting, and the utility proceeded to make plans to begin operation. One PG & E official lauded Diablo Canyon as the safest plant ever built.

Safe on paper, anyway. The licensing board appeared to rely primarily on what the utility told them, and the utility's best information was submitted in the form of blueprints. It must have been as much of a surprise to the licensing board and to the NRC as it was to top executives at the utility when one of PG & E's own engineers discovered, several months later in the fall of 1981, that the blueprints for the two reactors had been reversed by accident, which meant that the wrong reactor had been earthquake-proofed! This meant that the drawings used to locate pipes and their supports, as well as the numbers specifying pipe weights along the earthquake fault, were useless; in addition, "the seismic supports added to deal with the potential earthquake damage had been put on backwards; some pipes and equipment were supported too rigidly, others not firmly enough."[7] In other words, the volumes of data used to reassure an angry public in the otherwise sleepy college town of San Luis Obispo were invalidated by a simple mistake — an honest mistake to be sure, but one with massive potential consequences.

PG & E tried to save face, pointing out that at least the utility had promptly reported its mistake, and that one of its own engineers, John L. Horn, had made the discovery. This "vividly illustrates that no matter how embarrassing or costly an error may be, it will be reported," said senior PG & E vice president George A. Maneatis.[8] A long-time critic of the utility and of nuclear power, Governor Edmund G. (Jerry) Brown retorted that it didn't matter, since the engineer discovered the mistake, not as part of routine oversight on the part of the utility, but "out of simple curiosity, as an accident."[9]

The mistake made PG & E the laughingstock of the nuclear industry, although the potential consequences of an earthquake — the release of radioactivity, among other dangers — were no laughing matter. Public safety aside, even the cost of repairing the damage of such an accident would have run into millions of dollars, as shown by the sorry experience at Three Mile Island, whose damaged reactor remains idle years after the incident, while two governors, the federal government, and the utilities dispute who is going to pay the bill.

Defenders of Diablo Canyon at the NRC, the utility, and the trade associations representing the nuclear industry searched for an explanation for such a blunder, finally emerging with the answer: a failure in "quality assurance." Known by the initials QA, this referred to problems in management's oversight of the plant. At Diablo, management was lax in the development of careful processes under which many other reactors had been built and operated. Without these basic management tools, things were bound to go wrong. "At Diablo Canyon, communications between the utility and the seismic consultant went wrong," explained Robert Szalay, the vice president for technological and regulatory affairs at the Atomic Industrial Forum, the leading trade association of the nuclear industry. "The utility and the consultant were located across the street from each other, and they were passing the drawings back and forth. It was all too informal. The real issue was that, with the preoccupation in California with seismic issues, there was a breakdown in quality assurance procedures." But it is not management's "quality assurance" programs that the public relies upon for assurance of the safety of a nuclear facility. It is the assurance of the relevant federal agency, the NRC, which in this and similar cases was strangely silent.

On Capitol Hill, an enraged Rep. Morris Udall blamed the NRC for spending too much time on speeding up its licensing of reactors and too little time monitoring their safety. "I would hope that the commission will demonstrate the same vigor in correcting the defects in its quality assurance program that it has shown in seeking to expedite its licensing procedures," the Arizona Democrat said at a lengthy hearing, in November 1981, of the House Interior Subcommittee on Energy and Environment, which he chairs.[10]

For President Reagan's newly appointed NRC chairman, Nunzio Palladino, Diablo Canyon was a revelation, which marked a turning point in his own thinking about nuclear regulation. A former engineering school dean from Pennsylvania State University who had previously worked with an NRC licensing board, Palladino was known as an outspoken advocate of nuclear technology. His advocacy of the industry was one of the main reasons President Reagan appointed him to the chairmanship. Confronting the confused and indignant congressional subcomittee, Palladino allowed that his confidence in the industry was shaken, and that his few months on the commission showed him that "serious quality assurance breakdowns" existed throughout the industry as well as at Diablo Canyon.[11] "There are a number of utilities out there who got into something without realizing how different were the challenges from those of running conventional power plants," said Palladino. "Before Diablo Canyon, I might have been inclined to say it [the quality assurance system] is inadequate, but there are certainly serious questions raised about the seismic analyses that were performed, and hence the design features that were dependent on those analyses. And that sort of beclouds the high degree of confidence I had before this incident."[12]

Palladino was followed by the agency's director of operations, William J. Dircks, who admitted that since the Diablo incident, the agency had uncovered "serious quality assurance breakdowns with broad repercussions'' at four additional facilities.[13] Dircks blamed the utilities for retaining quality assurance staffs ''too small to maintain sufficient surveillance over the contractors' work.''[14] He itemized the causes of inadequate quality assurance: unqualified workers, falsified records, intimidation of inspectors, lack of authority, lack of communication, and poor to nonexistent procedures. But it was easier to blame the utilities than to accept responsibility for the NRC's own negligence in failing to provide adequate supervision. For its part, the agency is caught in the bind of regulatory ambivalence, its own self-image and public mandate too restricted to include meaningful oversight of utility management practices. ''We're just a limited audit operation'' is the operative phrase often repeated by top NRC officials when queried about their agency's lapses in the regulation of management.

Just why Diablo was such a rude awakening to NRC's management remains a mystery, since gaps in PG & E's management program had surfaced in the past. One example revealed that in 1980, 43 percent of the senior reactor operators and 36 percent of the remaining reactor operators had failed their qualifying exams, yet still worked for the company.[15] Similar rates of examination failure had been reported at Three Mile Island, whose accident had long since been attributed to ''human factors.'' The technology was sound; the only concern focused on who was operating it. Doubting Thomases, worried by these explanations, failed to take comfort in subsequent reports of cheating scandals involving operators anxious to pass their licensing examinations.

Embarrassed by the accumulation of mishaps, publicized through congressional hearings and extensive media coverage, the NRC finally suspended PG & E's operating license for Diablo Canyon. It was the first time in history that the government had suspended a utility's license to operate a nuclear reactor.[16] The agency also ordered an independent review of the plant's calculations on earthquake safety. Through its spokesman, PG & E expressed its disappointment at the suspension, still arguing that ''nothing has been discovered to date that would indicate the plant is not safe.''[17]

Despite Palladino's widely publicized promises to restore public confidence in nuclear energy, the NRC settled back into its old pattern of good will toward the utility, by allowing PG & E to select its own auditor to conduct an "independent review" of the blueprint fiasco. This was another instance in which both the NRC and the industry failed to appreciate the need to reassure the public. Only a high quality, independent assessment could have done the job. The agency ignored the pleadings of members of Congress, including Rep. George Miller (Democrat, California), who urged the NRC to select a "truly independent auditor." Miller labeled Diablo Canyon "one of the most troubling [matters] I've seen in my seven years in Congress . . . more serious than Three Mile Island."[18] Governor Brown, an early opponent of the reactor, tried to prevent the utility from selecting its own auditor, saying that any company picked by PG & E would be viewed as biased, no matter how fair the review.

As it turned out, the warnings were prophetic: not only was the reviewer viewed as biased, the firm actually was. Ignoring its critics, the NRC approved PG & E's choice of an auditor, Robert S. Cloud & Associates of Berkeley, California. As predicted, the auditor and the utility worked out a sweetheart relationship, in which the auditor sent its audit over to the utility — in effect, clearing the report with them first — before forwarding it to the NRC. "It was bound to happen," said Joel Reynolds, an attorney with the Center for Law in the Public Interest, representing the eight persons and groups challenging the Diablo license. "Cloud wasn't impartial," continued Reynolds. "How could it be? It was a small firm whose financial survival depended on PG & E."

The fiasco of the Cloud audit unfolded in late December 1981 to reveal a scenario similar to the way the Marx brothers might have handled the Watergate cover-up. At first, the utility denied having seen the report first, but when further investigation revealed Dr. Cloud's home telephone number on one version of the report, along with a watered-down version of the report finally submitted to the NRC, the case was overwhelming. The agency finally began an inquiry into Cloud's "independence" — a waste of time at that point, but a tacit admission of its initial errors in judgment. The real mistake the agency made was in allowing the utility to operate in a manner that amounted to self-regulation when its past history indicated the need for strong government intervention.

In the aftermath of the Cloud audit, numerous additional safety problems, called "design errors," began to surface. This led top NRC officials to finally level strong charges at the utility. There is something "basically wrong with the leadership at the utility," the NRC's director of inspection and enforcement concluded, somewhat belatedly. The NRC's regional director accused PG & E of "arrogance toward the commission," and Commissioner Victor Gilinsky said the Diablo incident called into question the company's "integrity" and "fitness to run a plant."[19]

Although the utility was not used to such harsh criticism from the NRC, it had long since accustomed itself to acting as if it were in a state of siege where the public was concerned. Perhaps its problems in dealing with political stress stemmed from its being forced to deal from the start with a higher level of public protest than that directed against most other plants throughout the country. The utility endured years of minor challenges, which reached a peak in 1979, when a crowd of twenty thousand protesters gathered at Cuesta College, near the reactor, and, joined by their governor, Jerry Brown, chanted "No on Diablo Canyon! No on Diablo Canyon!" The protests grew more serious after the mass demonstration, when fifty-eight antinuclear groups started training their members for the day when they would disrupt the opening of the plant through "nonviolent assault." They organized under an umbrella group called the Abalone Alliance, which took its name from the multicolored iridescent shellfish along the California coastline, many of whom had perished in 1974 in Diablo Cove after small amounts of copper were released into the sea form the plant's cooling system. Although PG & E spent about $10 million to replace the copper piping with titanium and save the abalone, the shellfish remained a symbol of the company's effect on the environment and a rallying cry for the antinuclear movement in California.[20]

The alliance trained thousands of people, whom it organized into what it called "affinity groups" — clusters of fifteen to twenty people, modeled after similar networks in the Spanish Civil War.[21] On September 14, 1981, their protest began in earnest, with three thousand protesters blocking the gateway and roads leading into Diablo Canyon, in an attempt to halt work on the plant. Bracing themselves for thirty thousand demonstrators were 162 highway patrolmen, five hundred National Guardsmen, assorted sheriffs' deputies, and even the Coast Guard. More protesters were expected, judging from newspaper headlines at the time, which said there were more media than protesters. The protesters were labeled by the *Washington Post* as "a quintessentially California happening of underworked TV actors and overgrown flower children." Their ranks swelled on September 21, when five thousand people, many with babies on their backs, swarmed past the gates of Diablo Canyon; this group was unrelated to the Abalone Alliance. In the end, after some sixteen hundred arrests, the protesters went home, their efforts in stopping the loading of fuel and other work on the reactor a failure.

What finally stopped the plant was not the protesters or the numerous legal attempts of the intervenors (people who challenge agency actions) to force the safety issues, but what former NRC commissioner Peter Bradford called "a first-rate screw-up." As outside consultants started looking more closely at Diablo, and their scrutiny intensified, scores of additional safety and management problems emerged. The blueprint error was just the tip of the iceberg. PG & E's quality assurance problems are rooted in its organizational structure, reported Richard Hubbard, representing MHB Associates, a San Jose consulting firm. Unlike other utilities, PG & E acted as its own architectural, engineering, and construction manager, instead of contracting out these functions. When you have a multiplicity of clients, Hubbard explained, they act as your quality assurance mechanism.[22] After its license was suspended, PG & E contracted out the management of the plant to a reputable firm, Bechtel and Co. "Even Bechtel was surprised by the number of mistakes, and they're in PG & E's camp," said Joel Reynolds. "It's like getting a top surgeon for a patient who's already dead. What can a surgeon do now? What can Bechtel do now?"

If not dead, Diablo lies on the operating table. Its license suspended, Diablo holds the dubious title of an NRC historical first, an unfortunate object lesson of uneven, ineffective regulation. The biggest surprise of all was the NRC's continuing surprise at the events at Diablo, despite all kinds of prior evidence pointing to PG & E's performance problems.

The NRC's reaction led logically to the question, where was the NRC while the plant was being built? Other questions soon followed. What kind of oversight was being provided that allowed a situation like Diablo to develop in the first place? And how could the regulators have allowed a utility of such questionable managerial competence to embark on such a high-risk venture without effective supervision?

In some instances, offense is really the best defense, and in the NRC's case it worked for a while. To offset criticism of the NRC's naiveté and lack of readiness, Palladino launched a campaign of candor, attacking the industry for its carelessness and the agency for its laxity. "During my first five months as NRC chairman, a number of deficiencies at some plants have come to my attention which show a surprising lack of professionalism in the construction and preparation of nuclear facilites," said Palladino in a speech to the Atomic Industrial Forum, shortly after the blueprint mix-up. "The responsibility for such deficiencies rests squarely on the shoulders of management." Palladino added that he did not mean to "absolve the NRC of its portion of responsibility at all. . . . Every deficiency that finds its way . . . into a plant or its operation . . . can be viewed as an NRC failure as well as an industry failure."[23]

Palladino achieved his immediate objective of staving off criticism, and his strategy was hailed as a public relations success. But the element of surprise in Palladino's speeches revealed an essential ingredient of what had gone wrong with nuclear regulation: far too much trust in the nuclear industry. By admitting at this point that its trust in the industry had been misplaced, the agency was in effect admitting that it had trusted the industry all along, and given it a great deal of latitude in making its own decisions.

As in all public relations gambits, it is often hard to sort out rhetoric from reality. If Palladino was traveling around the country talking about the agency's mistakes, would it not be reasonable to assume the agency would soon take corrective action? The answer was disappointing. In the Diablo case, the agency's early action gave way to a surprising reversal when the commissioners voted not to review an earlier decision by the licensing board that accepted the "seismic safety" of Diablo Canyon. Dissenting from that ruling, Commissioner Gilinsky explained that the other commissioners knew the board's decision was unsound, but the "prospect of reviewing it was so unsettling."[24]

At the same time it talked about safety the agency sent signals to industry indicating the reverse: that safety would take a back seat to speeding up the licensing process, which meant removing as many procedural impediments as possible. "There's a high priority given to streamlining," said Commissioner Gilinsky in an interview. "Just look at where the [agency's] Task Force on Regulatory Reform is housed . . . next to the chairman's office. I don't see any safety task force, or any task forces dealing with spent fuel or quality assurance around here."

"Only the commissioners are housed here," added Gilinsky, referring to the geographic nightmare of the NRC, whose ten offices are scattered around Washington and suburban Maryland. "Bureaucrats understand that language: the location of an office."

His colleague, Peter Bradford, offered further evidence of the agency's real priorities to a House subcommittee investigating Diablo on November 19, 1981: "We've had close to twenty meetings on expedited licensing since last winter. I would be surprised if we've had more than one or two dealing with quality assurance for specific plants."[25]

Additional inconsistencies between Palladino's statements and his actions also contradict the lessons of Diablo. As part of its "streamlining" program, the NRC has attempted to limit the role of intervenors by a series of procedural changes designed to make it more difficult and more expensive for them to participate in the licensing of nuclear reactors. Since outside groups have alerted the commission to safety failures in the past, it is difficult to justify the petty harassments of these groups by the commission, especially in view of the fact that no regulator or industry spokesman has ever substantiated, with concrete evidence, their oft-cited claim that responsible intervenors hold up the licensing process.

In the case of Diablo Canyon, delays were more accurately attributed to construction difficulties, added NRC requirements, and labor problems, not to citizen participation. In fact, PG & E was overly optimistic about the time it would take to complete the reactor; it exceeded its Diablo I schedule by eighty-two months prior to the Three Mile Island accident, and twenty-five months after that due to the seismic issue. Indeed, who would benefit from a speeded-up schedule while the earthquake issue was still being studied?

If the utilities and their suppliers had been able to build relatively risk-free reactors, there never would have been a problem. But this did not prove to be the case; and instead, widespread variations in competence shook public confidence in the industry as a whole. To be sure, the industry paid the price for the mistakes of the worst elements in its midst; but given such high-risk factors in nuclear energy, this was bound to occur. In fact, the industry itself functioned with the same complacency and misplaced trust as the government; its own "quality assurance" program was instituted only in the aftermath of Three Mile Island.[26]

Diablo Canyon was hardly unique. Mismanagement was unchecked by the federal agency responsible for its supervision. NRC's supervisory powers had all but atrophied, and the agency watched helplessly as a spate of accidents and near disasters undermined the fledgling nuclear industry from coast to coast.

To a large extent, the Diablo incident reflected the political environment of nuclear regulation, in which the marketplace virtually regulated itself. It was a decidedly nonadversarial environment, where decisions were "negotiated," not challenged, the very model of the business-government partnership promoted as "regulatory reform" by the deregulation advocates of the 1980s. To its critics, however, the partnership was not operating in the best interests of the public safety. As Diablo Canyon, Three Mile Island, and other incidents indicated, the NRC had taken on the appearance of a captive agency, dominated by the industry it was supposed to regulate. This weakness showed the need for a more adversarial relationship as a necessary check on an imperfect technology.

In the long run, Diablo Canyon demonstrated that the free market could be its own worst enemy. By pressing the regulators to trust them, the industry contributed to the atrophy of the agency's safety function, eventually endangering its own financial stability.

Diablo remains an unfortunate object lesson, a microcosm of all the regulatory problems that have beset the nuclear issue since the passage of the Atomic Energy Act in 1946 (amended in 1954). It shows how quickly the key objectives of effective regulation — to ensure the health of the industry, minimize its risks, and maintain public confidence — can be lost in a gutless regulatory environment.[27]

The Dual Mission of Development and Safety

To many, it seemed as if Diablo's problems were the problems of a regulatory process that had been derailed. To those who watched the development of nuclear regulation, however, the government's difficulties in sorting out its regulatory role vis-à-vis the nuclear industry were inevitable, the result of saddling the regulators from the beginning with the dual mission of developing and regulating the industry at the same time. In the excitement of the rapid growth, complexity, and constantly changing technology, the regulators became promoters of the nuclear industry. They advocated nuclear development while playing down their own safety function.

In a classic pattern, the regulators fell captive to the industry they were regulating; but more important, they were encouraged to continue in this pattern by their political masters, Congress and the President. Congress had already shown some signs that it was vaguely dissatisfied with having both promotion and safety regulation under the same roof. These qualms surfaced when it created the Atomic Energy Commission (AEC) in 1946, to regulate the military uses of nuclear power, and later, in 1954, when it expanded the agency to include the development of a civilian nuclear industry. Nothing was done about the problem until 1974, when Congress separated the functions into two agencies: the newly formed Nuclear Regulatory Commission (NRC), which would be responsible for ensuring public health and safety, as well as environmental protection; and the Energy Research and Development Administration (ERDA) — later to become a division of the Department of Energy — responsible for the promotion of nuclear and other sources of energy. But the habits of a generation were too hard to break by this time, and the NRC found itself still in the position of advocate as well as regulator.

Born in government laboratories, the nuclear industry grew up regulated, at first by the military, under whose leadership the atomic bomb was developed. Those who labored on the Manhattan Project, the first major effort leading to the development of the bomb, were drawn from private industry, from the military and civilian branches of government, and from the universities. Pressed by the urgency of the Second World War and protected by a veil of military secrecy, they created, in a miraculously short period of time, the bombs that were dropped on Hiroshima and Nagasaki, which President Truman credited with saving American lives and assuring the nation's final victory over Japan.

Many of the scientists and engineers who built the bomb, however, were distressed by the results of their research and haunted by a sense of responsibility for its human costs. Eager to turn these instruments of destruction to useful civilian purposes, they began urging political leaders in the late 1940s to support efforts to develop nuclear reactors that could produce energy and eliminate the fear of electricity shortages. Truman also indicated his concern about the future of nuclear power when he reportedly warned David Lilienthal, the first AEC chairman: "You have the most important thing there is. You must make a blessing of it or [pointing to a globe] we'll blow that all to smithereens."

These efforts prevailed, and President Eisenhower's Atoms for Peace program, announced in 1954, heralded a new era: the theoretical discoveries of Albert Einstein, Enrico Fermi, and Marie and Pierre Curie would be turned to peacetime uses. Nuclear advocates promised that harnessing nuclear energy would not only fulfill this country's needs but also serve a worldwide function. Nuclear energy would be "too cheap to meter," said former AEC chairman Lewis Strauss, in a statement typical of the optimism of the period.

The spurt of optimism accompanying creation of the Atoms for Peace program was reinforced by early successes. One year later, in 1955, a nuclear-powered submarine surpassed all records, and spawned plans for a nuclear-powered airplane, spaceships, and the construction of breeder reactors that would produce more fuel than they consumed. The submarine was built under the direction of Admiral Hyman Rickover, whose tireless efforts and management skill — an unusual mix of arrogance, strong leadership, political protection, and vision — were responsible for its success. To anyone familiar with Admiral Rickover's abilities, it was not surprising that the submarine's sister projects never materialized under different forms of leadership. In some ways, Rickover epitomized the model regulator, doing what regulators are supposed to do: protect the public, help the industry, prevent the industry from becoming too greedy, work efficiently, and never lose sight of the original set of goals. Rickover was unusual in his ability to control the peculiar mix of government and industry, and what he lost in popularity — particularly with the industry — he more than made up for in achievement. Mixed missions did not bother Rickover, who solved the conflict between safety and advocacy by according them equal status.

One of Rickover's distinct advantages was that, unlike the NRC, he had virtually total control over the nuclear subs, including design, manufacture, and allocation of funds. He also benefited from enthusiastic congressional support, which enabled him to operate in an environment relatively free from political controversy. Members of Congress believed Rickover's assurances on the safety of the subs; Rickover delivered on that promise; and eventually Rickover developed the enviable position of being free of the kind of hostile and suspicious oversight that has become routine today.

Although Rickover was able to extract the best from the military environment, and to benefit from it, it now seems clear that many of the present difficulties in nuclear regulation stem from its early marriage to the military, which is often characterized by the tendency toward secrecy, crisis management, rigid hierarchical control, and an aversion to public involvement. In adapting nuclear power to civilian needs, many of these traditions remained, with little effort to change them and no overt justification for their retention.

The aura of secrecy, for example, important for the national security in the 1940s, became a subject of considerable debate later on. "The reactor-licensing program was built by the same people who developed the bomb," recalled Peter Bradford. "They used the same excuse — national security — for the aura of secrecy in which they developed a process that legitimized the placing of reactors in communities all over the United States." There are seventy-four nuclear plants now in operation. Some, like the Indian Point reactor, near New York City, are close to major population centers, despite the explicit "remote siting" policy of the agency.

To some extent, the element of secrecy is still justifiable, since some of the materials used in civilian reactors — such as enriched uranium — are the same as those used in building bombs. In fact, one plant under contract with the Navy but regulated by the NRC has come under considerable criticism for not being able to account for the loss of some of its enriched uranium. Officials at the plant, located in Erwin, Tennessee, are unable to determine whether the uranium has been stolen, and possibly transported to governments unfriendly to the United States, or simply lost through sheer ineptitude.[28]

Reforms opened up the process of regulating nuclear technology to public scrutiny, but the old attitudes remained, not unexpected, since the personnel in charge of the process remained relatively constant, despite changes in the laws, the agency's organization, and the regulations. As the reasons for secrecy perpetuated the exclusion of the public, so did the ''doctrine of the expert.'' According to the rationale underlying this policy, the technology was too complex for most people to understand, and public policy decisions were best left to scientists and engineers more familiar with the field. That distinction between the experts and the public prevaded the mind-set of the nuclear regulators and continues to this day.

Unfortunately, many experts who never saw the relationship between public involvement and public support are completely baffled by the current antinuclear movement, many of whose adherents often confuse the peace- and wartime uses of nuclear technology. By 1982, the base of the antinuclear movement had expanded considerably, joining at many points both domestically and worldwide with the movement against nuclear proliferation. Atoms for Peace seemed remote, as the regulators and the industry struggled to make up for lost time and convince an ignorant public that nuclear power was safe, if properly managed. For a large segment of the public it was too late; their education had been ignored for too long, and they no longer believed those arguments.

From atomic energy's military roots also grew a tradition of crisis management, an acceptable and often necessary *modus operandi* in wartime. Unlike civilian problems, however, wars create emergencies largely outside the scope of national control, while nuclear emergencies like Three Mile Island are self-made. Questions like ''What could we have done to prevent these accidents from happening?'' were bound to emerge from a crisis-managed environment.

To some extent the regulators also adopted the hierarchical tradition of the military, a necessary component for the success of the Manhattan Project, but another matter when grafted on to a multiheaded civilian agency. Within both the AEC and the NRC, rigid hierarchies discouraged participation not only from the public but also from those within the agency with valuable contributions to offer. One nuclear engineer, Robert Pollard, resigned in frustration in February 1976 from the NRC, later appearing on CBS's ''60 Minutes'' to warn that the reactor at Indian Point was an accident ''waiting to happen.'' Now working for the Union of Concerned Scientists, Pollard argued that he was unable to make himself heard within an agency structured to screen out information it did not want to hear.

Two years later, in 1978, James S. Creswell, a thirty-five-year-old reactor inspector working at the NRC's Midwest regional office in Chicago, flew to Washington, at his own expense, to warn his superiors about a failure in the feedwater system at the Davis-Besse Nuclear Power Station in Ohio. The very failure that subsequently caused the reactor core damage at Three Mile Island apparently did not concern the agency at the time; Creswell was unsuccessful in persuading senior NRC officials to take him seriously. After fourteen months of effort, Creswell finally managed to get one NRC commissioner, John Ahearne, to request a report on the safety questions he had raised. But it was too late; the report was requested the very day after the accident at Three Mile Island. ''Worrying about the adequacy of nuclear plants and their safety systems was something that was supposed to be done by the hundreds of safety analysts at the NRC's headquarters, and not by a field inspector like Creswell, who was expected to be more of a bookkeeper than an engineer,'' wrote Daniel Ford in the *New Yorker*.[29] Ironically, Creswell later received a merit award of $4,000 for trying to alert the agency to his safety concerns, while two of his superiors, who had ignored Creswell, Victor Stello, director of the Office of Inspection and Enforcement, and Harold Denton, director of the Office of Nuclear Reactor Regulation, were given awards of $10,000 and $20,000, respectively, for their handling of Three Mile Island.

While the military influenced the development of nuclear power, there was also a strong tradition of civilian control built into the original mandates. A five-member commission ran the AEC, and the same pattern was followed at the NRC. But the decision to create the NRC as a solution to the historic ambivalence between nuclear development and safety addressed the problem on paper only. By the end of the 1970s, it became apparent to a variety of constituencies that the NRC still tilted toward promoting the nuclear industry at the expense of safety. The habits of a lifetime proved too ingrained to correct.

The Kemeny Commission, appointed by President Carter to investigate the Three Mile Island accident, for example, concluded that the NRC was still too preoccupied with licensing nuclear facilities to pay sufficient attention to safety issues, often erring "on the side of industry's convenience rather than carrying on its primary mission of assuring safety."[30] At the same time that the Kemeny report was issued, industry accused the report (along with a companion report called the Rogovin report) of undermining public confidence in nuclear power.[31]

Common Cause attributed the NRC's failure to separate itself from its predecessor to the retention of AEC personnel, many of whom came from the nuclear industry. The group's study showed that 279 top level NRC officials, representing 65 percent of the total, came from private companies under contract with the NRC.[32] The NRC not only inherited many of the AEC's personnel and programs, its first three chairmen had all worked for the AEC. To some extent, however, it would be unrealistic to think that, given the limited pool of talent in this highly specialized field, the agency would be able to recruit too far afield from its own and industry's ranks.

Only the stationery changed. One of the first official actions of the new agency was to adopt all the safety rules and policies of its predecessor. The mandate of the AEC, to foster the growth of the nuclear industry with minimal risk to the public, still prevailed; so much so that former Senator Abraham Ribicoff (Democrat, Connecticut) once remarked that it was "difficult to determine in the organization scheme . . . where the commission ends and the industry begins."[33]

The NRC also inherited the AEC's determination to speed the

commercialization of nuclear power. The AEC had predicted that one thousand reactors would be in full operation by the year 2000, a belief only reinforced by the Arab oil crisis of 1973–74. FREE US FROM OPEC — BUILD MILLTOWN 3 read one of the ubiquitous bumper stickers at a nuclear power site. The decision took on a life of its own, despite the oil glut of a few years later and new advances in alternative sources of energy. The most important factor contributing to the reduction in the demand for energy, however, was conservation.

The accident at Three Mile Island (TMI) forced a temporary change in policy, forcing the agency to place safety regulations at the top of its list of priorities. This new posture lasted for two years, during which many of the suggestions of the Kemeny and Rogovin reports were followed up. The Kemeny Commission pinpointed the TMI problem in the design of the reactor's control room, calling it unsuited to safe management by its own operators. The human factor, as it was called, led to the creation of an office of the same name, as well as to an "action plan" specifying what measures the agency was going to take to increase its performance in the area of safety regulation. Safety regulations trebled after TMI; there were now so many that the agency could not begin to rank them in the order of their importance.[34]

As it happened, the agency did not have the chance. When the memory of TMI receded, the political forces regained their traditional hold over the agency's policy making, and the old patterns reappeared.

Despite its uncomfortable role as an honest broker carrying out congressional and presidential directives — no matter how contradictory or inconsistent — the NRC is often the victim of political decisions over which it has minimal control. From Congress, for example, the NRC faces a battery of directives, leveled from at least nine different congressional committees with oversight jurisdiction over the NRC. Some took the agency to task for not licensing reactors fast enough; others called the NRC on the carpet for moving licenses through too swiftly while ignoring safety regulations. Regulators at the NRC who had also worked for the AEC suffered attacks of nostalgia, remembering the good old days in the 1950s and 1960s, when they enjoyed the uniform oversight — and protection — of only one committee, the Joint Committee on Atomic Energy, with whom they had developed a close and supportive relationship.

In the years following the passage of the amended Atomic Energy Act of 1954, Congress through the Joint Committee spoke with one voice, and that voice ordered an emphasis on development. Today, the Joint Committee's role has been taken over by the House Appropriations Committee through its Subcommittee on Public Works, which has jurisdiction over the NRC. Its chairman, Thomas Bevill (Democrat, Alabama), has taken a strong stand in favor of speeding up the licensing process, and his views appear now to prevail at the agency.

"The agency regards the House Appropriations Committee as the legitimate source of power," remarked Commissioner Gilinsky. "It is an important source of pressure. The bureaucrats, the staff, the chairman, and the commissioners cope with the other committees, but tend to regard Tom Bevill as their natural superior — much more so than the White House."

Former NRC commissioner Peter Bradford added that the emphasis now on speed in licensing was "not so much a product of Reagan but of Tom Bevill," whom Bradford labeled "sinister and heavy-handed," whose name was "mentioned five times as much as anyone else's." "The committee," said Bradford, "keeps bureaucrats jumping because of its control over the purse strings, while those who want to take short cuts use the committee as an excuse. The commission has to be responsive to Moffett and Udall, but tends to treat them as a nuisance, while Bevill is regarded as writing scripture."

Bevill makes no bones about the low esteem in which he holds the NRC, threatening budget cuts to force the agency into speeding up the licensing process. "It's a sad story," he said. "We've given them [the NRC] more personnel each year and they still haven't licensed a plant since July 1978. It's like pouring money down a rat hole."[35] Bevill estimates the United States needs two hundred more nuclear plants to become energy self-sufficient by the year 2000.

In looking to the White House for consistency, the agency has found little comfort; rather, it has had to deal with recent Presidents who have switched signals and indicated markedly different directions. The agency and its friends in industry suffered a shock when President Jimmy Carter, whose professional background as a nuclear engineer was cause for optimism, called nuclear energy a "last resort," when all other energy-producing technologies had been tried. With his typical ambivalence, Carter also made the safety advocates unhappy, accomplishing little in the way of appointments or organizational change to carry out his "last resort" statement to its logical conclusions.

When President Reagan took office in 1980, the trend reversed once more, with the President asking whether all these costly regulations were really necessary, and promising to help reduce delays in reactor licensing. "One of the best potential sources of new electrical energy supplies in the coming decades is nuclear power," he said in a statement issued by the White House press office. "Unfortunately, the federal government has created a regulatory environment that is forcing many utilities to rule out nuclear power as a source of new generating capacity. . . . Nuclear power has become entangled in a morass of regulations that do not enhance safety but that do cause extensive licensing delays and economic uncertainty."[36]

What policy directions can the agency expect from future Presidents? If public opinion polls are any indication, the agency faces another swing of the pendulum. A Harris poll, conducted in 1980, revealed that 84 percent of the American people believe that fundamental changes are needed in the regulatory process to keep the risks of nuclear power within "tolerable limits," while 57 percent favor a temporary ban on licensing nuclear plants.

As utility bills continue to soar, the public has also started to question the financial risks involved in choosing nuclear power as a primary source of energy. Far from being electricity "too cheap to meter," nuclear power has proved in some cases too expensive even to calculate. Estimates of the TMI cleanup alone, for example, run from $1 to $4 billion.

In an excellent article entitled "A Nuclear Fiasco Shakes the Bond Market" in *Fortune*, Peter Bernstein detailed the problems of the Washington Public Power Supply System (WPPSS), whose five reactors (two built, three under construction) have been idled by financial mismanagement. Known to its detractors by the unfortunate acronym WHOOPS, the utility has expanded its own group of opponents beyond the traditional antinuclear constituency to include bondholders, investment bankers, and consumers. In this case, the utility issued tax-exempt revenue bonds with "an incredible $6.8 billion in long-term debt outstanding — more than New York City owed when it was on the brink of bankruptcy in 1975."[37] By the time these bonds are retired, predicted Bernstein, "the electricity users of the Northwest will have paid a numbing $7.2 billion in principal and interest without getting a single kilowatt of electricity in return." Bernstein blames the utility for its problems. Even though WPPSS enjoyed the luxury of not having to deal with the steady confrontations from the antinuclear movement that plagued PG & E, the utility was unable to control the "lawyers who wrote slipshod contracts, managers who bungled, investment houses eager to sell more bonds and earn more commissions, and a feckless board of directors . . . utterly lost in the megabucks world of nuclear economics."[38]

In short, WPPSS could not control its own marketplace. Were the utilities and their customers really better off in the long run if they were untrammeled by the heavy hand of government regulators? Or could one suggest that what was good for the public safety and the public's pocketbook was also good for the industry? Did their interests coincide all along?

By 1982, all signs pointed to an industry in trouble, with no indications of an improved prognosis. *Life* magazine featured a story headlined "The Nuclear Industry Begins to Die," while the *New York Times* catalogued a litany of woes, describing the industry as "crippled by soaring costs, depressed energy demand, and public opposition . . . [with] little hope for a revival . . . for at least ten years, and possibly not until the next century."[39]

What the brief history of atomic regulation reveals is that the political decision makers went too far, too fast, with a technology that was still in its developmental phases. Despite an elaborate regulatory process, designed to ensure the unraveling of safety problems, the drive to apply the technology won out over the forces to contain it. Perhaps both the industry and the public would have been better off with a regulatory process that addressed both safety and development, with a dual mission that was not a competitive but a cooperative venture. For in the final analysis, a healthy industry depends on public support, with the regulators brokering that relationship.

Risk Management

"More people were killed at Chappaquiddick than at Three Mile Island," reads a familiar bumper sticker. It represents the popular version of the argument that despite the problems and the highly publicized failures, no lives have been lost at nuclear power plants.

"Even at Three Mile Island, what was expected in terms of the release of radioactivity was thousands of times less than what was predicted," said Donald C. Winston, media relations manager of the Atomic Industrial Forum. "Nuclear power technology," added his colleague, Robert Szalay, "is low-risk energy whose risks are comparable to other technologies."

Szalay's claim that nuclear energy is safe, clean, and cheap — relative to other forms of energy — has been verified by experts outside the industry. One of them, Canadian physicist Dr. Herbert Inhaber, measured the risks associated with coal, oil, nuclear power, wind, and solar energy, and concluded that energy systems like solar energy and wind were actually riskier to society than nuclear power.[40] Basing his calculations on cost-benefit analysis, Inhaber's findings were predicated on the assumption that while the risks associated with nuclear power were enormous, they were also unlikely. Following the Inhaber line of reasoning, other studies have shown the damage wrought on the environment from other sources of energy. The tall smokestacks of coal-fired utility plants, for example, produce the by-product acid rain, which has become a worldwide pollution problem and a serious bone of contention between countries and regions. Canada blames the United States for poisoning its lakes; Sweden accuses Germany of exporting its acid rain; and within the United States, the Northeast governors have banded together to seek ways to prevent the midwestern states from allowing their utilities to export their sulfur dioxide along with the prevailing winds.

On a smaller scale, risks associated with solar power also involve accidents, namely, serious falls suffered by do-it-yourselfers who install solar collectors on the roofs of their homes. Other risks involve mine accidents, oil rig explosions, gas leaks, and other problems associated with extracting the minerals needed for producing alternate sources of energy. Even wood-burning stoves, a back-to-nature energy alternative, have been widely criticized as hazardous.

The issue boils down to risk, and the management of risk — a problem neither the NRC nor any other participant has been able to resolve. The industry feels, with some justification, that the public demands "zero risk" from them, but looks less critically at other technologies, where at least some margin of error is tolerated. "Our critics," said Robert Szalay referring to Diablo Canyon, "feel that the technology is inherently impossible. Their goal is not to make Diablo safe but impossible."

But zero risk is not guaranteed, or even a goal, according to the enabling legislation of nuclear regulation. "The statute talks about achieving adequate protection, reasonable assurance, avoiding unreasonable risk," argued Leonard Bickwit, general counsel of the NRC, referring to the Atomic Energy Act. "The statute doesn't talk about zero risk, only about guarding against what is inimical to the public health and safety."

But the risk factor, and its application by the NRC to nuclear energy policy, form the crux of the nuclear debate: How much risk should be allowed, and who makes that determination? To the dismay of the nuclear industry, the NRC in its effort to appear independent has constantly changed the rules of the game — with disastrous consequences for the financial stability of nuclear energy. "If you so overregulate one particular industry as to continually reduce its competitiveness, you should also be looking at other technologies," said Szalay. "In the 1970s, regulatory requirements grew at a tremendous pace. This avalanche of requirements affects our ability to complete our designs in a timely and reasonable way."

As the NRC found more and more problems with reactor designs, they increased their demands on the industry. "There are thirty disciplines represented at the NRC," continued Szalay. "Each lobbied its own thing with tremendous power. One staffer would say, 'We know we're holding up your hearings, but I'd feel better if you just looked at this one thing.' When you start constructing a plant, there are thousands of criteria. Standards keep changing, and this is not done in a controlled way. There are pockets of individuals pressing their individual concerns without consideration of the whole." The result of all this, charged Szalay, has led to the wrong emphasis at the agency. "You should take care of the improbable, but not the almost impossible."

Superimposed on the technical responsibilities of the agency is an adjudicatory process, a multilayered set of hearings and negotiations that add considerably to the time it takes to put a plant in operation. Instead of the eight years it takes in Japan, France, or Belgium to build a nuclear facility, it could take fourteen years in the United States from start to finish, including the seven to ten years it takes for construction. Those extra years, argues the industry, come from misguided risk management, a Catch–22 nightmare in which every time the NRC finds another safety hitch, the whole industry has to go back and deal with it. The backfitting required by continual changes in safety requirements becomes difficult, expensive, and often technologically impossible once a reactor nears completion. The alternative, ripping the plant apart and starting over from scratch, is financially prohibitive.

This problem is partly the fault of the companies producing nuclear reactors; they have been reluctant over the years to submit to a standardization of nuclear plants that would make the process more streamlined and predictable. "Every company wants to custom-build its own plants," said Joseph Fouchard, the director of the NRC's Office of Public Affairs.

When financial risk begins to compete with safety risks, the process of making hard choices takes over. "We're fooling people if we say in setting safety standards that we're ignoring economic concerns," said the NRC's Bickwit. "Something other than pure safety, namely, economics, is at work here and ought to be at work here. Economics is an interest you ought to take into account in formulating public policy."

Factoring economics into risk management becomes a political problem when economics wins out, as it frequently does in the process known as regulatory tradeoffs. Critics of the NRC say that the dominance of financial considerations enjoys something of a tradition at the agency. An early memo from former NRC chairman Joseph M. Hendrie, written in 1972, suggests the agency's priorities as something along the order of "what's good for General Electric is good for the country." Hendrie's memo was written in response to a memo from Dr. Stephen H. Hanauer, one of the chief technical advisers at the AEC, who warned nine of his colleagues of the serious safety risks involved in the type of containment structures — the giant circular buildings used to house the radioactive material in nuclear reactors — built by the General Electric Company. Hanauer wrote that since "recent events have highlighted the safety disadvantages of pressure-suppression containments . . . I recommend that the AEC adopt a policy of discouraging [their] further use."[41]

In his response, Hendrie indicates that although he agreed with Hanauer that "dry containments" were superior to the G.E. variety, he rejected his advice to deny General Electric the permits to build them. No scientific reasoning to rebut Hanauer's health and safety concerns accompanied the rest of Hendrie's answer, which addressed instead his economic concerns: "Reversal of this hallowed policy . . . could well be the end of nuclear power. It would throw into question the continued operation of licensed plants, would make unlicensable the G.E. and Westinghouse ice condensor plant now in review, and *would generally create more turmoil than I can stand thinking about.*"[42]

Hendrie, who was later replaced as NRC chairman following the TMI debacle, reflected the general reluctance of nuclear regulators to intervene too vigorously, particularly when they felt the health of the industry was at stake. Few officials today would react as openly as did Hendrie, who probably never dreamed of the Freedom of Information request that eventually brought his memo to light. But similar actions and inactions have indicated the agency's ambivalence when confronted with the choice between safety and economics. This appearance of ambivalence, characterizing the agency's attitude toward risk, has produced widespread criticism of its ability to regulate in the interest of the public safety. In addition to the incidents at Diablo, Three Mile Island, and Davis-Besse, many other "events" have occurred, pointing to some of the very real risks associated with nuclear power. To cite a few of the better-known incidents:

- At the Robert E. Ginna plant in Rochester, New York, on January 25, 1981, a tube in the steam generator plant (built by General Electric) burst, producing seven hundred gallons of radioactive coolant per minute. Fortunately, the problem lasted only one day.

- At the Zimmer plant, on the banks of the Ohio River, forty miles east of Cincinnati, the absence of an adequate quality control program led to such serious breakdowns in job performance in the early 1980s that criminal charges were pressed. Welders were converting materials to their own personal use, making belt buckles and selling them. Lax construction procedures led to valves being rusted shut or welded into systems; improperly mixed electrical cables, constituting a serious fire hazard; and beams being installed that did not appear on the designs for the plant. By 1983, construction on the plant was halted indefinitely by the NRC.

- Similar construction problems exist at the Commanche Peak site, and at Marble Hill in southern Indiana; while seismic problems plague another California plant, San Onofre. Experts have also questioned the strength of the containment building at the McGuire plant near Charlotte, North Carolina, and emergency evacuation plans are still troublesome for plants like Shoreham on Long Island.

- The fire at the Tennessee Valley Authority's Browns Ferry plant on March 22, 1975, remains one of the most serious accidents affecting a nuclear power plant. In what was later discovered by NRC inspectors to be routine practice by employees, a worker was using candles to check for air leaks in an inflammable sealant when the cables caught fire, a rather primitive practice in an electronic age. Similar fires occurred at the Peach Bottom plant in 1965, at Indian Point in 1971, and twice at San Onofre. In addition to the damage they cause to the cables, these fires can also cause failures in the reactor's safety system.

- At Indian Point, which is within a fifty-mile radius of about 10 percent of the entire population of the United States, the problems Robert Pollard warned about finally occurred, four years after his departure. On October 17, 1980, an employee of the Consolidated Edison Company, the utility in charge of Indian Point, found radioactive water ankle deep on the containment floor, with steam rising in an area near the reactor, indicating more leakage. Mechanical problems with the pumps continued to defy any solution, six months later causing another spill; this time, eight thousand gallons of slightly radioactive water drained into the Hudson River.

- At Three Mile Island, one-half of the senior operators failed all or part of their relicensing examination. Of the twenty that were tested, the vast majority were ordered to undergo retesting because of widespread cheating on the examination. Two shift supervisors actually confessed to cheating on their licensing examinations. At San Onofre, sixteen of eighteen operators failed their licensing tests.

- Finally, in 1979, Three Mile Island came within one hour of a meltdown, the most feared of all nuclear accidents. The danger produced by a meltdown could involve the sudden release of lethal, radioactive material, up to one hundred tons in solid, liquid, gaseous forms in a typical power plant, much of which could enter the environment and endanger people within a hundred-mile radius of the plant, depending on which way the wind was blowing. The failure of the emergency core cooling system, intended to guard against meltdowns, recalled past warnings from AEC and NRC research scientists about its efficacy. Much of the core of the TMI–2 reactor was destroyed by this accident, to a point at which it is probably beyond repair. When scientists got their first televised look inside the TMI reactor three years later, they concluded that the damage had exceeded their original estimates, and that an almost complete meltdown had taken place inside the core.[43]

In the period following TMI, the NRC worked very hard to restore its tarnished image as a protector of the public safety, in a sense benefiting from the scare caused by the accident. In its most important product of this period, its 1982 "action plan" to deal with unresolved safety issues, the agency offered a noteworthy goal: to scientifically assess the safety risks in order to regulate more effectively. The plan identified 133 "generic" problems — those affecting all current plant designs — and unresolved safety issues.[44] Couched in the jargon of "probabilistic risk assessment," the plan sets forth specific numerical guidelines for dealing with risk, including a determination of the number of deaths attributable to nuclear accidents, and the risks of "delayed mortality," or the chances of getting cancer at a later date from exposure to radioactivity. The admission that minimal risk did exist at nuclear plants represented a new direction for the agency, as well as a tacit admission that it had been less than perfect at previous efforts at risk management. (In fact, in 1978, the agency withdrew its own endorsement of a 1975 study that concluded that the risks of death from a nuclear accident were unlikely.)

Far more interesting about the NRC's new plan was not what it said but what it specifically excluded: the chilling statistic that the actual lives at risk numbered thirteen thousand. That is, in the event of an actual nuclear accident, thirteen thousand lives could be lost. In his dissent from the action plan, Commissioner Bradford called the exclusion of this figure from the report a "sad mistake," especially since the "commission staff does not dispute the validity of this calculation."[45] Bradford wondered whether this conscious omission reflected the NRC's "past regulatory overprotectiveness of nuclear power that has helped to bring the technology into disrepute today."[46] Commissioner Gilinsky explained that the commission was unwilling to display these numbers because of its tendency to "distrust" the public's good sense.

In another study, released on November 1, 1982, the NRC again withheld the worst-case death and damage estimates, which were far worse than any previous data. The commission concealed the figure that an accident at certain high-risk atomic power plants could result in a death toll of one hundred thousand lives and cost over $300 billion. The agency justified its decision to withhold the report for more than six months, and then to selectively withhold some of the data, on the grounds that the probability of such an accident was very low, less than the possibility of a jumbo jet crashing into a football stadium during the Superbowl.[47]

Very often, the public's reaction to risk has influenced the NRC's policies on risk management, to the detriment of the agency and the industry. Fearing public hysteria, the agency often tends to stonewall when it should be candid, and to withhold information at the expense of the public's right to know.

Not true, argues Joseph Fouchard, who detailed some of the constraints under which the agency operates. For one thing, the agency denies permits to plants it deems unsafe, determining through lengthy reviews at the two major stages (site selection and operating license) whether a plant will pose an undue risk to surrounding populations. "People forget about the plants that never got construction contracts, such as Greene County, Baltimore Gas and Electric Company [denied for population reasons]," he said. "This kind of news doesn't reach the public. By the time a case reaches the hearing stage, it looks like we're [the agency] acting as advocates." Fouchard added that in 1975, the agency shut down twenty-one plants suspected of pipe-cracking problems. Again, no publicity appeared to applaud the agency's safety vigilance. "Five or six years ago," said Fouchard, "the safety issue was nil."[48]

To some extent, the agency still operates under the very real constraint of depending too heavily on the utilities and the vendors, which means it ultimately accepts industry's calculations as well as its primary role in setting the levels of tolerable risk. Numerous critics, including the General Accounting Office, have noted that the NRC has relied too often on self-evaluations conducted by the utilities — an inevitable result of overlapping personnel. Exploring the roots of this problem over the years, a Rand Corporation report concluded in 1977 that "the nuclear power industry was . . . willing to take risks somewhat larger than the public was willing to accept."[49]

The Oak Ridge National Laboratory issued another study in 1982, which indicated that the NRC's risk estimates were far too low, and that an accident as bad or worse than Three Mile Island could be expected every ten to fifteen years. The Oak Ridge study identified 19,400 failures at nuclear plants between 1969 and 1975; of these failures, 169 held the potential of causing a serious accident. "What we discovered," said Richard Bernero of the NRC's Division of Risk Analysis, which had commissioned the study, "is that in some cases events were showing a higher probability than we had predicted." One example was small leaks of cooling water, which occurred more often than expected.[50]

Both the Kemeny and Rogovin reports introduced another significant element for understanding the agency's efforts at risk management: the absence of a centralized data bank. Properly managed, an information system with the capability of processing the experience of all the operating reactors would catch failures in equipment early enough to prevent similar "events" from occurring in the future. Had such a capability existed, the accident at Davis-Besse might have been averted; the owners of other Babcock and Wilcox reactors alerted; and Three Mile Island prevented. Instead, one lone NRC employee, James S. Creswell, struggled with a bureaucracy that ignored him and the information he had to offer.

The NRC still has no real system for encouraging employees to follow Creswell's example, although Fouchard argued that the NRC had instituted a "program of professional dissent, an open-door policy by which employees could go directly to the commissioners." After all, he added, "we didn't fire Basdekas," referring to an NRC safety engineer who had written an article, published on the Op-Ed page of the *New York Times,* attacking the NRC and warning of the likelihood of future meltdowns.[51]

Others within the NRC question this "open-door policy," maintaining that loyalty and a "don't rock the boat" philosophy prevailed instead. One NRC official, who declined to be quoted, said that one example of this premium on loyalty was that "people do not leave the NRC; they defect." In any event, there appears to be, at this point, little evidence of a program of responsible dissent on the order of a management-imposed, highly publicized system within the agency, with specific rewards and incentives for those who display a sense of courage in uncovering safety problems.

The real problem with the NRC's reliance on industry's estimates of risk, however, is that the industry is insured against the worst consequences of risk by the government itself. In enacting the Price-Anderson Act, in 1957, the government gave the nuclear industry an extraordinary gift: it limited the liability of the industry to $560 million in the event of an accident.[52] The act also prevents businesses and home owners from purchasing insurance to protect their property against damages from a nuclear accident. The act has been extended twice, and its figures bear no relation to the cost of an accident, which by government estimates could cost billions of dollars. More important, it absolves the nuclear industry of responsibility for its own mistakes and releases it from other kinds of constraints, such as liability laws, that keep other industries in check. The Price-Anderson Act, and the unwillingness of Congress to repeal it, have been described by the group Critical Mass as a "massive, unprecedented subsidy for the nuclear industry" and, as Three Mile Island has demonstrated, a "travesty of justice for Americans," especially for the consumers who may eventually have to pick up the tab through their utility bills.[53]

The act also represents an early admission by government and by the industry that lobbied for the act that nuclear technology is, in fact, potentially dangerous as well as expensive. In protecting the industry from undue risk, the government ended up doing industry a disservice in the long run; the net effect of its policy only discouraged industry from adopting its own fail-safe systems. In effect, the government actually provided the disincentives for what were later regarded as serious lapses in quality assurance, in a peculiar form of public-private sector partnership that did not work well for either side.

"Things would have been better," said Commissioner Gilinsky, "had this [nuclear technology] been handled totally within the government or entirely in the free market. We turn this over to sixty-five utilities of varying sizes and capabilities, and a lot of them are not prepared. We're still going through the painful process of upgrading them. Our people in the regions go after the companies; they sit down with management and hold enforcement meetings. Some of these cases bring good results, and the companies are relieved that somebody snapped them out of their dangerous mode. The plant people are also glad when the NRC cracks down, because it forces the companies to give them extra resources.

"We're still recovering from the mistakes of the 1960s," continued Gilinsky. "The agency still emphasizes reactor design, instead of the more important safety problems, which focus on the soft spots: ongoing maintenance of the reactors and operator training.''

The consequences of these policies are now being played out at Three Mile Island, where no one wants to pick up the $4 billion cleanup bill. After failing get the federal government to pay, the utilities took the unusual step of banding together and suing the NRC for the money, on the grounds that the agency was negligent in failing to warn them of the defects of the Babcock and Wilcox reactors previously indicated by the accident at the Davis-Besse plant. In effect, the industry was suing the regulators for not regulating them adequately! An ironic twist in the prevailing regulatory reform environment, where the rule makers are more often attacked for regulating too much.

In the complaint, which represents the clearest attack to date of the NRC's management of risk, the utilities charge that ''the NRC negligently or wrongfully failed to warn licensees of other B & W [Babcock and Wilcox] supplied nuclear plants, including Met Ed [Metropolitan Edison], of defects and hazardous conditions in plant components, systems . . . of which the NRC, in the exercise of due care, should have known as a result of its investigation of a similar incident . . . at the Davis-Besse nuclear plant . . . and . . . other 'precursors' of the TMI-2 accident.''[54]

''The NRC should have known,'' the complaint continued, ''that its failure to notify other licensees, including Met Ed . . . would create a serious and immediate danger of core uncovery and potentially catastrophic injury to life and property.''[55] In addition, the NRC's negligence or wrongful conduct contravened duties imposed on the NRC by statute and regulations.[56]

In one of the most damning statements of all, the utilities accuse the NRC of allowing the marketplace to regulate itself: ''The NRC negligently or wrongfully approved B & W [Babcock and Wilcox] analyses contained in topical reports, including those for small-break loss-of-coolant accidents, even though those analyses were dangerously defective and failed to comply with NRC regulations. In approving the analyses, the NRC violated agency regulations.''[57]

The NRC now faces a real crisis in its management of risk: a feeling on the part of many that in a contest between economics and safety, the agency will lean toward the financial health of the industry. Local and nationally based groups regularly express their discontent, based largely on the belief that they are the guinea pigs, the subject of an experiment that went too far and too fast for its own and the public's good. The result is that the NRC is confronted with anger over inadvertent risk, anger at the idea that the agency and the industry together have put the public in a position of jeopardy over which it had no control.

The NRC's Response to Public Discontent

Stung by public criticism, the Nuclear Regulatory Commission decided to have less of it. Their method: to erect barriers to public participation in the decision-making process. To the NRC, as well as to the industry itself, public critics were "kooks," to be ignored, excluded, or diverted. Never mind that it was the public critics who first raised the safety issues at Diablo Canyon, Three Mile Island, Black Fox, Turkey Point, Seabrook, and Vermont Yankee.

Under the rubric of "expediting the licensing process," the NRC under Palladino's leadership began, in 1981, to propose a series of exclusionary rules, some of them deceptively minor. Their effect was to restrict the limited set of legal tools now available to outside groups. These rules would consolidate the NRC's already considerable control over who participates at every stage of the process: in the granting of construction permits, operating licenses, and interim work authorizations. Supported for the most part by the nuclear industry, these "reforms" were also encouraged by the Reagan administration, in keeping with its efforts to dismantle the regulatory process. In this case, however, instead of eliminating regulations, the dismantling took place through writing new regulations.

The changes seem petty, but they are far-reaching. One of the proposals would limit an outside group's right of discovery to fifty questions.[58] Since a typical application for a license in a contested case can run into thousands of pages, a limit of fifty questions would pose serious problems for any group attempting to address serious safety issues. The application to restart the undamaged reactor at Three Mile Island, for example, has already exceeded twenty-two thousand pages.

Another "reform" would determine who can participate and who cannot by imposing requirements based upon technical expertise. Under this system, groups would have to submit documentation substantiating their claim that a genuine issue exists; the licensing boards would then decide whether the claim is legitimate. In effect, the rule forces groups to prove their case even before there is a case, a rule without precedence in administrative law or in jurisprudence.[59]

These "reforms" would freeze out, by fiat and by professional pressure, those outside the nuclear fraternity. "Intervenors don't have nuclear degrees," said Joseph Fouchard, justifying these exclusionary policies, a return to the reliance on "expertise" that has so often proved inadequate. It would appear that Diablo Canyon, Three Mile Island, and other problem plants have not shaken the agency's faith in its own expertise and infallibility, or driven them to expand their circle of experts. At the very least, including the doubters in their midst would limit the NRC's liability, so that in the event of accidents the regulators could say they left no stone unturned.

Other "reforms" also seem petty, except for the intent: more thorough exclusion. One proposed rule puts financial barriers in the path of participation by requiring groups to send materials by express mail — an expensive way to do business. Considering the difference from regular mail service of only one or two days, expediting delays can hardly be the reason behind this move, particularly in view of the ten- to fourteen-year delays in plant construction and licensing that Palladino and his supporters seek to reduce. The rule does make sense from one point of view: to make it too expensive for hard-pressed environmental groups to challenge the agency.

The commission also voted to prevent intervenors from raising alternative site issues, a surprise in view of past criticisms of the NRC's siting policies, which placed many reactors near major population centers.[60]

"It's the typical arrogance of the NRC," said Ellyn Weiss, a young attorney who handles the legal challenges for the Union of Concerned Scientists and the Natural Resources Defense Council. "They lump together the UCS, the NRDC, and the Jane Fondas. They feel there is nothing to be gained by listening to their critics; they have no appreciation for public participation. The industry regards public participation as a little minefield that the law requires them to tiptoe through."

Even those within the agency are witnessing some erosion of their right to question safety issues through a proposed reform known as *sua sponte*. This would limit the right of members of the licensing board to raise safety issues on their own accord, even though they would still have the power to dismiss contentions they believe are invalid.[61] Although this restriction will speed up proceedings, it will undercut the agency's own technical capability, namely, its safety boards, whose members are supposed to conduct tough, aggressive hearings, their expertise another check on public safety questions. In effect, the NRC is treating some of its own employees as "intervenors."

These proposals reflect a deep distrust of public participation dating back to the AEC, whose leaders were even more blatant in their efforts during the 1950s and 1960s to discourage the public from raising safety issues. According to Elizabeth Rolph, who studied the agency closely during this period, "the nuclear industry and the regulatory staff saw the intervenors primarily as a product of poor public relations."

"Rather than seeing in them," Rolph wrote, "the reflections of legitimate public concern and changing public values that demanded substantive response, they saw technically uninformed people who needed to be taught how risk free and beneficial nuclear power indeed was."

The members of the AEC rationalized that since their technology was beyond the scope of ordinary people, outsiders could not contribute responsibly to licensing proceedings, and therefore there was no reason to include them. This led to the development of a closed shop, in which staff reports and documents were not distributed to the public. It also led to the routine minimizing of information about nuclear risks, through what Rolph called such "cosmetic tricks as relabeling the HAZARDS EVALUATION REPORT, the SAFETY EVALUATION REPORT."[62]

Dismantling America

Isolated in its own rarefied environment, the AEC in 1969 and 1970 tried to extend its independence from public involvement to the law itself, declaring the agency exempt from the National Environmental Protection Act's provision requiring environmental impact statements. For what reason? Was nuclear energy not part of the environment? This time, however, the agency had traveled too far along the path of regulatory isolation, and, in the famous case of *Calvert Cliffs Coordinating Committee v. Atomic Energy Commission*, the court invalidated the agency's position.[63] The AEC then revised its regulations and required environmental impact statements in future reviews of proposed nuclear plants.

The AEC and its successors perpetuated a regulatory environment that was essentially shortsighted, as later events were to demonstrate. Both the Kemeny and Rogovin reports identified the lack of public confidence as a serious problem in nuclear regulation, encouraging the agency to make up for lost time by facilitating, not discouraging, the public's right to know. The Rogovin report went even further, recommending the creation of an Office of Public Counsel, to provide help for intervenors, and funding them for licensing and rule-making procedures. In the continuing conflict over efficiency versus participation, the Rogovin report chose participation, recommending increased rule making to achieve this goal despite added costs.

Representatives of the agency and the industry, for the most part, disagreed. Intervenors have adequate opportunities for participation, they argued; their contributions range from mildly helpful to frivolous; and, on balance, there is more to be gained from restricting rather than expanding their opportunities to make an impact.

"You have to create a threshold where you separate out where the intervenor and the group has something, and where they are wasting time," said NRC counsel Leonard Bickwit. "The NRC's new rules will raise that threshold to prevent contentions that are utterly groundless [the larger category] and contentions in which the intervenors don't have the guns and ammunition to prosecute them adequately." Pressed for an example of such a time waster, Bickwit offered the following illustration. In the licensing of the Allen's Creek facility, one individual questioned why the commis-

226

sion had not looked into "biomass farming" as an alternate source of energy, since in the conversion process of "biomass farming" the same amount of energy could be reproduced without incurring the risks of nuclear energy.[64]

"This contention was allowed in," continued Bickwit, "because we have a lower threshold than other agencies." To Bickwit, this low threshold diverts valuable staff resources from more productive activities, a view shared by many of his fellow regulators. "Why did the staff have to go through the process to prepare a summary disposition motion on a matter in which the contention obviously isn't going anywhere?" he asked. "The staff has taken the position that discovery is consuming too much of its time and resources; it delays licenses, and keeps them from things they regard as more important than answering discoveries."

Bickwit added that the commission's goal in enacting these reforms was to "shield staff resources and speed things up." Anything that hastens the process along, he said, will inevitably "curtail intervenors."[65]

Others at the NRC claim there are adequate opportunities for the public to make an impact throughout the process. The problem is, they argue, the public has not demonstrated much interest in the past. "I remember one public hearing in an auditorium in Germantown," recalled Fouchard. "No one came and no one gave a damn. At another hearing in Georgia, the janitor was the only one there."

Donald Winston of the Atomic Industrial Forum offered examples from his own recollections documenting the wasted time common to the adjudicatory process. "I sat in on the hearings of a $2 billion plant in Houston," he said. "Citizens groups there were questioning the amount of water the plants would need, questions that had been decided three years ago, involving whether there would be enough water left for the farmers. The consortium running this plant was paying 16 percent interest on the money it had borrowed to invest in this plant. At the $1 million a day it is costing when these plants are left idle, they will soon be out of business.

"That's the aim of these groups," he added. "To run these plants out of the market."

Many share his alarm, fearing that investors will abandon ship after looking closely at the increasing political problems and the cumbersome regulatory process. "The regulatory process is so lengthy, complex, and unpredictable," said Fritz Heimann, an attorney for the General Electric Company, in a lecture at the Massachusetts Institute of Technology, "that it is inconceivable that any utility will start another nuclear plant under present ground rules. It means subjecting a multibillion-dollar investment to a process whose outcome may not be known for ten to fifteen years and which is likely to require hundreds of millions of dollars in additional costs."[66]

Theoretically, the process is open to the public at all stages, starting with the initial application for a license to build a plant, which is available in the document room of the local public library. The public can also participate at successive stages in the process: site selection, when the safety evaluation report (SER) and environmental impact statements (EIS) are issued; and at the public hearing prior to construction. Hearings are currently adjudicatory in nature, which means they are similar to court cases but are more limited than judicial rights in the areas of cross-examination and discovery.

The process itself has come under considerable criticism recently as an inadequate vehicle for nuclear regulation. An adjudicatory forum — particularly for those in the scientific community — is not suited to dealing with complex technical issues, which scientists feel should be negotiated among scientists, who are better equipped to deal with the problems of nuclear technology. A courtroom setting, even for the quasi-judicial administrative hearing, is still an adversary proceeding in which there will be winners and losers.

The leading intervenors reflect the typical lawyer's view that the adjudicatory process protects them against arbitrary decision making. They say that only legitimized confrontation will unearth all the facts necessary to make rational decisions. Otherwise, issues are negotiated behind closed doors, and the participants tend to take short cuts and to make deals, often at the expense of the public safety. "It would be like the old days at the AEC, when the licensing process was conducted totally by the lunchtime lawyers," recalled Anthony Roisman, a public interest attorney who has represented intervenor groups and has served on the Rogovin Commission. "These lunchtime lawyers, so named because they did all their business over lunch, would get the AEC technical people and the industry people together, and they'd work everything out.''

Roisman went on to say, "You should pay intervenors on the same premise that they send a canary down a mine before miners go in. They'll find the mistakes for you because they're looking for them.''

Like the canary in the mine, intervenors have uncovered important safety issues at a number of sites, among them:

• Diablo Canyon, where intervenors raised the seismic as well as other safety issues as early as 1973.

• The Seabrook plant, where intervenors (including the attorney general of the state of Massachusetts) questioned why there were no plans to evacuate the sixty thousand people who use the beaches adjacent to the plant on any given summer day.

• The Black Fox plant in Oklahoma, where intervenors pointed out the failure of what was then regarded as ''non-safety-related'' equipment and later turned out to be the very problem of stuck valves that contributed to the accident at Three Mile Island as identified by both the Kemeny Commission and the NRC's Special Inquiry Group.[67]

• Vermont Yankee, in New Hampshire, where intervenors in the early 1970s took their objections all the way to the Supreme Court. They were the first to question the disposal and management of nuclear waste, a problem that did not seem to worry the industry or the AEC at the time, but is very much of an environmental problem in the 1980s.[68]

• Turkey Point, in South Florida, where the intervenors successfully fought through changes in the applicant's plans to store its radioactive steam generator assemblies in a dirt-floored facility.[69]

The NRC's primary justification for harassing intervenors — that they hold up the licensing process — was challenged by a background paper issued in 1979 by the Congressional Budget Office, which reported the results of an extensive study of 211 reactor projects to determine the real sources of delay. The study found the longest delays in the construction phase, identifying 80 percent of the total amount of delay reported for reactors under construction as due to "events or decisions in the private sector unrelated to the regulatory decisions of the NRC."[70] In other words, intervenors were not the real problem; causing most of the widely publicized delays were construction problems, labor problems, and financial problems. Public interventions, said the report, accounted for some delays, but those only amounted to "short periods of time."[71] And although a few interventions were obstructionist, many were "instrumental in publicizing important safety and environmental issues," which at most would delay a project no more than six months.[72]

Yet, the NRC is moving ahead to limit the role of the intervenors, making them scapegoats for other problems. An enigma? Not really, if you look at the political pressures on the agency.

"We're under strong pressure from the Appropriations Committee to kick all the environmentalists in the ass and get them out of here," explained Commissioner Gilinsky. "We've also got pressure from within the agency from the technical people, who are naturally hostile to the adjudicatory process. They think it is not the right way to decide issues.

"A lot of what they are doing to intervenors is wrong," added Gilinsky, "particularly when you realize that intervenors are really weak. Many of the stronger intervenors got sucked into government during the Carter administration, and went elsewhere after his defeat. Outside of Diablo, where you have the state coming in, there are no potent intervenors. It's a myth that they're holding back the industry; it's a lot of malarkey."

To some extent, if intervenors hope to function in the anti-regulatory environment of the 1980s, they will have to join with political forces to enhance their own clout. As Diablo showed, the entry of the governor and the state of California contributed significantly to the legitimacy of the protest and to its eventual outcome. At the Seabrook plant, in New Hampshire, the intervention of the attorney general of Massachusetts on evacuation plans eventually forced the NRC to sit up and take notice, recalling Senator Clinton Anderson's warning to the nation's governors, in the late 1950s, to watch out for their states in proceedings involving the siting of nuclear plants. History also shows that intervenors can increase their chances of success when someone famous joins their ranks. An early case involving the siting of the Malibu plant in 1963 brought the protests of five intervenors, including the comedian Bob Hope, who owned property near the proposed reactor. They argued that the seismic activity in that area presented a potential danger to the community. After four years, the commission rejected the recommendations of its own board (Atomic Safety and Licensing Board) and staff and returned the design to the utility for further evaluation — tantamount to quietly shelving the license request. The number of references to Bob Hope in the AEC's records has led to the conjecture that he was a force "to be reckoned with."[73]

Meanwhile, intervenors without clout struggle against the very real barriers being quietly raised against them. Limiting their rights may streamline the process and address the concerns of those impatient with lengthy, legalistic procedures. But the process is not going to change. It will still have what seems like an interminable number of steps and the basic framework guaranteed by the Administrative Procedure Act. What will be lost is the sense of equity and fair play that has characterized administrative law. The deck will be stacked.

"Limiting intervenors intended," charged Ralph Nader, "to cripple public participation in the licensing process." This is leading to "less thorough safety work, reduced reactor inspections, and a restricted public role . . . by limiting access to important safety information." These proposals, he added, "will try to destroy many years of administrative procedure designed to invite and respect the public's concerns and insights."[74]

The new rules limiting the right of the public to participate became so blatant in their exclusionary intent that in the early fall of 1982, the chairman of a three-judge panel inquiring into the safety of two reactors at Indian Point resigned, accusing the NRC of not allowing opponents of the plant to present their side of the case. Judge Louis J. Carter charged that the new procedures were "contrary to the precedents of the law" and "incompatible with my sense of fairness."[75] The rules he found most disturbing involved requiring witnesses to testify about the probability of an accident, rather than allowing them to arrive at this information through cross-examination. Judge Carter labeled this an "unfair and heavy burden" for intervenors. The *New York Times* editorialized that Judge Carter's departure further undermined the credibility of the Indian Point inquiry. "Nuclear power is a political issue, not just a question of whether the plumbing works. In a process like the Indian Point inquiry, form counts as well as substance. The purpose of weighing the safety of the plants is not just to satisfy the commissioners but the public too."[76]

Undoubtedly, there are many ways in which the licensing process can be speeded up while still benefiting from the public's contributions. Alan Rosenthal, head of the Atomic Safety and Licensing Appeals Board, who is generally regarded as thoughtful on the subject, advocates tougher adjudications as a way to reduce delays. This way, issues like "biomass farming" could be thrown out quickly without diverting valuable staff time yet still allowing for more valid safety-related questions.[77]

But certain questions will still remain unsolved, as they do in any exclusionary act: who will do the deciding, and by what criteria will they evaluate what is important and what is not?

Several industry and NRC representatives offered another solution: encouraging the public to participate at earlier stages in the process — at the site selection stage, or at the early site review — when it is easier to solve problems, rather than at the operating license stage, when industry may have already invested up to $1 billion in the plant. At that later point, the utilities, the vendors, and the agency have invested so heavily in the plant that they will fight regardless of the obstacles. "Once they get that hole in the ground," said one NRC official, "there's no going back."

Yet intervention at the site selection stage has recently been rendered moot by new rules preventing challenges to site selection. It is also unrealistic, according to the Natural Resources Defense Council and the Union of Concerned Scientists, because of the difficulties both groups have experienced in trying to get information from the agency early in the process. At hearings before the NRC, these two groups identified the "single factor most responsible for inefficiency and wasted time . . . as the failure of the NRC staff to produce its basic review documents, the SER [Safety Evaluation Report] and the EIS [Environmental Impact Statement] until months after the outset of the adjudicatory process."[78]

The most credible argument against the intervenors goes to the heart of the adversary system: that, for the most part, the intervenors are "antinuke," and their real mission is to drive the nuclear industry out of business, not merely to call attention to safety problems. From his statements, for example, it is clear that Robert Pollard, of the Union for Concerned Scientists, would rather see the adoption of alternative sources of energy. "It is an inherently dangerous technology," he has said of nuclear power, with risks "comparable only to a nuclear war." Pollard regards Three Mile Island as "the worst possible accident I can imagine without killing somebody," adding that it was still possible to have an "accident of unprecedented proportions."

It is no wonder that, faced with these opponents, the industry and the agency tend to stonewall, a strategy guaranteed to alienate a much larger public, as recent trends indicate. At Three Mile Island, for example, the voters in a nonbinding referendum in 1982 flatly turned down the restart of TMI-1, the undamaged reactor, by a two-to-one margin. The fight against the referendum to restart the reactor was led by Kay Pickering, operating out of a dingy, two-story clapboard tenement several blocks from the governor's mansion in Harrisburg. Pickering's success was most notable in view of the disparity of resources. As she described her campaign strategy, Pickering emphasized the group's financial difficulties, including a debt of $60,000 to $70,000, of which only $3,000 was spent on the referendum. The utilities' expenditures, on the other hand, totaling $257,000 on ads alone between September 1981 and April 1982, according to a Harrisburg newspaper, made little difference in the final result.[79]

At Three Mile Island and Diablo Canyon, the disparity of resources became less important as public awareness increased. Willingly or not, the public has realized that they do participate in some form. In the case of Three Mile Island, they will pay the cost of the cleanup, through higher utility bills, or through higher state, local, and federal taxes.[80] They participate through their pocketbooks, their morale, and their physical and mental health.[81] Abridging their right to participate early in the game exacts a high price, according to former NRC commissioner Peter Bradford, the "first casualties [being] truth and other people's money."[82]

If the NRC under Palladino's leadership continues to frustrate

233

meaningful participation within the system, the public may increasingly resort to the more unchanneled variety of participation: lawsuits, referendums, and mass demonstrations.[83] These outlets, accompanied by the harsh glare of publicity, hold up the licensing process far longer than the few extra months it might take for cross-examination and discovery. Including the public early in the process might avoid these difficulties later on, and help solve the much larger issue of the crisis in public confidence, stemming from such ongoing evidence as the Kemeny Commission's conclusion that the NRC favored the industry almost all of the time in its decisions.

Further exclusions of the public from NRC deliberations can only fuel, with some justice, the public's suspicions that the agency and the industry have something to hide. Too many recent incidents have already shown what was successfully concealed before Three Mile Island: the high risks of nuclear energy; the tendency to often ignore those risks in the haste to build reactors; the uneven quality of utilities and manufacturers; the financial weaknesses of the industry; and the continual victory of development over safety. The biggest secret of all emerged after Three Mile Island and Diablo Canyon: in spite of its awareness of the unsolved technological problems, the government had recommitted the nation to nuclear energy.

To work well in the long run, the partnership between government and business must expand to include a third partner: the public. Without the public's support, policies tend to boomerang, as they have in the field of nuclear energy, where both public safety and the financial health of the industry have suffered immeasurable harm.

The absence of credible federal control — the only mechanism for guaranteeing public involvement — remains the most serious problem to date, one that is not being addressed by the "regulatory reform" theories of the 1980s. "Cost-benefit analysis, and White House review of rulings, do little to improve public confidence in the independence of the NRC or its ability to act quickly," editorialized the *Washington Post*.[84] Not only does the nuclear power issue demonstrate the dangers of inadequate and unresponsive regulation, it also shows the dangers of regulating with defective theories.

"With its present organization, staff, and attitudes," concluded the Kemeny report, "the NRC is unable to fulfill its responsibility for providing an acceptable level of safety for nuclear power plants."[85] Not much has changed since this report appeared in 1979, because meaningful reform can only be addressed by strengthening the public side of the regulatory environment.

Nuclear regulation is admittedly a difficult and complex task, because it raises scientific and technical issues that are on the threshold of knowledge. It also raises difficult moral and ethical questions, almost biblical in scope, in which the possibility of an accident with potentially enormous consequences must be weighed against its low probability. It is clear, however, that neither the industry nor its difficulties will go away. The problem now is how to control the development of this revolutionary technology in the best interests of society.

The nuclear issue has become the most important contest in the broader debate on environmental regulation: nuclear power risks are more serious than acid rain, hazardous waste, or any other pollutant; costly mistakes involving nuclear power may have consequences that exceed current estimates. Whatever form it takes, nuclear technology and our experience with it present a convincing case for effective and credible government intervention at all stages — economic, managerial, and scientific — of its development.

The case of the nuclear industry demonstrates that if government in partnership with the public does not become deeply involved in the development of new, potentially destructive technologies, those technologies simply will not be allowed to develop at all. Vigorous regulation that meets objective standards is seen by the public as assurance that these industries will not be allowed to expand without adequate attention to public safety and, to a lesser extent, fiscal responsibility. Once the public loses confidence in the regulators — as in the case of the NRC's ability to regulate the domestic nuclear industry — the industry itself appears all but doomed. Its only hope for survival is the emergence of a strong, independent NRC.

7

The Risks of Laissez Faire

When does the operation of the so-called free marketplace become predatory?
— Hobart Rowen, the *Washington Post*

It's destructive and it's cruel, but that's the way the market functions.
— Alfred Kahn, former chairman, Civil Aeronautics Board

THE RUSH TO DEREGULATE is proving increasingly costly to the business community, which had campaigned long and hard to "get the government off our backs." At a time when major competitors abroad are subject to increasing government regulation, which has succeeded in gaining public confidence in their products, many American industries left to their own devices are producing shoddy products that have driven away customers and ultimately threatened the very existence of the industries themselves. Witness the automobile companies, facing competitors whose governments regulated quality control. Will they ever recoup their losses both at home and in the international marketplace?

Without regulation by the federal government, industries will become increasingly subject to conflicting state regulations, which will impose additional burdens in the form of new costs and increasing uncertainty. Industries will also suffer because the absence of uniform national standards will create a no man's land of legal responsibility, depriving them of the ability to defend their actions and their products by pointing to compliance with federally accepted procedures.

In the absence of effective regulation in many areas, and the rush to hasten deregulation in others, a disaffected public is increasingly turning to the courts to seek damages. It is a pattern that has spelled disaster for a number of industries. As the drug companies, the asbestos manufacturers, and others afflicted by the proliferation of product liability litigation are finding out, the burdens of the free market can far exceed an individual company's capabilities and resources for self-protection. Indeed, the old argument that the threat of lawsuits was preferable to government regulation in keeping products safe and business honest has proven false. Only in the case of the nuclear industry, where government limited the liability of individual companies by law, was some measure of protection afforded from the increasing trend to resort to legal remedies as a way of filling the regulatory vacuum.[1] Other industries were given no such protection, and they soon discovered that the absence of effective regulation is as bad for business as it is for the public.

One company, the Denver-based Johns-Manville Corporation, filed for bankruptcy in 1982 under the pressure of lawsuits filed by individual employees disabled by working with asbestos produced by the company. Called one of the biggest industrial bankruptcies in American corporate history, the bankruptcy was declared by company officials to be in the best interests of its stockholders, employees, and creditors, since the protection of Chapter 11 of the federal bankruptcy law at least froze all lawsuits pending against the company (16,500 at that time, with 500 new lawsuits filed each month). The nation's largest producer of asbestos, ranking 181 on the Fortune 500 list, Johns-Manville claimed it was in otherwise healthy condition, reporting its net worth at $1.1 billion.[2]

The Risks of Laissez Faire

But even a company as financially sound as the Manville Corporation cannot sustain an unlimited onslaught of lawsuits. In the first half of 1982, the company spent $8.6 million on asbestos litigation, and faced a potential price tag of over $2 billion — or nearly twice its net worth.[3]

As a result of the bankruptcy filing, the price of Johns-Manville stock fell by 35 percent in the only day of trading following the bankruptcy announcement, and the company lost its coveted place as a component of the Dow Jones Industrial average — a position it had held for fifty-two years. The price rebounded, however, several weeks later.

The subject of these lawsuits was work place safety, a responsibility assumed by the company in the absence of a regulatory presence. In the case of asbestos, a definite link had been established between asbestos fibers and lung cancer, a crippling and often fatal lung disease known as asbestosis, and cancers of the gastrointestinal tract, larynx, and kidney. Over the last forty years, an estimated twenty million people have been exposed to asbestos fibers, making asbestos "the greatest single source of occupational cancer," according to Dr. William Blot of the National Cancer Institute. Researchers at Mount Sinai Hospital in New York have calculated that five thousand cancer deaths linked to asbestos will occur annually at least until the end of the century.[4]

While filing for bankruptcy will leave the company protected for a limited amount of time, no one yet knows what will happen to the tens of thousands of plaintiffs seeking damages from Johns-Manville as well as other asbestos manufacturers. UNR Industries, a Chicago steel products firm, also filed for bankruptcy after confronting seventeen thousand lawsuits. At last count, there were tens of thousands of lawsuits pending against 250 other asbestos producers.

Asbestos is not the only "toxic time bomb" facing industry; there are lawsuits involving benzene (an industrial solvent), vinyl chloride (used in plastics), formaldehyde (formerly used in home building), and PCBs (polychlorinated biphenyl, a component of electrical equipment). The potential for increased litigation is enormous, considering that the Occupational Safety and Health Administration (OSHA) has identified two hundred toxic chemicals in the work place.[5]

239

Although it has turned out to be a bonanza for lawyers, liability law is a useless remedy for the long-term solution of regulatory problems like work place safety.[6] An outgrowth of the common law concept of torts or wrongful damage, it is increasingly apparent that liability law has created both confusion and inequity. In many cases, companies have had to pay large damage awards even when they have proven they had not acted negligently; large awards are sometimes granted by sympathetic judges and juries who may base their decisions on who seems most able to pay.

The situation has reached such crisis proportions that the *Wall Street Journal* called it "unproductive liability," arguing that the explosion of product liability "litigiousness" has inhibited product development, by diverting resources to legal costs, and raised the cost of product liability insurance.[7]

The costs to the companies far exceed their ability to pay over the long run, and threaten their very existence. In one case alone, a jury awarded a seventy-two-year-old woman an award of $2 million, including $1 million in punitive damages.[8] If this process continues, not only will all asbestos companies file for bankruptcy, but they will take their insurers with them as well. In self-protection, insurance companies are following the procession into the courts, arguing over who will pay the billions of dollars in asbestos-related claims.[9]

It would be ironic if the courts ended up as the policy arbiters on asbestos, as they have on so many other controversial regulatory questions: cotton dust, nuclear waste, and air bags, to name some of the issues that ended up in the judicial branch for temporary resolution. In the final analysis, Congress will have to deal with these issues, as it has already begun to do in discussions on limiting the liability of asbestos companies. But if it goes that route, the public will only tolerate limiting industry's responsibility if there is a tradeoff attached: a strong regulatory system.

The Taxpayer and the Regulatory Bail-Out

Plagued with troubles, many companies have turned to the federal government to come to their rescue, claiming that since many of

The Risks of Laissez Faire

the asbestos victims were working in World War II shipyards, the government should share some of the responsibility. "The tort system is unworkable," said John A. McKinney, president of Manville. Since the government is partly responsible, he suggested, let "us all participate by putting up the pool that pays these people [who] have a disability." [10] This solution involves the creation of a trust fund financed by contributions from industry and the government, and run by a board of experts, who would determine who would be entitled to compensation. [11]

The evidence is scattered but the direction is clear: the public will pick up the tab for industry's mistakes and the government's regulatory mistakes, just as it always has in the past.

What else can government do? In terms of its checkbook, government is the only last resort. Who else but the public treasury has the resources to clean up the ravages of toxic waste and excessive work place pollution, or assume the long-term medical costs of chronic illness? Government has responded accordingly: with decency, humanity, and at tremendous cost to the taxpayer. Looking back, it was federal and state governments that paid for the environmental ravages of Kepone in the James River, toxins at Love Canal, and many other less publicized chemical accidents, in addition to the nuclear accident at Three Mile Island. Setting a pattern for the future, Congress accepted in the taxpayer's name the biggest responsibility of all, cleaning up toxic waste sites, with the passage in 1980 of the "superfund" — a five-year, $1.6 billion program. A similar fund, the Black Lung Disability Trust Fund, was also created by Congress to compensate victims of black lung disease.

With an eye on programs like the superfund, as well as other publicly financed trust fund programs, some interest groups and their attorneys have begun to press Congress to bail out their industries. Spearheading one such effort is the Asbestos Compensation Coalition, an organization of nine asbestos manufacturing companies that is pressing Congress to pass asbestos compensation legislation. The bill would compensate workers suffering from asbestos-related diseases with funds contributed equally by companies and the federal government. [12]

This time, though, some members of Congress are balking, influenced perhaps by the fate of the Black Lung Fund, which, in spite of its modest appropriations, has run up enormous deficits in the last few years. Rep. George Miller (Democrat, California) favors putting the entire onus on industry, and has proposed legislation that would require the industry to set up its own compensation fund. Miller's bill shifts government's role, in this conflict, away from its Santa Claus image and back into a regulatory mode. The government should not be asked to "come into this situation and bail out companies from multibillion-dollar liabilities of their own making," said Miller's staff director, John Lawrence. "The liability of the federal government is unknown and therefore limited. And why the federal government, which has cut millions of dollars for health benefits for the elderly, would turn around and willingly accept billions of dollars in liabilities from industries that have already been found legally responsible is beyond me."[13]

Congress is also considering an even more ambitious new fund to compensate all victims of toxic pollution, this one recommended by a panel of legal experts representing four of the country's most prestigious legal groups.[14] The plan would open up a virtual Pandora's box of unlimited federal financial responsibility, only partly offset by provisions that would make it easier for victims with large claims to sue industry for damages.[15]

Government has no choice. It must protect its citizens and help those who have suffered the consequences of inadvertent risk. But, in effect, government will pay for its own absence of regulation, and for the negligence that comes from leaving regulation to the marketplace. The asbestos cases, along with those of their companion industries, clarify once and for all the costs of not regulating, raising the question of whether this situation could have been averted by a workable regulatory system: one that protected industry from the unlimited damages of litigation at the same time that it protected the worker from industry's unrealistic claims to self-regulation of work place safety.

The Market as Predator

While the asbestos companies coped with excessive litigation, other industries in the throes of economic deregulation were beginning to have second thoughts. The airline industry is a case in point: it slid almost immediately from record profits in 1978 — the year the Airline Deregulation Act was passed — to financial difficulty, which included two bankruptcies and lots of red ink for many of the nation's major airlines.

With big government formally written out of the picture, the marketplace took over with a vengeance. The immediate losers were some of the larger airlines, which started to expand their routes without sufficient resources or adequate markets. Airline executives saw deregulation as a ticket to increased profits (most of them strongly supported unraveling the process that had governed their industry since 1938), and immediately pursued the new opportunities available to them.

The experience of Braniff International was the most dramatic example of what could go wrong. Fearing competition from its major competitors, Braniff chose to expand quickly, opening up dozens of new routes within the United States, Europe, and Asia, and slashing fares by an average of 40 percent. During the same period, other airlines were also moving fast to beat out the competition. Close at Braniff's heels was American Airlines, which had moved its headquarters from New York to Dallas, Braniff's home base; American soon matched Braniff's fare cuts on domestic routes.

The rate war between American and Braniff was described by the *Wall Street Journal* as a "bleeding contest," destructive to both airlines, and disastrous for Braniff, which filed for bankruptcy in May 1982.[16] Braniff followed by only a few months the demise of Laker Airways, a British company also known for its fare cuts and rate wars.

Some industry analysis worry that the Braniff experience will become a common pattern under deregulation: an excessive fear of competitors that propels executives toward management decisions unsupported by market conditions. In Braniff's case, this fear factor led to overexpansion, overcapacity, and price cutting. Similar battles are shaping up among airlines seeking to dominate the routes to New York, Denver, Los Angeles, and Dallas.

The skies have also turned unfriendly for United Airlines, which posted an operating loss of $148.8 million for 1981, down from an operating profit of over $300 million in 1978 — the year deregulation went into effect.[17] Two additional major airlines, TWA

243

and Pan American, also reported operating losses during 1981 that surpassed the $100 million mark — in addition to the now defunct Braniff, which lost $160.6 million.[18] By the first quarter of 1982, the picture was bleak: the industry was settling into one of the worst financial periods in its entire history.

While many of the larger airlines are drowning in red ink, some smaller airlines — previously barred from the marketplace by regulation — have taken advantage of the new system to expand both their routes and their profits. Called industry's "upstarts," these airlines have increased their share of the market by an astounding 66 percent, refuting some of the early critics of deregulation who warned that the larger airlines would dominate the skies. From May 1980 to May 1981, Piedmont increased its share of the market by 24 percent; Frontier Airlines, by 15 percent. The most dramatic growth was experienced by US Air; once an obscure airline restricted to routes in the Appalachian mountain region and now one of the nation's twelve largest carriers, US Air reported an operating profit of over $74 million for the first three quarters of 1981.[19]

In the short run, the smaller carriers found themselves at a distinct advantage. Unburdened by inventories of large, wide-bodied aircraft, they could take advantage of current market conditions and rely on the smaller jets, avoiding the problem of empty seats that has plagued the larger airlines. Newer airlines also had lower labor costs: the pilots flying United's 737 jets make twice the $30,000 salary earned by pilots working for New York Air. Labor costs vary widely at all levels of employment, with the unionized airlines falling rapidly into a competitive disadvantage vis-à-vis their nonunionized counterparts. Large airlines also found that the managerial advantages of their size were being more than offset by their enormous overhead costs, which in addition to the aircraft included investments of millions of dollars in maintenance facilities, airport gate equipment, and computer equipment, plus the cost of all the added personnel involved in their maintenance. The "upstarts" merely lease the equipment and crews, a decided advantage in a fluctuating marketplace.

An additional uncertainty entering the picture relates to safety. Although the Federal Aviation Administration (FAA) — the agency responsible for air safety — was not deregulated, there have been suggestions that economic deregulation is related to a decrease in airline safety. Flight 90, the disastrous Air Florida crash in December 1981, is a case in point. Just minutes after takeoff, the jet airliner plunged into the icy waters of the Potomac River, killing most of the passengers and all members of the crew. An ill-fated combination of bad weather and an inexperienced flight crew was given as the major reason for the crash; failures in the deicing equipment added to the visibility problems leading to the pilot's error in judgment.

"It was the inexperience of a crew flying jet airplanes in winter weather," concluded Professor Fred Thayer, a specialist in airline deregulation at the University of Pittsburgh. "How do you get to that situation? By telling little airlines to fly routes they've never flown before, into airports where they've had no experience. On larger airlines, pilots are assigned to fixed routes, where they get trained. They know about weather and about airports. By the time a pilot becomes a captain he's been in that kind of weather hundreds of times."

Opening the floodgates to inexperienced airlines through rapid deregulation will exacerbate these safety problems, according to Thayer, who also pointed out the correlation between leasing equipment and airline safety. "There is a lack of coordination," Thayer continued, "when smaller airlines rent equipment — as Air Florida demonstrated with its lack of familiarity with deicers — that contributes to the institutional inexperience that permeates the system."

Together with the airlines, the consumer also finds himself coping with uncertainty and upheaval, in the form of often wildly fluctuating air fares, as well as in reduced service to many parts of the country. True, the promise of reduced fares — one of the most compelling arguments for deregulation — has been realized; but these fares tend to be found only on the popular tourist routes, like New York to Miami, or the coast-to-coast routes, where rate wars have driven fares even below the airlines' actual operating costs. Most important, getting to East Succotash and paying for the service has become much more difficult, as airlines drop unprofitable routes, leaving whole communities bereft of service, while making up the deficits from their rate-war routes by tripling prices on others.

The effects have been felt by more than individual consumers of airline services. Some cities have faced serious disruptions when businesses departed along with the airline service, although to some extent that void has been filled in other cities by commuter airlines. In addition, many firms dependent on traveling salesmen complained of much higher travel costs.

Deregulation shares responsibility for upheavals in the airline industry with a host of other developments, a fact often cited by supporters of deregulation. A worldwide recession contributed to a decline in passenger traffic, as did the sharp rise in the price of jet fuel in the last decade, high interest rates, the air traffic controllers' strike, and additional labor problems. Although these problems may cumulatively even outweigh the effects of deregulation, the nagging possibility remains that regulation may have blunted their effects. Instead, destructive rate wars and route wars assaulted an industry accustomed to a protected environment. The results were swift: the airline industry jumped enthusiastically into the free market, where it quickly met a series of financial disasters. Whether the real villain was recession, fuel prices, or deregulation is still uncertain; but the fact still remains that the industry plummeted from record profits in 1978, the year deregulation went into effect, to a condition of uncertainty so chaotic by 1982 that the industry's credit worthiness reached record lows.[20] In fact, Chase Manhattan withdrew from the group of banks financing Pan American, forcing the airline to sell one of its subsidiaries and look for new sources of credit. The effects have even extended to travel agents — burned by the Braniff experience — who may soon begin to book passengers only on airlines they regard as sound, a policy that can only accelerate the problems of United, Pan American, and some of the other financially troubled airlines.

In the period before deregulation, uncertainties as troublesome as these would have been rare, with the Civil Aeronautics Board (CAB) picking up the slack. The system put the agency in the role of marriage broker, coaxing weaker airlines into mergers with stronger partners, as when Delta absorbed Northeast Airlines in the late 1960s. CAB tinkering in the form of distributing lucrative routes and fare increases could also stave off financial disaster for troubled airlines.

Current difficulties have not swayed deregulation stalwarts, who still maintain that the old system was all wrong: it was inefficient in controlling the marketplace, and companies failing to meet the rigors of the marketplace deserved to go out of business. "It's destructive and it's cruel, but that's the way the market functions," said Alfred Kahn, one of the architects of airline deregulation under President Carter, warning against a return to "cartelization."[21] "What the airlines need is a good bankruptcy," remarked James C. Miller III, before a group of businessmen, when he was still at the Office of Management and Budget, and before the Braniff and Laker bankruptcies. Immediately following those bankruptcies, President Reagan's chief economist, Murray Weidenbaum, echoed Kahn and Miller's assessment, saying that the Braniff closure gave the country "an opportunity to show that we really believe in a free enterprise system of profit and loss." He added that he was "unaware of any organized effort in Washington to do anything other than express regrets."[22]

Weidenbaum was wrong — at least about organized calls for re-regulating the airline industry. The labor unions were angered by the thirty thousand jobs lost since airline deregulation went into effect, and by the absence of regulations protecting their benefits. Mandated by a labor protection clause in the Airline Deregulation Act, rules protecting some worker benefits had already been proposed by the Carter administration but were apparently put on permanent hold by the Reagan administration in its effort to decrease federal regulation.[23]

Another group disappointed by the return to the free market are the travel agents, who are anxious to maintain their regulated status, which guarantees their position as the only outside distributors of airline tickets. "There is deep concern in Congress and elsewhere that deregulation isn't what it was cracked up to be," said the president of their trade association, Joseph R. Stone.[24] In fact, two bills calling for the re-regulation of the airline industry were introduced in Congress in 1982, four years after the original legislation was passed.

Even some members of the industry who had previously supported airline deregulation are now calling for help. Ed Daly, president of World Airways and a former advocate of deregulation, has asked the CAB to regulate fares again, because his airline is being victimized by what he called the "disastrous and completely irrational" rate wars.[25]

Daly's call for help illustrates the major fallacy of airline deregulation — indeed, behind most attempts at radical regulatory change, for that matter. That is the assumption by the policy's liberal and conservative formulators that the marketplace will operate rationally, because the captains of industry will make rational decisions.[26] But experience has shown that many segments of the industry did fail to act rationally in the immediate aftermath of deregulation, creating chaos for the industry as a whole. "When does the operation of the so-called free marketplace become predatory?" asked economics reporter Hobart Rowen.[27]

Another unchallenged assumption characterizing the thinking of the leaders of airline deregulation — mostly economists — was that regulation and efficiency were antithetical. Although regulation can work to promote inefficiency, the fault lies more within the purview of the agency and its management practices than with the principle of regulation itself. A glance at the highly regulated yet extremely efficient transportation systems of some Western European countries bears out this point.

Those who maintain their allegiance to deregulation argue that it is better for the industry and for the public in the long run; but no one seems to know how long that will be, and who else will suffer in the process. Deregulation proponents foresaw neither the extent of the upheaval in the airline industry, nor the inability of management to cope with such sudden change. Deregulation was a high-risk venture, with the costs far higher than even its opponents predicted.

Airline deregulation was typical of the radical approach for getting government out of the marketplace. It is conceivable that it may eventually result in more efficient, less costly service, but that remains an open question. In the meantime, the landscape is still being littered with corporate wreckage, the result of uncertainty and the high risks of such radical surgery.

A similar return to the free market was also charted for the trucking industry in the Motor Carrier Act of 1980, but the Interstate Commerce Commission — perhaps with its eye on the airline experience — has slowed down its implementation considerably. Also, the Teamsters and the trucking lobby present more formidable political opposition than do most of the participants in other areas of economic deregulation. An entirely new set of uncertainties stalks the telecommunications industry, whose deregulation is proceeding rapidly under Mark Fowler, chairman of the Federal Communications Commission.

Even banking deregulation, which began without much controversy, ran into some stumbling blocks associated with the rush to deregulate. Like airlines and trucking, the plans made sense on paper. Former Representative Henry S. Reuss, Democrat of Wisconsin, who as banking committee chairman led a successful crusade that culminated in the Financial Deregulation and Monetary Control Act of 1980, said in an interview that "we had set up such a crazy system of highly specialized institutions that our financial system was showing rigor mortis. We moved to break down some of those barriers between institutions, and let the Savings and Loan Associations make a wider variety of loans, and allow banks to do some of the things hitherto reserved to investment bankers."

But by 1983 several bank failures and an unpredictable marketplace led some highly respected leaders of the financial community to express their reservations. "I see a tremendous amount of new pressures, movement, and instability," warned Richard Pratt, chairman of the Federal Home Loan Bank Board, the government agency that regulates federally insured savings and loan institutions. The government had created an "explosive" imbalance, he continued, by giving banks new freedoms without establishing safeguards to ensure that they act responsibly.[28]

Henry Kaufman, an economist with the investment banking firm of Salomon Brothers, called for the "re-regulation of financial institutions," on the premise that they "perform a unique role involving both public and private trust." The need for government protections became even more evident after observing the risk-taking behavior of the banks in the marketplace, said Kaufman in a speech before the National Press Club on March 10, 1983: "Under deregulation, financial institutions become highly entrepreneurial, particularly if they sense that they will be bailed out and not held accountable for the ultimate risks.'' Despite widespread disagreement over how to address these problems, even advocates of deregulation now believe that some kind of controls — perhaps organized by the marketplace — need to replace many of those that have been eliminated in the government.

The real problem with economic deregulation is that the transportation system, the airwaves, and the banks are national resources, affecting many segments of the population with no immediate connection to the affected industries. A bankrupt airline can leave a city without adequate air transportation, damaging that city's ability to compete in the business community and reducing the quality of life for its residents. In that sense, the traditional lines between economic and social deregulation become blurred. A bankrupt airline, the development of a ghost town, and the closing of a company represent upheavals with such enormous impact that some measure of public protection is more than justified. And who else but a public agency can serve as the ultimate arbiter, stabilizing the kind of erratic market conditions that brought about the creation of these agencies in the first place?

Granted that these agencies may themselves become ossified: inefficient, captives of the industry they are supposed to regulate, or corrupt. But, in the last analysis, it is probably better to reform them through public pressure and improved management than to dismember them when their basic functions are still needed. With the consequences of deregulation so far-reaching, perhaps reform should occur more gradually, in order to provide more stability for the industry and greater protection for the public.

Coping with the Regulatory Vacuum

As business failures, crushing litigation, and uncontrolled competition continue to emerge from poorly conceived and hastily implemented deregulation, some business leaders have begun to call for a reversal of the trend to dismantle the regulatory process. They are just beginning to realize that what was intended as a gift to the business community has instead turned out, in many respects, to be a shortsighted policy damaging to their own economic interests. What is encouraging about this development is that it will eventually balance the political equation, which up to this point has been weighted heavily toward deregulation in any form. Indeed, in some areas, industry has teamed up with its former adversaries, the public interest groups, to stave off further deregulation.

The alcoholic beverage industry has recently joined with its public interest counterparts to oppose the Reagan administration's effort to dismantle the agency that regulates them: the Bureau of Alcohol, Tobacco, and Firearms in the Department of the Treasury. Originally conceived as a gift to the industry, the Reagan administration's plan turned the bureau's functions over to the Customs Service, thereby easing industry's burdens while saving the government $11.5 million annually. "Our intention is to have a minimal amount of compliance with the [Federal Alcohol Administration] act," said Robert Powis, deputy assistant treasury secretary for enforcement.[29] He explained that dismantling the office would lead to decreased enforcement of the laws governing licensing, unfair trade practices, labeling, and advertising.

Ironically, the Reagan administration expected the same level of applause from industry that it had received for dismantling the environmental, health, and safety agencies. To its surprise, the reverse occurred. It appeared that no one in the administration had consulted the wholesalers — the brewers, the distillers, and the vintners — before unveiling the policy, assuming that any form of deregulation would be eagerly accepted by business.

Not in this case, though. "We were dumbfounded," said Douglas Metz, executive vice president of the Wine and Spirits Wholesalers of America, expressing an almost unanimously held sentiment.[30] For Metz and others in this industry remembered all too well what things were like before federal regulation, when the free market governed. In those days, the marketplace was controlled by gangsters like Al Capone, and the industry was "rife with monopolies, criminals, and unethical promotions used to encourage the consumption of alcohol."[31] Eventually public opinion toward the industry grew so negative that the forces supporting prohibition were able to pass an amendment to the Constitution prohibiting the sale of alcohol, which was not repealed for thirteen years.

Fearing a reenactment of its unsavory history, the industry rightly resists any efforts at federal deregulation. It also dreads the inevitable political overkill: specifically, that federal regulation would be replaced with far more onerous and restrictive state regulations — especially in the Bible belt states. From the point of view of efficiency as well, the industry would much rather deal with one set of federal regulations than with fifty separate sets of state regulations.[32]

There are also signs that even the easing of environmental regulations has begun to backfire, provoking pockets of protest from the business community. Some companies that have complied with Environmental Protection Agency (EPA) regulations by making huge investments in pollution control now find themselves at a distinct competitive disadvantage vis-à-vis companies that have not complied. Instead, their competitors dragged their feet, held on to their capital, hired teams of lawyers to fight the regulations, and waited for political solutions to their problems.

The Bacardi Corporation, the world's largest rum producer, found itself in this disadvantageous position. Since 1979, the company had spent more than $10 million to clean up the water pollution from two distilleries in Puerto Rico. The ground rules read that Bacardi would build up its treatment plant on condition that the government would require the rest of the industry to comply with its strict antipollution standards. After Reagan took office, the EPA began to consider easing regulations to permit Bacardi's major competitors to continue dumping large amounts of molasses residue, used in the manufacture of rum, into the Caribbean. Under heavy pressure from Bacardi's competitors, as well as from the governor of Puerto Rico, the administration ignored the earlier agreement with Bacardi, justifying its actions on the basis of the island's adverse economic conditions.[33]

In effect, the government penalized Bacardi for complying with the law, and rewarded the firms that had consistently refused to invest in pollution control. The government also sent an implicit message to the business community, that it is wiser to invest in attorneys specializing in dilatory strategies than to comply with the law.

The Risks of Laissez Faire

Complaints similar to Bacardi's began flowing in from a variety of other industries, particularly those involved in disposing of hazardous waste — oil refiners and steel manufacturers. Again, "without firm scientific evidence, the agency [EPA] is rewarding those companies that failed to comply," argued Clement B. Malin, government relations manager for Texaco.[34] Together with Exxon and several other large oil companies, Texaco has also criticized an EPA proposal that would ease regulations to permit smaller oil refineries to use more lead in gasoline than the larger companies are allowed. The larger companies are then placed at a distinct disadvantage by having already made substantial investments in modernizing their facilities in order to comply with the clean air laws. Their complaints are echoed by the steel companies, who are worried about similar regulatory proposals that will reduce their competitiveness, as well as by a coalition of landfill companies who argue that a new EPA "loophole," giving landfill operators who have not invested in up-to-date equipment more time to comply, amounts to preferential treatment and extra profits for those companies.

What industry failed to predict in the rush to deregulate were the political vicissitudes, the switch in regulatory approaches that left some companies at a distinct disadvantage. Not only is this policy of abrupt deregulation patently unfair on its face; it will also make government's job more difficult in the future. How will the EPAs of the future get companies to comply with their regulations when the lessons of the past so clearly point to the financial benefits of avoidance?

Facing similar disruptions from the federal government's attempt to deregulate, the states have begun to echo the business community's complaints. A subtle switch in tone has been heard from state officials, who often mirrored the antiregulatory posture of industry but are now calling for a renewed federal presence. Many object to the sudden shift in the environmental area, where within a very short time states have been given responsibilities well beyond their fiscal and managerial capabilities. By 1982, nearly half of the EPA's programs had been turned over to local control, with EPA administrator Anne Gorsuch promising to "make good on the idea of equal partnership" with the states by delegating 75 percent of all environmental programs to the states by 1984.[35] Twinning the administration's deregulation objectives with its "new federalism" program has enabled the administration to cut back existing environmental enforcement and licensing programs through budget cuts, agency reorganization, personnel shifts, and rewriting key regulations. The use of executive power has been enormously effective in achieving these goals quickly, leaving state officials and their client groups to cope with the consequences.

Many state officials complain that the rollback of federal regulations has led states to seek to attract industry by competing over which can produce the least onerous regulations. "When the Feds walk away from the problem, businesses ask, 'Why stay in your state? Why not go to another state with very lax standards?' " said Norman H. Nosenchuck, director of the Division of Solid Wastes in the New York State Department of Environmental Conservation. "This is a real problem. Here in New York we value our quality of life." In the case of hazardous waste management, he noted, "without federal action for appropriate national standards, stringent requirements on industry by an individual state could lead to the loss of existing industries from that state to other states that accept land burial." But industry sometimes alleges "overregulation" as a justification for a move that has other causes, such as cheaper labor or better transportation.

Mistakenly, the state officials believed that the decentralization of power would be accompanied by the resources needed to administer these environmental programs. This did not occur, leaving the states with increased responsibilities at the same time that they confronted sharp cuts in federal funding, accompanied by fiscal austerity at home. The full impact of this development is yet to be felt, but early signs point to a bleak future. Indiana officials reported that "without more federal and state aid, it was forced to trim its clean air program to the bare bones, placing as much of the burden upon industry as possible." Faced with similar financial problems, Pennsylvania closed nearly half of its forty-six environmental enforcement offices, and New York threatened to pull out of the business of hazardous waste control if federal help did not arrive soon.[36] Finally, the National Governors Association released a study warning that only a few states would find the fiscal resources to compensate for the reduction in the federal presence.

254

The Risks of Laissez Faire

In effect, the shift to the states will mean that in some states, environmental protection will shrink to the point of oblivion, with obvious implications for the future of the environment, while in other states local governments will gear up to meet the new challenges.

Most ironic of all, it now appears that federal deregulation has not really stemmed the flow of regulations, as the states slowly step in to fill the void. In a one-year period, from 1980 to 1981, proposed state regulations doubled, from twenty-five thousand to fifty thousand.[37] How does this square with the claims of the Reagan administration that federal regulations have been reduced by half?[38]

Some business organizations that originally welcomed regulatory diffusion, believing that they had more political clout in state capitals than in Washington, now regard the issue differently. It was all well and good for the federal government to ease regulations involving the work place and the marketplace, they believed — but not if it meant state and local governments moving in to fill the vacuum.

"If you're a major manufacturer and distributor of products in interstate commerce and have to be worried about conflicting regulations not only of the fifty states but also of local jurisdictions, you have a nightmare," said Jeffrey H. Joseph, vice president for domestic policy of the Chamber of Commerce.

Thomas W. Ball, vice president of State and Federal Associates, a group that keeps track of such matters, reported that one third of the Fortune 500 companies now have state government relations officers to keep on top of state regulations, a new growth industry. "With the states, you've got fifty tiny little governments, each with its unique character and set of problems, and 7,400 legislators, each trying to carry out the wishes of their constituents," he noted.

States are also promulgating their own environmental regulations as well as those involving food labeling, product liability, energy, and worker safety. "One of the reasons why the Environmental Protection Agency was created in the first place was because there were too many dissimilarities among the states," said Lawrence B. Cahill, a management consultant with Booz-Allen & Hamilton. "Some oil shale facilities and electric utilities are now required to get fifty permits."

255

Dismantling America

Business now confronts a maze of conflicting standards and bureaucracies that could wreak havoc on interstate commerce, as well as on the long-term planning of individual firms. Already, the giant chemical companies are trying to figure out how to deal with the different hazardous chemical packaging and labeling requirements passed by New York, West Virginia, and several other states. In fact, after ten states and two localities promulgated standards of their own, the chemical industry reversed its position of opposing a federal standard and pressed the Office of Management and Budget to adopt a standard that already has been approved by the Labor Department.

Within two weeks after the Tylenol murders, in 1982, the pharmaceutical manufacturers — fearing fifty different state regulations — pressed the Food and Drug Administration to pre-empt the field and mandate tamper-proof jars for over-the-counter drugs. Perhaps in the future, local environmental regulations will determine where companies locate (and relocate), as well as the quality of the new technology, all as a result of the regulatory Balkanization inundating the "free" marketplace.

8

There's No Such Thing as a Free Market

The world only goes forward because of those who oppose it.
— Goethe

THE RUSH TO DEREGULATE is a return to the law of the jungle. Ultimately, it would remove protections against the industrial excesses of the past, and return us to the nineteenth century — when child labor was commonplace, the work place was a threat to life and limb, *caveat emptor* was the prevailing consumer doctrine, and the nation's waterways were becoming public sewers.

The marketplace reigned supreme, as the nation concentrated on the need to industrialize. Maggots on meat were considered minor inconveniences, for example, when compared with the availa-

257

bility of meat, the jobs created by the packing plants, and the profits derived from meat production. Unprotected by fire regulations, teen-age girls worked in tinderbox sweatshops that clothed the nation, while miners died in uninspected shafts, extracting the minerals that fueled a growing nation.

In the rush to industrialize, all other values were subordinated to technological progress, and even the first efforts at regulation were geared toward furthering the process of industrialization. The nation's industrial power, its fledgling steel and coal industry, and an intercontinental railroad, all had to be built and nurtured — at any cost. The protections that we take for granted today were nonexistent then, because for all practical purposes there was no protector: government was subordinate to industry. Factory owners did not have to worry about inspectors from the Occupational Safety and Health Administration (OSHA) checking the safety of the scaffolding. Tire manufacturers did not have to worry about the National Highway Traffic Safety Administration measuring the depth of treads, or the quality of the rubber. Advertisers did not have to worry about substantiating their claims before a skeptical Federal Trade Commission (FTC). The important thing was to build, grow, manufacture, and sell.

In time, however, the nation's industries grew so powerful that they no longer required the nurturing needed in their formative years, and the public began to question the sacrifices that had accompanied this growth. Many of industry's most blatant excesses aroused a public outcry that demanded legislative action. Congress responded by creating agencies empowered to protect consumers, workers, air, water, food, and drugs.

Curiously, industry itself was a major beneficiary of the social regulations emerging from these agencies. The new regulations gave the public more confidence in American products and a respectability that industry had not previously enjoyed. More significantly, the early regulations established monopolies, destroyed competition, and limited industry's legal liability, by enabling companies to argue that they were not negligent because they were living up to federal standards. An additional advantage for business was that federal regulations that superseded those of the states afforded still further protection for business by freeing individual companies from the burden of complying with fifty different sets of standards.

But when the regulators began to protect the public rather than industries, "regulation" became a dirty word. Federal regulatory agencies found themselves in a continual state of siege, culminating in an all-out attack by two Presidents, several Congresses, and leaders in both political parties, united in their commitment to erode federal protections in a misguided effort to help American industry recover in a shaky economy. They have been successful in the last five years in unraveling many of these protections, propelled by groups of "Neo-Darwinists," who envision a marketplace untrammeled by regulations as a guarantee of industrial growth and renewal.

Everyone is a loser in this dismantling of the regulatory process, industry as much as the public. Was any industry better off before it was regulated? Was the meat packing industry better off before government intervened to ensure sanitary standards? The current woes of the nuclear industry may be traced in large measure, as we have shown, to a lax regulatory system and its inability to maintain safety measures sufficiently rigorous to ensure responsible growth and instill public confidence.

It is ironic that these regulations are becoming unraveled at a time when American manufacturing standards are being assailed the world over. The downgrading of quality control in the automobile industry in the early 1970s, for example, led to short-term profits and long-term disaster, a pattern repeated by other American industries. But manufacturing standards are protected by the governments of America's chief overseas competitors. The Japanese, faced with a lack of public confidence in their products, initiated national standards that overcame the bias against products "made in Japan." Thus, while American manufacturers claim that federal regulations place them at a competitive disadvantage, Japan and Western European countries believe that regulatory controls helped business by increasing public confidence in their products. What American business regards as rampant consumerism has been elevated to national policy in nations that are now edging the United States out of world markets. These nations correctly identified consumer and business interests as mutually reinforcing, especially in highly visible and highly competitive industries. "The French regulatory system assures consumers the world over that when they purchase a French wine they will receive the quality they expect," argues Robert Reich, former director of policy planning at the FTC, who believes that consumer protection should be part of a national marketing strategy. "Similarly, Sweden's Board for Consumer Policies has established rigorous standards for product grading . . . that have earned Sweden a reputation for quality automobiles, vacuum cleaners, and hand tools. . . . And West Germany has pioneered exacting standards for product performance and consumer information, thereby boosting its world sales of cameras, furniture, and household appliances." [1]

The critical question is whether an advanced technological, democratic society can flourish — or even exist — in a climate reminiscent of the Social Darwinism of the late nineteenth century. The Social Darwinists twisted the theory of the natural selection of the species to fit the socioeconomic environment. They believed in the survival of the fittest, whom they identified as those with the power and the resources to build industrial empires. Their latter-day descendants do not, however, believe in total laissez faire. They have successfully campaigned for government intervention on their behalf, and support the regulatory agencies when they help them consolidate their gains. Regulation became anathema to them only when it appeared to be at cross-purposes with industry, and began to emphasize protection of the work place, marketplace, air, water, and people's health.

Today's Neo-Darwinists carry out their legacy in a variety of imaginative ways, creating in effect a new set of rights to be used for their own purposes. One of these new rights could be called the right to pollute, and was bestowed in a set of rules proposed by the Environmental Protection Agency (EPA) in 1982. [2] Under this rule, a manufacturer whose factory emits pollutants that are below allowable limits could sell, lease, or give to another company a pollution credit that would enable the recipient company to pollute in excess of EPA standards. In effect, industry is being invited to stake its claims to unpolluted air, while government has identified a new form of private property — the air — proposing that it be "saved, sold, traded, or deposited in special banks." [3] But is air a commodity to be bought and sold on the open market? And if it is, should not the profits be shared among the nation's 220 million citizens? Obviously, air is not a commodity, to be entrusted to the mercies of the free market, even if the government says it is. The policy is a sham, another of the spurious ideas of the Neo-Darwinists' vision of regulatory "reform," the sum total of which places a heavy mortgage on the nation's limited sources.

Another bogus right developing under the Neo-Darwinists' policy rubric would allow companies to sell products abroad that have been banned in this country.[4] This is chauvinism run rampant, putting the United States in the *de facto* position of placing a higher value on American lives than on the lives of other nationals. Hazardous chemicals already have found markets abroad, with disastrous results for local populations either unable to read the instructions on the containers, or unaware of why they have been taken off the market in the United States.[5] Americans naive enough to feel immune from these problems would think twice if they knew how often these banned chemicals returned to their own dinner plates in the imported foods fertilized by these substances.

Under the Neo-Darwinism that has prevaded current regulatory thinking, new rights are rapidly developing under the rubric of "reform" or "reindustrialization" that tend to obscure the values that legitimize government's intervention in the marketplace: the protection of the public.

Tracking the Public Mandate

A news story prominently featured on the front page of the *New York Times* announced that a private firm, with only seven employees, had just launched its own spacecraft at a fraction of what it would cost the government. The project was named Conestoga, after the covered wagons used by the pioneers, and in that spirit its promoters hailed a new era in space exploration and technological innovation. Speaking from the command center, located in several house trailers and surrounded by a cattle fence, the company's chairman, David Hannah, Jr., a Texas real estate developer, promised to give the National Aeronautics and Space Administration

(NASA) some real competition, by using the technology developed by the nation's space agency but making it more economical.[6]

Readers of the news story marveled at this new advance in "reprivatization" — turning over to the private sector what had formerly been within the province of the government. They pondered its implications: the superior efficiency of private industry; its ability to eliminate red tape; and the potential for decreasing taxes as well as public expenditures by attracting private capital for space exploration.

The cost factor was so central to this event that few thought about its larger implications. Who is going to regulate this activity? Indeed, how could a private company take the initiative to build and launch its own private rocket?[7] If a hundred other companies followed suit and began sending up their own missiles, what would be the effect upon air traffic? Upon weather satellites? What if one of these companies decided to take foreign policy into its own hands and fire its rockets at a foreign country? Even the most bellicose antiregulatory rhetoricians would think twice before turning over NASA's functions to the private sector, or before permitting private companies to launch rockets willy-nilly without deferring to government intervention.

The rocket incident shows what can happen when the wrong questions — who pays and what does it cost? — are repeatedly asked at the expense of two other vital questions. Who suffers and who governs? The public has been lulled into a false sense of what is important, so much so that it is jeopardizing its future health and security.

This is probably what happened in Peking, where a crash program to industrialize left the city devoid of birds, grass, and shrubs. Now described as an "ecological basket case," Peking in April is the same as Peking in winter, "bald and birdless." The air is so bad that bicycle riders are forced to cover their faces with surgical masks to avoid breathing coal dust, and raw sewage and industrial waste have so contaminated the city's water supply that a glass of water "could pass for a test tube of toxic chemicals," among them "harmful amounts of mercury, cyanide, cobalt and benzene." EPA scientists who measured the air quality found it six times more toxic than what was considered safe, which explains the prevalence of chronic bronchitis, known by foreign residents as "Peking lung."[8] Of course, in Peking there is little in the way of public input to force a reversal of such misguided government policies.

The problem is that the rush to deregulate is so pervasive that the public may not see the forest for the trees — until, as in Peking, there aren't any trees. Yet while the President and Congress proceed to dismantle the regulatory process at a rapid pace, without significant opposition, poll after poll reveals public support for the principles of regulatory protection, particularly in the areas of health, safety, and the environment. The polls even reveal the public's willingness to pay the costs of cleaning up. There is also evidence of public dissatisfaction with the growing uncertainties emerging in the deregulation of the telecommunications, banking, and airline industries.

The noted pollster Louis Harris reported to Congress in 1981 findings that indicated "just how committed the American people are in their resolve not to cut back or relax existing federal standards on air pollution."[9] According to Harris, "not a single major segment of the public wants the environmental laws made less strict." Specifically, "by 80 to 17 percent, a sizable majority of the public does not want to see any relaxation in existing federal regulation of air pollution." In addition, "by a resounding 65 to 32 percent, a substantial majority says they are opposed to any constraint on human health standards on cost grounds."

"This message on the deep desire of the American people to battle pollution is one of the most overwhelming and clearest we have ever recorded in our twenty-five years of surveying public opinion," said Harris, in a statement buttressing his findings. There was no doubt in his mind as he attempted to alert members of Congress to the political consequences of dismantling environmental regulation. Even under grilling by Rep. John Dingell, chairman of the Subcommittee on Health and the Environment, Harris stood his ground, warning that clean air was one of the "sacred cows," and that the voters were saying, "Watch out. We will have your hide" if you "keelhaul that legislation."[10]

The current deregulatory frenzy thus may prove as politically damaging to its champions in Congress as it is physically harmful to the public at large. Imagine the public outcry and scalp hunting after the first environmental crisis attributable to the dismantling of the regulatory process.

In other areas of deregulation, a separate Harris poll showed similar opposition to unraveling the regulatory process, but not as dramatically as the figures in the environmental area.[11]

- By 66 to 31 percent, a majority opposed cutting back on the enforcement of employee safety regulations by the Occupational Safety and Health Administration.

- By 59 to 32 percent, a majority opposed cutting down the scope and enforcement powers of the Consumer Product Safety Commission.

Public disapproval of Reagan's regulatory appointments also was reflected in the responses to questions dealing with who was doing the deregulating. By 64 to 28 percent, a majority opposed the practice of "putting people who formerly represented mining, timber, oil, and gas companies in charge of what happens to federal lands," a direct reference to public dissatisfaction with the pronouncements of Interior Secretary James Watt.[12]

Watt was among several Reagan appointees who viewed their roles as dismantling the agencies whose laws and regulations they had sworn to uphold. He was a throwback to the tradition of placing the regulatory agency in the hands of the very interests that its leaders were appointed to regulate.

Why such a disparity, then, between what the public wants and what the public allows its leaders to do? The Reagan administration entered office, its leaders believed, with a mandate to deregulate, a task it has successfully achieved in hundreds of ways. "I don't think they have a mandate," argued Gus Spaeth, former chairman of the Council on Environmental Quality. "Who on earth would want to abandon control of hazardous waste disposal to the free market?"

But public sentiment often contradicts itself. The Harris poll found not only a high level of support for social regulation but also widespread support for the deregulation of business, with 61 percent of the respondents agreeing with the statement that "after all the years that federal regulation of business has kept growing, we need drastic action like this to cut it back." Harris interprets this as a strong "mandate to get government off business's back," albeit accompanied by "doubts about some of the specific proposals."[13]

The real answer to this paradoxical state of affairs lies in the gap between the public's lack of understanding of the regulatory process and the political realities of that process. While the American public overwhelmingly supports clean air, worker safety, and other goals of regulation, it has only a rudimentary perception of the government apparatus involved in ensuring those protections. A League of Women Voters poll in 1982 was almost more revealing in this respect than the clean air polls, because it tested the level of public education and found it seriously wanting, the regulatory process a complete mystery to an overwhelming majority of Americans. Half of those sampled failed to name a single regulation that affected them, and 47 percent thought that Congress wrote regulations. Only 17 percent correctly identified the executive branch as having responsibility for writing regulations, while 10 percent said the courts wrote regulations. Of the remaining half that could name regulations that had an impact on them, only 6 percent identified the EPA.[14]

The public's ignorance has made it relatively easy to unravel the regulatory process; the task of dismantling is that much more effective if conducted in the cracks, between an unsuspecting public, on the one hand, and a political leadership that knows too well what it wants to do in the area of deregulation. In this political environment, accountability is confused, as the public fails to identify who is to blame for the recent results of deregulation: dirtier air and water; an increase of carcinogens in the environment; increased risks of radiation exposure at nuclear power plants; increased uncertainty in the marketplace; and increased risk in the work place. Yet these are the trends that have developed in that vast gulf between the public's real mandate to government — to maintain its regulatory role — and the public's low level of awareness in the area of how to maintain the protections essential to the country's health and welfare.

Buying into Regulatory Reform

The numerous regulatory reform schemes promoted in recent years all share one thing in common: they tend to weaken the regulatory environment instead of streamlining and strengthening it. Most of them also fail dismally in coming to grips with the real regulatory problems of health, safety, and market stability, and even though they are offered in the guise of "reform" and "relief," their architects are deceiving themselves as well as the public about what these policies will accomplish.

Regulatory reform has turned out to be an exercise in national self-deception because of the singularity of its dominant goal: short-term relief for business. By itself, the goal is worthy; as a method of pushing aside other objectives, it is self-defeating.

Regulatory reform also has relied too heavily on several assumptions that have already been proven highly questionable. One of these, that the marketplace is a better regulator than the government, has not been borne out by the facts in most of the important areas of social regulatory involvement, as well as in some of the economic areas.

Leaving work place safety and health to the textile mills did nothing for the lungs of the workers, who finally realized that "flexibility" was not in their best interest. Permitting the nuclear industry to dominate the regulatory process for so many years damaged the long-term economic health of the industry and undermined public confidence in the safety and cost efficiency of nuclear energy.

Cost-benefit schemes, which are the basis for the bulk of White House reform activity, represent another example of basing policy on false assumptions, namely, that forcing agencies to undertake lengthy cost-benefit analyses for all major regulations will lead to better government. It has indeed led to fewer regulations and decreased enforcement activity, a worthy objective if society understands and accepts the consequences that have accompanied those "reforms": an increase in miners' deaths; an increase in the release of poisonous chemicals into an already overloaded environment; and numerous other undesirable social outcomes.

266

There's No Such Thing as a Free Market

No matter how you spell "relief," the regulatory reform packages introduced by the last two Presidents have led to the same objective: to get away from the command and control form of regulation, and return to a system of looser standards that will reduce costs and increase efficiency. On paper they all look good. The EPA's much touted "bubble concept" allows company managers to increase pollutants from one source and decrease them from others, as long as the total amount of pollution stays within the "bubble" and does not exceed clean air requirements. Other EPA "reforms" are similarly innovative in terms of decreasing costs and encouraging industry to participate more actively in regulation.[15] In the area of worker safety, the Carter administration promoted "performance standards" to replace command and control regulations: respirators in the work place were one example of "flexibility" that allowed companies to avoid the more expensive method of cleaning up the air in factories.

The enthusiasm for regulatory flexibility hit a new peak with proposed Federal Aviation Administration (FAA) regulations that would allow each airline to decide how it would meet federal safety standards. Called regulation by objectives (RBO) by FAA administrator J. Lynn Helms, the plan promises to give the airlines more independence without compromising basic safety. It also will wean the industry away from safety standards at the same time that it is losing its system of economic regulation. Critics fear disruptions similar to those caused by the unraveling of the economic regulations, one of them warning that RBO would remove public scrutiny from the process, as well as congressional oversight. "Unfortunately," said one analyst, "crashes or enforcement investigations are the ultimate test of whether RBO is going to work."[16]

With the results of these reforms becoming increasingly evident, one wonders why Congress has followed the executive branch's lead in its own efforts to restructure the administrative process. The congressional regulatory reform bill basically copies President Reagan's executive order, adding layers of cost-benefit analysis to regulation writing, and making the process even more technical and unwieldy. The reason is simple. Congress, like the executive branch, has been seduced by cost-benefit ratios, and has made little or no effort to question this perspective.

Dismantling America

Political imperatives also have swayed Congress in its approach to regulatory problems. Following the lead of the executive branch, Congress now tends to address the most vocal element of the business community in its attack against regulation, and has responded by opening up its own opportunities to exert control over the agencies. The legislative veto, struck down by the Supreme Court, would have given Congress the power to veto individual regulations after they had been issued by the agencies. Had Congress been serious about providing genuine oversight over the thousands of regulations pouring out of the agencies, it would have had to increase its staff and resources to a level well beyond what the public would be willing to support. Instead, Congress would probably have concentrated on the "sexy" issues, as well as the issues that increased its leading backers. And although the legislative veto was promoted as a vehicle to expand congressional oversight, its real impact would have been felt in the growing number of opportunities for powerful groups to affect the administrative process through the Congress.

The legislative veto would also have put Congress in a more politically vulnerable position, with members held personally accountable for the thousands of regulations issued by the regulatory agencies. Thus, whereas Congress originally gave authority to regulatory agencies because it often was unable to reach compromises on controversial issues, it would have been unable to dodge those issues. In the same manner, presidential intervention in the regulatory process is also politically dangerous, because it involves the President in many controversies he would best ignore. President Carter's brief involvement in the cotton dust issue suggests the perils of presidential involvement in the regulatory process.

Events in the FTC's short history of operating under a legislative veto are testimony to increased congressional obeisance to the wishes of the Political Action Committees and the special interests they represent. Congress vetoed an FTC rule requiring used car dealers to list a car's known defects before attempting to sell the automobile. The rule seemed innocuous, even in its attempt to improve the ethics of the marketplace; but the lobby representing the used car dealers, which had contributed more than $800,000 to congressional campaign coffers, made a more powerful case before

268

Congress than the unorganized purchasers of used cars.

Caveat emptor will not only become the watchword for those buying automobiles; it should also become part of the lexicon for those involved in the wholesale purchase of regulatory "reform."

A Question of Governance

Regulatory "reform" asks too few questions, and then acts on the basis of incomplete answers. The dominant question — who pays? — would be legitimate except for the fact that it crowds out other questions and in excluding them produces distorted results. In assuming that industry pays, the "reformers" neglect the larger question of "Who pays in the long run?" — a question that would produce more accurate answers and reveal that the costs are really shared by a much wider population, a population that has up to now been relegated to the periphery of regulatory policy decisions. In addition, "Who pays?" means more than monetary costs; the social costs of deregulation can be far more extensive and damaging, especially to future generations.

A change in the questions asked must now occur unless the public wishes to mortgage its future and the future of its children and grandchildren with the heavy burdens incurred by the dismantling of regulatory protections. "Who suffers?" or "Who will be harmed from the relaxation of a set of regulations?" should be reintroduced more substantively into the process to correct the excesses that have turned the clock back to a preindustrial era. Consider the risks incurred by textile workers breathing in cotton dust every day of their working lives, by miners working in uninspected mines, by people living near unevenly regulated facilities like Three Mile Island, by ordinary citizens drinking tap water in a city whose industrial plants have been given the green light by EPA to relax the processing of toxic wastes.

The measure of a modern and responsible society is the extent to which we ask these questions and the extent to which we care about who will suffer or who will benefit from these misbegotten

269

"reforms." Who will benefit, ultimately, from proposed Department of Labor regulations that relax restrictions on the child labor laws? Will our society become stronger as a result of allowing fourteen-year-olds to work longer hours at subminimum wages? Who will benefit from the recent upsurge in mine deaths, or from new federal regulations that would no longer require hospitals to inform poor people that they will be cared for without charge? The answers are obvious, but it is significant that the questions are never raised by policy makers who worship the new regulatory deity, the cost-benefit ratio — a theory that lacks both vision and humanity. The victims of these misguided regulatory policies — an expanding constituency — must press decision makers in Congress and the executive branch to reject this narrowly based theory they call reform, and to begin asking the relevant questions that will rebuild a stable and effective regulatory presence.

The foundation of regulatory reform rests with Congress, whose laws spawned many of the controversial regulations in the first place. But so far, Congress has presented the public with a mixed bag. At times, Congress passes socially progressive laws, but then retains the power to eviscerate those laws through devices like the legislative veto. What emerges are mixed mandates, confusing to the agencies and to the public. Bureaucrats struggle to discern congressional "intent," then get into trouble when they implement it. In the case of the FTC, the agency proceeded to do its job on the basis of very specific mandates from Congress, spelled out in appropriations hearings and in the law. When political pressures began to overwhelm Congress, the members forgot about the mandate and quickly clamped down on the agency through the imposition of a legislative veto and punitive budget measures. In effect, the agency was blamed for following the job description set forth by Congress. Congress's solution was to switch mandates through legislative devices, rather than changing the statute, which would involve a public admission that it was retracting its social policies.

Congressional oversight can be equally confusing in other areas. In the field of nuclear energy, at least nine committees and subcommittees wield oversight power, a legislative fail-safe that should enhance the public safety. But, instead, the regulators face cross-pressures from this plethora of watchdogs, some urging licensing speed-up, others pressing for increased safety measures.

The search for the elusive legislative mandate ends at the doorstep of the appropriations process, where Congress's real intentions are uncovered. How much is Congress willing to appropriate for the implementation of a law? How much can an agency spend in the process of enforcing those regulations? How large are the agencies created by Congress to improve the environment, reduce risks, and ensure the safety of the work place? Here, too, the numbers are instructive. Is it really possible for an agency like the FTC to police American industry on an annual budget of $73 million?

Congress can participate more creatively in regulatory reform by shifting its own focus and making a serious attempt to stop the swing of the pendulum. Instead of joining the lynch mob, and unraveling regulation for its own sake, Congress has ample opportunity through the oversight process to manage what is already on the books, carefully selecting what deserves to be deregulated from the vast majority of regulatory protections. Instead of merely responding to angry pressure groups, Congress can examine on an individual basis those areas of regulatory activity causing the most distress and attempt to correct them, slowly and incrementally, without producing the upheavals that have emerged from the last five years of regulatory "reform." For Congress knows better than anyone how easy it is to dismantle, and how many years it will take to rebuild those protections.

Congress also has the opportunity — and the obligation — to alert the public to the value of regulatory protections in an industrialized country, as well as to what society would be like without them. If the public is going to take involuntary risks, it should be aware of those risks, as well as their long-term costs. Congress rose to that occasion when it brought to public attention the wayward direction of the EPA under the Reagan administration.

Congress will refine its management of regulatory activities as the public becomes more aware of the legislative role, particularly its tendency to rely on the quick fix: the catchy program; the ambitious legislation that raises hopes without providing the resources for fulfilling those hopes. In the future, Congress will have to write laws that it is prepared to back up, instead of burdening agencies with difficult regulatory tasks without the personnel or financial resources to achieve them. At the same time, it must avoid laws that inflict impossible burdens on state and local governments, universities, and businesses lacking the resources to fulfill their mandates. Legislators should also be taken to task more strictly to define what they mean, in order to avoid the extremes of political conflict that have resulted from vague mandates like a "safe work place whenever feasible." But these are all problems that are remedied by experience and a leadership with a collective memory reaching back far enough to absorb the lessons of the past. For Congress's role in regulatory reform is too important to ignore. Unlike the White House, Congress benefits from having a more open process, being more accessible on a day-to-day basis than the executive branch: its hearings are, for the most part, open to the public; its deliberations on the floor are public; and its votes are a matter of public record.

Only the federal government can take the lead in the management of regulation, because government is the only thing that stands between an increasingly affected public and a mercurial marketplace. In this context, it is wise for the President to retain some central power over the coordination and management of the regulatory process. But the vehicles by which Presidents Carter and Reagan have assumed control have lent themselves to abuse, providing the impetus for dismantling valuable regulatory agencies and their protective functions. The extent of recent presidential dominance over the regulatory system undermined the system of checks between the agencies and the President, a balance originally intended to prevent the types of abuses now common throughout government.

Although centralizing the management of regulation under one roof makes good sense from the point of view of efficiency, it also means concentrating power in the hands of one person who can use it for a variety of purposes. President Reagan is a case in point, showing what happens when a President is willing to maximize this power. President Carter laid the groundwork through his executive order creating the Regulatory Analysis Review Group (RARG), and Reagan's advisers "hit the ground running," to use their own words. The Reagan administration succeeded in dismantling many social regulations, primarily through hiring regulators who could be trusted to delay regulatory controls; through budget cuts that undermined the agencies' basic missions; and by allowing the Office of Management and Budget (OMB) to bury any remaining regulations that managed to break through those formidable barriers.

Ironically, increased presidential control over the regulatory process has long been urged by a spate of blue-ribbon presidential commissions, many of whose recommendations have been taken seriously, judging from recent trends. Presidential dominance of the independent regulatory commissions also has expanded through building up the role of the chairmen and by linking them and their agendas more closely to the White House. What has not been fully taken into account is the extent to which this development depends on the President himself, and the ease with which he can channel the process to his own political needs and priorities, not to mention what the presidential capture of the agencies has done to undermine the judgment and technical expertise of agency heads. How many regulators today would resist White House pressure the way OSHA administrator Eula Bingham did when she stood her ground on the cotton dust rules?

There is still a good argument to be made for OMB to remain as the lead agency in this field. But OMB is losing credibility with the public because of its emphasis on cutting costs, its primary mandate, as well as its tendency to hold secret meetings with affected businesses and then deliver regulatory "relief." This perverts the administrative process and creates a long-term problem for OMB, which is otherwise a highly professional agency capable of making a real contribution to regulatory reform. To recover its credibility, OMB could open up to some degree its coordinating activities with affected industries and interest groups, creating in effect a sunshine provision to alert the public to the content and the existence of these activities. This would increase the public's trust in the executive branch's role in regulation, and legitimize its role in the process at the same time. The regulatory process itself is open. Should not the role of the White House be more open as well, especially in these highly controversial decisions? Indeed, the long-term credibility of the agencies has rested on their accessibility to the public and to a wide constellation of interest groups. In addition to its coordinating role, OMB's own decision-making process should be more open, a reversal of its current practice, through which regulations tend to disappear into the infamous OMB "black

273

hole,'' only to surface under congressional subpoena, in court, or not at all. This only serves to anger the public, to enshroud regulation in secrecy, and to cloud OMB's image as an effective and fair arbiter. Opening up the process may be less efficient than ''hitting the ground running,'' but decisions will be much improved as a result.

The development of research guidelines for recombinant DNA vividly demonstrated the advantages to business and to the public of an open process. At the beginning, the issue showed all the signs of becoming the same kind of long-term political controversy as nuclear energy. Research advances in biotechnology were accompanied by the public's fear of its potential dangers — with visions of three-headed monsters roaming the sewers. When the National Institutes of Health (NIH) entered the picture, its leaders sought to avoid these pitfalls. Instead of following the typical policy of excluding nonscientists from the decision-making process, Donald Frederickson, the NIH director, opened the doors to all the conflicting interests — citizens' groups, companies involved in recombinant DNA research, universities, scientists, and public officials. The difficulties of holding what he called a ''town meeting on molecular biology'' were far greater at the outset than they would have been with a more limited constituency. But opening up the process also dispelled much of the fear, and increased the long-term public acceptability of this new technology.[17]

Like Congress, the President can also take a leadership role in encouraging regulation in the public's interest. Recently, executive leadership has been effective only in dismantling the process. The exhortation of presidential adviser Murray Weidenbaum to regulators, ''when you have nothing to do, undo,'' is really a shortsighted approach, because it encourages decision makers to unravel without thinking of the consequences and assumes that all regulation is bad. Instead, he should have inspired the regulators to manage more effectively, to correct the inevitable problems in the regulatory process, and not to throw out the baby with the bath water. Simply ''undoing'' regulations is a mindless approach to government that can only lead to poorly conceived public policy. Indeed, the rush to deregulate has shown in almost every instance that radical change is costly for the public and industry alike. The costs of economic deregulation to the airlines were immediately visible, and led to doubts in other industries about how they would fare. The costs of social deregulation will take much longer to determine. With consequences clearly so far-reaching, perhaps such changes, when needed, should occur slowly, to provide more stability for the industry undergoing change and more protection for the public. Similarly, regulations should be formulated slowly and openly, with maximum participation by both the public and industry, to ensure widespread acceptance and minimal disruption.

The goal is not a plethora of regulations; quantity does not guarantee quality. The goal is government protection against abuses that threaten our health, safety, and lives. Without a shift to constructive policy making in the regulatory arena, the rush to deregulate is a high-risk gamble for the politicians who have championed its cause. It is a theory without vision, without humanity, and without conscience — a false panacea that will create more problems than it cures — and it should finally be recognized as such. One outbreak of a serious epidemic caused by lax medical or drug regulations would not only cost lives but also destroy careers, discredit political organizations, or lay the groundwork for a regulatory system far more onerous than the one so many groups are now anxious to dismantle. One mine disaster traced to inadequate inspection and lax regulations, one major nuclear accident, could have devastating political consequences. To recommend taking regulation out of politics would be naive; the political system created the regulatory process, and remains fully capable of reforming the system as well as working within it. But the politics must be more open, more balanced, less negative, and encompass larger segments of the affected public. There is little doubt that, in the long run, the nation will return to its regulatory senses. One hopes that it will not require a major tragedy to begin its restoration, and that business, labor, and political leaders will close ranks behind a rigorous, well-managed regulatory process. For we all face the same hazards, and share the same hopes for ourselves and our children and grandchildren, who will inherit our follies along with our triumphs.

The deregulation frenzy in the early 1980s was symptomatic of widespread frustration with government, and led to the dramatic curtailment of its size, scope, and responsibilities. The regulatory community was a major victim as those in power forgot the original reasons for its creation. Each regulation and each regulatory agency addressed a specific problem with a solution representing years — decades in many cases — of careful development. But in dealing with the more controversial of these problems, the political leadership found it more attractive to use the ax than the scalpel. Forsaking a selective approach, the President and Congress made wholesale reductions in regulatory power, gutting regulations rather than initiating better management procedures. Regulations were unraveled, personnel dismissed, budgets cut. Agencies responsible for protecting the public found themselves unable to do so. The decision was political, managerial, and symbolic as well as substantive. It also was misguided.

For regulation is the connective tissue of a civilized society. As technological and scientific advances lead us into unknown worlds with unimaginable dangers, society needs more protection, not less. This means more government regulation, intelligently crafted, skillfully managed, and sensitively enforced. It means a new appreciation of government's role, born of a new sophistication in public attitudes. Finally, it means a shift in our national values to assure the public's protection in an increasingly hazardous world, and a realization that the power and resources to achieve that goal can be provided only by government.

Acronyms

AEC	Atomic Energy Commission
CAB	Civil Aeronautics Board
CEA	Council of Economic Advisers
COWPS	Council on Wage and Price Stability
CPSC	Consumer Product Safety Commission
CRS	Congressional Research Service
DOE	Department of Energy
DOT	Department of Transportation
EEOC	Equal Employment Opportunity Commission
EPA	Environmental Protection Agency
ERDA	Energy Research and Development Administration
ERISA	Employee Retirement Income Security Act
FAA	Federal Aviation Administration
FCC	Federal Communications Commission
FDA	Food and Drug Administration
FERC	Federal Energy Regulatory Commission
FTC	Federal Trade Commission
HEW	Department of Health, Education, and Welfare
HHS	Department of Health and Human Services
MSHA	Mine Safety and Health Administration
NASA	National Aeronautics and Space Administration
NFDA	National Funeral Directors Association
NHTSA	National Highway Traffic Safety Administration
NRC	Nuclear Regulatory Commission
NRDC	Natural Resources Defense Council
OFCCP	Office of Federal Contract Compliance Programs
OMB	Office of Management and Budget
OSHA	Occupational Safety and Health Administration
OTAA	Office of Trade Adjustment Assistance
RARG	Regulatory Analysis Review Group
SEC	Securities and Exchange Commission
USDA	United States Department of Agriculture
WPPSS	Washington Public Power Supply System

Notes

Chapter 1. Silent Partner (pages 1 – 37)

1. *Forbes*, January 15, 1972, p. 24.
2. Roger Williams, Letter to Mr. Joe Quilici, Chairman, Select Committee on Economic Problems, Montana House of Representatives, December 19, 1980, p. 1.
3. The U.S. share of the world copper market dropped to about 19 percent in 1981, from 35 percent in 1950. *Wall Street Journal,* September 16, 1982, p. 56. This article from the *Wall Street Journal* on the state of the ill fortunes of the copper industry does not even mention regulation as a contributing factor.
4. *Business Week,* April 14, 1977, p. 50.
5. *Business Week,* June 28, 1980, p. 58.
6. Letter to Senators John Melcher and Max Baucus, and to Reps. Ron Marlenee and Pat Williams, November 4, 1980, p. 3.
7. *Washington Post,* June 29, 1982, p. A2.
8. Remarks of Charles L. Schultze, chairman of the Council of Economic Advisers, before the Commonwealth Club of California, San Francisco, April 13, 1979.
9. In their media campaign against the FDA, the drug companies found unlikely allies in a small group of drug consumers: those who are victims of serious but rare diseases, who need but cannot obtain the "orphan drugs," drugs that are too costly to produce and research because of their limited use. Television star Jack Klugman, who plays a crusading medical examiner on the NBC series "Quincy," made an appearance with a nineteen-year-old victim of Tourette syndrome before a House subcommittee investigating this issue to help dramatize the seriousness of the problem. At the same hearing, Lewis Engman, president of the Pharmaceutical Manufacturers Association, suggested that the FDA accept foreign governments' clinical studies in order to avoid "the duplication of research which has already been done abroad," and to stimulate further research. *New York Times,* March 10, 1981, p. A16.
10. *Washington Post,* February 8, 1981, p. G2.
11. The advertising industry was responding to a report issued by Timothy Muris, director of the FTC's Bureau of Consumer Protection, arguing for a partial relaxation of the agency's regulation of false and deceptive advertising. The report indicated that advertisers should not be required to complete all the tests now necessary before making a claim as long as they had a "reasonable basis" for that claim. "I don't subscribe

to the view that a lie is okay if nobody is hurt," said Howard H. Bell, president of the American Advertising Federation, in response to the report. Prior substantiation of claims, he continued, "has had a salutary effect on protecting the marketplace — consumers as well as advertisers — making sure that competitors don't make false claims to unfairly gain a share of the market." See the excellent article on the subject by Caroline E. Mayer, *Washington Post,* November 12, 1982, p. A29.

12. For an excellent analysis of this "absurdist, mind-boggling licensing scheme," whose "driving" purpose appears to be restrictive entry, see Jonathan Rose, "Controlling Clip Joints — The Arizona Story," *Regulation,* July/August 1980, pp. 37–40.

13. *New York Times,* May 4, 1981, p. B9.

14. Lester Thurow, *Zero-Sum Society,* New York: Basic Books, 1980, p. 123.

15. P.L. 93–637.

16. The U.S. Court of Appeals for the District of Columbia voided the Reagan administration's rescission of the air bag rule on August 4, 1982, ordering the auto companies to start putting air bags or automatic seat belts in cars beginning in 1983. The decision was upheld by the Supreme Court on June 24, 1983.

17. Murray L. Weidenbaum, *The Future of Business Regulation,* New York: AMACOM, 1979, p. 4.

18. A recent court decision handed down on January 29, 1982, by the U.S. Court of Appeals for the District of Columbia ruled that a legislative veto of an independent agency was unconstitutional (*Consumer Energy Council of America v. FERC,* no. 80–2184). Upheld by the Supreme Court, this could affect nearly two hundred laws, all of which contain legislative vetoes, in such diverse areas as immigration, arms sales, pesticides, foreign trade, federal salaries, and the sale of nuclear fuel. A prior court ruling in the ninth circuit declared a congressional veto over an executive agency unconstitutional (*Jagdish Rai Chadha v. Immigration and Naturalization Service,* U.S. App., no. 77–1702). The Supreme Court agreed.

19. Montana Senate Committee on Economic Problems, December 19, 1980, pp. 1–3.

20. Ibid.

21. See note 6.

22. Letter dated November 20, 1980.

23. Letter dated April 27, 1979.

24. News release, October 2, 1980.

25. Associated Press, October 28, 1980.

26. "Questions and Answers regarding Anaconda's Smelter and Refinery Decision," The Anaconda Company, October 6, 1980.

27. EPA, *Environmental News,* March 19, 1981, pp. 1–2.

28. Ibid.

29. "Since you [Pertschuk] arrived at the FTC," the memo reads,

Notes

"the commission has decided *not* to issue *rules* in the following areas — notwithstanding real problems identified by the staff." The memo goes on to list the nine areas, which included auto repairs, prescription drug advertising, insurance cost disclosure, advertising by veterinarians, cellular plastics (advertising and labeling), household plant labeling, pesticide advertising, prescription drug generic substitution, and food phase 3.

30. *New York Times,* June 4, 1981, p. A22.

31. For an analysis of this area of regulatory activity, see Bruce A. Ackerman and William T. Hassler, *Clean Coal/Dirty Air,* New Haven: Yale University Press, 1981.

32. The politics of deregulation has also clouded the traditional boundaries between social and economic regulation found in most textbooks. Where would the regulation of nuclear reactors fit into this traditional scheme? Nuclear safety, regulated by the Nuclear Regulatory Commission, affects the economic state of the industry, as well as the health, environment, and safety of the affected populations. As airline deregulation has shown, even the more clear-cut economic regulatory systems have spilled over into the social realm, particularly in terms of their effects. See chapter 7 for a discussion of airline deregulation. Indeed, the most controversial of the regulatory disputes involve regulations that fall within both categories. The funeral rule and children's television advertising, two highly controversial issues at the Federal Trade Commission, involve the regulation of specific industries, with very definite social impacts.

Chapter 2. Capturing the Regulators (pages 39 – 71)

1. In addition to his business and acting background, Reagan also wrote a nationally syndicated column. See Ronald Reagan, "Nailing the Regulator," Special Weekly Column, King Features Syndicate, August 10, 1979.

2. The regulatory agencies are divided into two basic categories: independent and executive branch agencies. Both types of agencies issue regulations, and share similar functions in terms of scope and power; indeed, the regulatory agencies issue more rulings than the courts and the legislature combined. The major difference is that the independent agencies are accountable primarily to Congress, while the executive branch agencies answer directly to the President. There are twenty-two independent agencies, among them: the Nuclear Regulatory Commission, the Federal Communications Commission, the Federal Trade Commission, the International Trade Commission, the Securities and Exchange Commission, the Interstate Commerce Commission, to name a few. They are headed by multi-

membered commissions, with the commissioners named by the President and submitted for congressional approval. In that way, the President shares power with Congress; his power limited by the fact that the terms of the commissioners do not run consecutively with the President's. The executive branch agencies are directly under White House control, although Congress through budgetary oversight can make an impact on their decisions. Executive branch regulatory agencies include the Occupational Safety and Health Administration, located in the Department of Labor; the Environmental Protection Agency, an executive agency headed by a subcabinet level administrator; the Army Corps of Engineers, in the Department of Defense; and the Social Security Administration, in the Department of Health and Human Services, to name several of the better known of the more than ninety executive agencies inside the executive branch that have been given the power by Congress to issue regulations ranging from strip mining to economic development. Some agencies find themselves in peculiar administrative arrangements that do not fit neatly into either of the two categories. The Federal Energy Regulatory Commission (FERC), for example, is an independent agency, but is located within an executive branch agency, the Department of Energy. An excellent source of reference on the regulatory agencies is the *Federal Regulatory Directory,* published annually by Congressional Quarterly Press.

3. The Administrative Procedure Act was amended thirty years later: 5 U.S.C. 553 (1976).

4. Martin Tolchin, *New York Times,* January 17, 1979, pp. A1 and D17. Since Jackson, the President's power to fire and control officials in the administrative agencies has been considerably refined by Congress and the courts, both of which clearly differentiated between the executive branch and independent agencies. In *Myers v. United States,* 272 U.S. 52 (1926), for example, the Court ruled that the President could remove subordinate appointees without congressional consent, pointing out that as a postmaster, Myers clearly fell within the jurisdiction of the Chief Executive. Several years later, the Court clarified the difference in the removal power in *Humphrey's Executor v. United States,* 295 U.S. 602 (1935), which involved an independent regulatory commission, not under the direct control of the President. In this case, the Court ruled that the President did not have the right to remove without cause a member of the Federal Trade Commission, pointing out that Congress in granting rule-making and adjudicatory powers to the FTC intended to insulate its decision makers from political interference.

5. Much of the material involving RARG and the Carter experience originally appeared in the following article: Susan J. Tolchin, "Presidential Power and the Politics of RARG," *Regulation,* July/August 1979, pp. 44–49.

6. Schultze, an economist from The Brookings Institution, was a well-known advocate of alternatives to regulation. His book, *The Public Use of*

Notes

Private Interest (Washington: The Brookings Institution, 1977), is a classic in its field.

7. The cotton dust case was later decided by the Supreme Court, which ruled in favor of the tighter standards advocated by OSHA, in *American Textile Manufacturers Institute v. Donovan,* 452 U.S. 490, 101 S. Ct. 2478, 69 L. Ed. 2d 185 (1981).

8. *Natural Resources Defense Council et al. v. Schultze et al.,* U.S. District Court, D.C., Civil Action no. 79.

9. An unpublished memorandum from the Justice Department's Office of Legal Counsel, prepared in January 1979, for Interior Secretary Andrus, supports this view. The memo dealt with the legality of consultations between the CEA and the Department of the Interior over rule-making hearings under the Surface Mining Control and Reclamation Act (the Strip Mining Act). It concluded — not surprisingly, since the Justice Department is also part of the executive branch — that in rule-making hearings there was "no prohibition against communications within the executive branch after the close of the comment period on these proposed rules. Nothing in the relevant statutes or in the decisions of the D.C. Circuit suggests the existence of a bar against full and detailed consultations between those charged with promulgating the rules."

10. For a more thorough discussion of cost-benefit analysis as applied to regulation, see chapter 4.

11. "Materials on President Reagan's Program of Regulatory Relief," Office of the Press Secretary, June 6, 1981, p. 97.

12. "OMB: The Role of the Office of Management and Budget in Regulation," House Subcommittee on Oversight and Investigations, Committee on Energy and Commerce, June 19, 1981, p. 97.

13. The administration asked the independent agencies to comply with the executive order voluntarily, but as of this writing only the Federal Trade Commission under the leadership of James Miller III indicated it would comply. As more Reagan appointees fill positions in the independent agencies, it would not be unreasonable to expect more agencies to join the FTC in submitting to the executive order.

14. 46 Fed. Reg. 13,193 (1981).

15. DeMuth, a Harvard professor, replaced James Miller as head of the OMB regulatory reform effort. Hopkins heads the regulatory analysis division.

16. Sea turtles are protected under the Endangered Species Act of 1973. See "Regulations Modifying Threatened Sea Turtle Resuscitation Procedures," National Marine Fisheries Service, National Oceanic and Atmospheric Administration, 46 Fed. Reg. 43,876 (1981).

17. Executive Office of the President, Office of Management and Budget, List of nongovernment groups represented, along with the subject and date, accompanying a letter from James C. Miller III to Rep. John Dingell, April 28, 1981.

18. Ibid.

19. OMB: The Role of the Office of Management and Budget in Regulation,'' House Subcommittee on Oversight and Investigations, Committee on Energy and Commerce, June 18, 1981, p. 103.

20. Ibid., p. 105.

21. Ibid., pp. 110–12.

22. *Washington Post,* November 1, 1981, p. C7.

23. Paperwork Reduction Act of 1980, Pub. L. No. 96-511, 44 U.S.C. et seq. (1980), and the Regulatory Flexibility Act, Pub. L. No. 96-354, 5 U.S.C. 601 et seq. (1980).

24. *Sierra Club v. Costle,* 657 F. 2d 298 (D.C. Circ. 1981).

25. Ibid., pp. 212–20.

26. Nan Aron and Charles Ludlum, "Undermining Public Protections — The Reagan Administration Regulatory Program," Alliance for Justice, 1981.

27. *Sierra,* p. 207.

28. "An Analysis of Constitutional Issues That May Be Raised by Executive Order 12291," Report Prepared for the Use of the House Committee on Energy and Commerce, U.S. Govt. Printing Office, June 15, 1981, p. 71.

29. Ibid., p. 54.

30. See note 3.

31. Office of Management and Budget, "Executive Order 12291 on Federal Regulation: Progress during 1981," April 1982.

32. Although many previous presidents had tried. Proof of their efforts is the number of commissions created by the Chief Executive to study ways to bring the agencies more directly under presidential control, all under the rubric of administrative reorganization. See Herbert Kaufman, "Emerging Conflicts in the Doctrines of Public Administration," *American Political Science Review* 50 (December 1956): 1057–73.

Chapter 3. Dismantling America (pages 73 – 109)

1. *Natural Resources Defense Council, Inc. v. United States Environmental Protection Agency,* 3d Cir., No. 81-2068, Brief for Petitioner, pp. 4–7. See 683 F. 2d 752 (1982).

2. S. Rep. No. 95-370, 95th Cong., 1st Sess. 58 (1977). Cited in *Natural Resources,* p. 11.

3. H. Rep. No. 95-139, 95th Cong., 1st Sess. 18 (1977). Cited in *Natural Resources,* p. 11.

4. The lawsuit resulted in *NRDC v. Costle,* 12 E.R.C. 1833 (1979).

5. *Natural Resources.*
6. Ibid., pp. 13–14.
7. Ibid., p. 16. Part of the dispute centered on a technicality: whether these regulations would be considered major or minor rules. If, as EPA originally argued, they were designated minor rules, they would be exempt from regulatory review under the executive order; if major, they could in OMB's view be indefinitely suspended under the executive order.
8. The Administrative Procedure Act, 5 U.S.C. 551 (1946), and the case law developed under it, clearly delineate what constitutes a rule, and what procedural requirements govern the processes by which those rules must be developed, including advance notice by the agency of its intent, as well as opportunities for meaningful participation by outside groups and a concise explanation for final agency actions. Only in "calamitous circumstances" can an agency act without notice and comment, according to the decision in *Nader v. Sawhill,* 514 F. 2d 1064 (1975), which concluded that a combination of the Arab oil embargo and price increases in domestic crude oil made agency procedures "impractical."
9. *Natural Resources,* p. 19.
10. Ibid.
11. Ibid., p. 33.
12. Ibid., p. 36.
13. Nan Aron and Charles Ludlum, "Undermining Public Protections — The Reagan Administration Regulatory Program," Alliance for Justice, 1981, p. 62. Two other significant reports appeared, each critical of the Reagan regulatory "reform" effort on substantive and methodological grounds. The highly respected Conservation Foundation, the most conservative of the environmental groups, issued its *State of the Environment 1982* (Washington, 1982). Sharply critical of the Reagan administration, the study concluded that "the effect of the Administration's policies on environmental institutions has already been dramatic and promises to become even more evident." The report also reaffirmed the federal government's role: "the federal government risks a great deal of its legitimacy as a protector of public health and safety if it refuses to assume those responsibilities for which it is best suited" (p. 429). The General Accounting Office issued a report the same year, faulting OMB's use of cost-benefit analysis for regulatory decision making on methodological grounds. See General Accounting Office, "Improved Quality, Adequate Resources, and Consistent Oversight of Regulations," Report to the Chairman, Senate Committee on Governmental Affairs, GAO-PAD–83–6, November 2, 1982. The report also recommended that OMB conduct its oversight activities in the open.
14. *New York Times,* April 5, 1982.
15. *Washington Post,* March 21, 1982, p. A6.
16. *Washington Post,* July 10, 1982, pp. A1 and A6.
17. *Washington Post,* September 22, 1981, p. A19.
18. At this writing, the rule is pending in the courts.

19. *Washington Post,* September 26, 1981, p. A9.

20. *Washington Post,* October 24, 1981, pp. A1 and A24.

21. The issue was brought to court, and on June 24, 1983, the Supreme Court upheld the court of appeals decision to void the Reagan administration's rescission of the air-bag rule.

22. *Washington Post,* November 1, 1981, pp. H1 and H3.

23. Ibid. After the USDA issued its proposed regulations on July 31, 1982, the agency received sixteen hundred comments. Department of Agriculture, Food Safety and Inspection Service, "Standards and Labeling Requirements for Mechanically Processed (Species) Product and Products in Which It Is Used," 46 Fed. Reg. 39, 274–351 (1982). The final rule was issued one year later, on June 29, 1982. The rule eliminates the requirement that meat products containing powdered bone bear labels specifying the percentage of powdered bone on the package. Instead, the product can include the powdered bone on the label under its disclosure of the amount of calcium in the product.

24. Robert Crandall, "Has Reagan Dropped the Ball?" *Regulation,* September/October 1981, p. 15.

25. Ibid.

26. *Christian Science Monitor,* October 28, 1981.

27. *New York Times,* October 15, 1981. The actual reduction in the EPA budget from fiscal year 1982–83 was $125 million, or a 12 percent reduction. Personnel went from 9,821, down to 8,645 planned for 1983. The administration asked for $209.5 million for 1983, $127.8 million less than its 1981 appropriation. In actual dollars, this represents a reduction. Ninety-eight percent of the cuts are in funds allotted by the agency for outside research, or two-thirds of its research. See Lawrence Mosher, "More Cuts in EPA Research Threaten Its Regulatory Goals, Critics Warn," *National Journal,* April 10, 1982, pp. 635–39.

28. Although on December 16, 1982, the House of Representatives cited Gorsuch for contempt of Congress for refusing to turn over documents on the agency's hazardous waste program. She said she was following White House orders. The bipartisan House vote was 259–105.

29. *Legal Times,* October 26, 1981, pp. 8–9.

30. *New York Times,* January 29, 1982, p. A12.

31. Linda E. Demkovich, "Critics Fear the FDA Is Going Too Far in Cutting Industry's Regulatory Load," *National Journal,* July 17, 1982, pp. 1249–52.

32. All quotes on page 95 are from *Business Week,* December 28, 1981, pp. 55–57.

33. Weidenbaum was referring to a case involving benzene in the work place, later decided by the Supreme Court in July 1980 (*Industrial Union Dept. v. American Petroleum Institute,* 448 U.S. S. Ct. 2844, 65 L. Ed. 2d 1010 [1980]). The decision invalidated the OSHA benzene standard, faulting OSHA with failing to adequately establish that benzene posed a "significant" enough risk to warrant federal intervention.

34. *Los Angeles Times,* July 31, 1977, p. 9.
35. *National Journal,* March 14, 1981, p. 424.
36. *Wall Street Journal,* February 12, 1981.
37. Crowell advocated cutting down what he called "old lumber," arguing that this policy would have certain benefits, while not causing substantial harm to the forests. See John B. Crowell, Jr., "Remarks Prepared for Delivery at the Western Forestry Center," Portland, Oregon, Department of Agriculture, January 19, 1982.
38. *Washington Post,* January 8, 1982, p. A21.
39. *Wall Street Journal,* July 10, 1981.
40. A riveting article on the effects of strip mining under the Reagan administration written by Dale Russakoff appeared in the *Washington Post,* June 6, 1982, pp. A1 and A8.
41. *National Journal,* February 28, 1981, p. 267.
42. The statute governing hazardous waste is the Resource Conservation and Recovery Act. *New York Times,* February 22, 1982, p. A14.
43. For an excellent study of the backgrounds of the key Reagan regulators, see Ron Brownstein and Nina Easton, *Reagan's Ruling Class,* Washington, D.C.: Ralph Nader, 1982.
44. *National Journal,* March 31, 1981, p. 475.
45. Ibid.

Chapter 4. Particles of Truth
(pages 111 – 141)

1. Bernadino Ramazzi, *A Treatise on the Diseases of Tradesmen,* quoted in *AFL-CIO v. Marshall,* 617 F. 2d 636 (1979), pp. 13–14.
2. *American Textile Manufacturers Institute v. Donovan,* 101 U.S. 2478 (1981), p. 5.
3. Ibid., p. i.
4. Ibid., p. ii.
5. The phrase is written into the act creating the Occupational Safety and Health Administration, Pub. L. 91–596 (1971), which went into effect on April 28, 1971.
6. A popular name for byssinosis coined by Ralph Nader.
7. *American Textile,* p. 7.
8. P.L. 91–596.
9. "Perspectives on Current Developments: The Cotton Dust Case," *Regulation,* January/February 1981, p. 5.
10. Mark Green and Norman Waitzman, *Business War on the Law: An Analysis of the Benefits of Federal Health/Safety Enforcement,* rev. 2d ed., Washington, D.C.: The Corporate Accountability Research Group, 1981, p. 108.

11. Susan J. Tolchin, "Presidential Power and the Politics of RARG,"
Regulation, July/August 1979, p. 45.
12. See note 9.
13. 43 Fed. Reg. 27,384 (1978).
14. This meant that "permissible exposure levels for different segments of the industry be structured according to cost-effectiveness considerations. . . . OSHA had agreed to prescribe levels that varied from 0.2
to 0.75 milligrams for different stages of cotton processing." *Regulation,*
January/February 1981, p. 5.
15. *AFL-CIO v. Marshall,* pp. 13–14.
16. *Industrial Union Department v. American Petroleum Institute,* 448
U.S. 607, 100 S. Ct. 2844, 65 L. Ed. 2d 1010 (1980).
17. *American Textile,* p. 11.
18. Ibid.
19. Ibid., p. 10.
20. Ibid., pp. 16–17.
21. Ibid., p. 17.
22. *AFL-CIO v. Marshall,* p. 36.
23. *New York Times,* June 19, 1981, p. D5.
24. Based on a standard definition of cost-benefit analysis, which requires the "systematic enumeration of all benefits and costs, tangible and
intangible, whether readily quantifiable or difficult to measure." Quoted
from E. Stokey and R. Zeckhauser, *A Primer for Policy Analysis,* New
York: W. W. Norton, 1978, p. 134; and cited in the cotton dust decision,
American Textile, p. 15.
25. *American Textile,* pp. 17–18.
26. Ibid., p. 18.
27. During the congressional hearings on the Reagan regulatory reform program, specifically Executive Order 12291, two of the order's principal architects demonstrated occasional ignorance of which statutes required cost-benefit analysis, and which specifically prohibited it. A few
extracts from the hearings indicate the embarrassing results:

DINGELL: Can you tell us . . . whether you did any research to find out which of
           these [acts] were subject to this cost-benefit analysis and which were
           not, before the orders were issued?
MILLER: The answer is no.
DINGELL: Well, you seem to be in the rather anomalous position of having an
           order which you defend vigorously but not being able to tell us who
           might think on the basis of their own research that it applies to them.

At that same hearing, which followed the Supreme Court decision, the
Reagan appointees still insisted with total disregard of the court decision
that cost-benefit analysis would be applied to OSHA regulations.

GORE: Are you going to insist that OSHA apply a cost-benefit test to new reg-
           ulation issued pursuant to section 6(b)5 of OSHA?

Notes

MILLER: Yes . . . in the following sense: first, to the degree that the decision is relevant . . . and, second, the executive order requires certain analyses be done with respect to the lowest-cost way of meeting any given objective.

"OMB: The Role of the Office of Management and Budget in Regulation," House Subcommittee on Oversight and Investigations, Committee on Energy and Commerce, June 19, 1981, pp. 149–50.

28. *American Textile,* p. 22.

29. Ibid., p. 28.

30. Ibid., p. 60.

31. Ibid., p. 25.

32. Ibid., p. 26.

33. Ibid., p. 39.

34. Throughout this section, cost-benefit analysis will be referred to as both a method and a theory, where appropriate. To be sure, it is utilized in both contexts. As a theory, it can be distinguished from classical models of politics, where consensus prevails as the decision rule. Instead, cost-benefit analysis substitutes economic efficiency as the rule (in maximizing the net present value of the benefits); and as such it tilts the normative preference to efficiency. In addition, the logic and normative biases of cost-benefit analysis as a theory inexorably lead to a methodological framework, which includes 1) objective function, 2) choice set, 3) constraints, 4) classification of subjects and costs, 5) their valuation with prices, 6) discounting of present values, and 7) summation as a ratio of net benefit. For several excellent references on this issue, see Robert H. Haveman and Julius Margolis, eds., *Public Expenditure and Policy Analysis,* Chicago: Rand McNally, 1977; U.S. Congress, Joint Economic Committee, *The Analysis and Evaluation of Public Expenditure: The PPB System,* 91st Congress, First Session, 1969; Jesse Burkhead and Jerry Miner, *Public Expenditure,* Chicago: Aldine Atherton, 1971; and E. J. Mishan, *Cost Benefit Analysis,* New York: Praeger, 1971.

35. The Food and Drug Administration, for example, held up for more than eighteen months regulations dealing with infant formula, while it went through the motions of conducting extensive cost-benefit analysis. See chapter 3 for details. See also "Infant Formula: The Present Danger," unpublished committee hearing, House Subcommittee on Oversight and Investigations, Committee on Energy and Commerce, March 11, 1982.

36. Executive Order 12044 (Carter) and Executive Order 12291 (Reagan). See chapters 2 and 3.

37. Robert DeFina and Murray L. Weidenbaum, *The Taxpayer and Government Regulation,* St. Louis: Center for the Study of American Business, Washington University, March 1978.

38. Julius Allen, "Costs and Benefits of Federal Regulation: An Overview," *Congressional Research Service,* LOC Report no. 78–152 E, July 19, 1978, pp. 16–17.

Notes

39. Ibid.

40. Michael H. Brown, "The Price of a Life," *New York Magazine,* March 10, 1980, pp. 28–32.

41. Ibid.

42. Costs to the government under the Federal Coal Mine Safety and Health Act of 1969, known as the Black Lung Benefits Act, 30 USC 901 et seq.

43. "Approaches toward Valuation of Human Life by Certain Federal Agencies," U.S. General Accounting Office, cited in a letter to Senator Thomas F. Eagleton (Democrat, Missouri) from Morton A. Myers, director, November 9, 1981.

44. Ibid.

45. Methodological changes in cost-benefit analysis receiving attention were introduced by the U.S. Army Corps of Engineers. In recent regulations, they have substantially reduced the admissible range of benefits that can be included in the calculation, and have increased the discount rate. Both have had the effect of discouraging public investment.

46. Mark Green, "The Faked Case against Regulation," *Washington Post,* January 21, 1979.

47. "Approaches toward Valuation," p. 2.

48. Stephen Rhoads, "How Much Should We Spend to Save a Life?" *Public Interest* 51 (Spring 1978):78.

49. Amitai Etzioni, "How Much Is a Life Worth?" *Social Policy,* March/April 1979, p. 4.

50. Quoted in an article on cost-benefit analysis by reporter Philip Shabecoff, *New York Times,* November 7, 1981, p. B28.

51. "Approaches toward Valuation."

52. The phrase is the title of an excellent book by Guido Calabresi and Philip Bobbitt, *Tragic Choices,* New York: W. W. Norton, 1978.

53. Rhoads, p. 91.

54. James W. Singer, "Should Equal Opportunity for Women Apply to Toxic Chemical Exposure?" *National Journal,* October 18, 1980, pp. 1753–55. See also *New York Times,* January 5, 1979, pp. A2 and D8.

55. Use of the female pronoun is based on current data linking reproductive risk primarily to females. Representatives of women's groups have argued, however, that current research will soon show reproductive risks associated with male workers.

56. A body of literature in economics and political science has developed around the theory of public goods. Mancur Olson, in *The Logic of Collective Action* (Cambridge, Mass.: Harvard University Press, 1965), points out that people are not inclined to actively promote the securing of public goods; nor do they avoid public bads. See also Garrett Hardin's work on the "commons," a metaphor of a medieval English village in which cattle owners, by overgrazing their cows on the "commons," ruined the pasture for everyone. Garrett Hardin, "The Tragedy of the Commons," *Science,* December 13, 1968, pp. 1243–48.

57. Senate Governmental Affairs Committee, Press release on regulatory reform, March 27, 1980, pp. 1–2. See also the report itself: "Benefits of Environmental, Health and Safety Regulation," Senate Committee on Governmental Affairs, 96th Congress 2d Session, March 25, 1980, Washington: U.S. Govt. Printing Office. See also Nicholas A. Ashford, "Alternatives to Cost-Benefit Analysis in Regulatory Decisions," *Annals of the New York Academy of Sciences* 363 (April 1981):129–38.

58. December 1979, pp. 1210–11.

59. *New York Times*, June 27, 1981, p. 9.

60. David L. Bazelon, "Science and Uncertainty: The Regulation of Health Risks," Paper delivered at the Health Policy Forum, Harvard School of Public Health, May 4, 1981, pp. 7–8.

61. This is well documented in an article by Kenneth W. Clarkson, Charles W. Kadlec, and Arthur B. Laffer, "Regulating Chrysler out of Business," *Regulation*, September/October 1979, pp. 44–51.

62. Bazelon's decision, subsequently overturned and remanded by the Supreme Court, faulted the NRC for failing to "come to grips with the limits of its knowledge" and giving "no serious response to criticisms brought to its attention. No technical oversight within the agency was demonstrated, and no peer review by the expert community at large was possible." See David L. Bazelon, "Risk and Democracy," Address delivered to the National Academy of Engineering, Washington, D.C., November 1, 1979. See also Judge Bazelon's decision in the Vermont Yankee case, *Natural Resources Defense Council, Inc., and Consolidated National Intervenors, Petitioners v. United States Nuclear Regulatory Commission and United States of America, Respondents, Baltimore Gas and Electric Co., et al., Intervenors*, 547 F. 2d 633 (1976). The Supreme Court remanded the case back to the Court of Appeals for the District of Columbia. See *Vermont Yankee Nuclear Power Corp. v. NRDC*, 435 U.S. 519 (1978), and NRDC, 685 F. 2d 459 (1982).

63. David L. Bazelon, "Science and Uncertainty: A Jurist's View." Paper delivered at Duke University, October 29, 1980, p. 5.

Chapter 5. High Noon at the FTC
(pages 143 – 188)

1. The agency was created with the enactment of the Federal Trade Commission Act of 1914. It was preceded by the formation in 1898 of the Industrial Commission, created by Congress to study the monopolistic behavior of corporations. The commission recommended that a federal bureau continue its information-gathering functions, leading to the creation of

the Bureau of Corporations, which joined what was then the Department of Commerce and Labor, in 1903.

2. *Federal Regulatory Directory,* Washington, D.C.: U.S. Govt. Printing Office, 1980, p. 297.

3. Known as the Magnuson–Moss Warranty — Federal Trade Commission Improvement Act, P.L. 93–637. The legislation also encouraged greater public participation in rule making.

4. Michael Pertschuk, Unpublished transcript of a lecture series scheduled for the fall of 1981, pp. 1–20. Later published as *Revolt against Regulation: The Rise and Pause of the Consumer Movement,* Berkeley: University of California Press, 1982.

5. Ibid.

6. Ibid.

7. Ibid.

8. *Incentive Marketing,* September 1977, p. 35.

9. Quoted in the *Los Angeles Times,* June 16, 1980, p. 19.

10. *Philadelphia Inquirer,* October 1, 1978.

11. Robert Sherrill, "Jousting on the Hill — Skewering the Consumer's Defender," *Saturday Review,* March 29, 1980, p. 18.

12. By way of illustration, he brought up what he called the green plant case, which he said indicated the potential for abuse created by giving staff members too much power and discretion. "A staffer in Seattle had bought a plant for his office," Josephs recounted, "and the plant died. He thought this was a conspiracy on the part of the plant industry so that people would keep buying plants; he also thought that plants should have care instructions tacked onto the pot. . . . He then went down to Florida, where he chaired hearings. The growers were getting very concerned. The FTC covered up, saying the real issue was toxicity: What would happen if the children ate the plants? The issue was kept alive till 1978, when Pertschuk, at a Press Club luncheon, announced the investigation was over; the FTC was getting rid of unnecessary regulation! . . . It's iatrogenesis . . . the cure that kills. If a green plant is unfair, what else is?" concluded Josephs. Responding to the green plant case, Albert Kramer, head of the FTC's Bureau of Consumer Protection, angrily defended the FTC. "The staff suggested a plant labeling rule," he recalled. "My office said no. The commissioners agreed it was silly and the case was dropped." What angered him most, he added, was that the chamber used cases like this to set its own agenda and its lobbying priorities, which in effect fanned the flames of business resentment against the agency. After all, the case was dropped and the issue permanently shelved — proof that the system of checks and balances within the agency worked to weed out the "unfair" from the frivolous. (Green plants were on Reich's humility update list.) But the case did linger on for three years, from start to finish, from the time a young staff member first set eyes on his dying office plant, to Pertschuk's announcement that the FTC was capable of sorting out useless

regulations. The FTC's dismissal of the green plant case discounts the short-term effects on an industry, which are not unlike the effects on a stock merely from the rumor that it is scheduled for investigation by the SEC. The legal costs, the element of uncertainty, and the bad publicity are impossible to calculate in terms of the damage to an industry. Although the green plant case did more political damage than economic, it made the case against the FTC stronger and more politically salable later on, when it was easier for members of Congress to vote against the beleaguered agency.

13. *Newsday,* May 29, 1980, p. 8.

14. One of the major cases forming the legal basis for this kind of intervention is the 1972 Supreme Court decision in *FTC v. Sperry and Hutchinson,* 405 U.S. 233, 244 (1972). The language in this case gives the FTC a broad mandate to declare illegal conduct that is "immoral, unethical, oppressive or unscrupulous," while admitting that this congressionally mandated standard is elusive. The earliest application of the unfairness doctrine, like the kid-vid case, involved children, who were determined to be an especially "vulnerable" group, on the basis of which the FTC banned certain techniques for marketing candy to children. See *FTC v. R. F. Keppel Bros.,* 291 U.S. 304 (1934). In the case law that has built up since the *Keppel* case, the courts set three basic guidelines for determining unfairness: (1) whether a practice offends public policy, (2) whether a practice is immoral, unethical, or unscrupulous, and (3) whether a practice causes injury to consumers or to businessmen.

15. *Washington Post,* April 6, 1981, p. A14.

16. For an excellent study of the FTC's involvement with the tobacco industry, see A. Lee Fritschler's *Smoking and Politics,* 3d ed., Englewood Cliffs, N.J.: Prentice-Hall, 1983.

17. The tobacco companies also were involved with the FTC during the same period in a long, drawn-out investigation of their advertising techniques, the FTC seeking to determine whether their advertising was unfair *and* deceptive. After fifteen years of struggle, the end loomed in sight. A court order finally directed the tobacco companies to comply with the FTC's request for evidence, with the agency agreeing to compromise and settle for a minimal number of documents at the initial stage. All but one company complied with the subpoena and with the FTC's offer of limited documentation, giving the FTC anywhere from two hundred pages to a box full. The one exception was the Kentucky-based Brown and Williamson Tobacco Company, whose annual sales of Kools, Belairs, and other brands grossed $1.8 billion a year. Riding the crest of the then current anti-FTC fervor, Brown and Williamson loaded up a truck with seven tons of documents, and tried to deliver it, in July 1979, on the doorstep of the FTC. A former FTC lawyer, Bill Baer, now with the law firm of Arnold and Porter, recalled the confusion of that morning: "Brown and Williamson decided not to comply with our offer of limited production, where we would look at what they gave us and decide whether we needed more, and instead

decided to hype it up and exaggerate the fact that they were fighting it. They tried to get the press to cover it, with mixed results: they had big stories down in Louisville.''

18. *Washington Post,* March 23, 1980, p. E6.

19. An interesting coda to the kid-vid rule and the involvement of the tobacco companies emerged in the form of a little known rider to the act inserted by Senator Ford for the benefit of the tobacco companies. The preceding fall, the FTC had released the results of a Roper survey indicating that bans on smoking in public buildings might hurt cigarette sales. The agency had acquired the survey from the tobacco companies as part of the information subpoenaed by its investigation of cigarette advertising. In response to a *Wall Street Journal* article about the survey, on October 23, Senator Ford wrote a letter to Pertschuk vowing to prevent the FTC from issuing such documents in the future. He succeeded. The act prohibited the FTC from releasing any information gathered in law enforcement investigations. See Bill Fulton, ''The Paper Curtain Congress Ready to Curb Release of FTC Business Data,'' *National Journal,* April 12, 1980, p. 595.

20. The other involved whether the FTC should become involved in agricultural cooperatives, an amendment that also went against the agency because of the hostility engendered by an antitrust case launched by the FTC against Sunkist.

21. Jonathan Alter, ''It's Your Funeral,'' *New Republic,* March 1980, p. 8.

22. Jessica Mitford, *The American Way of Death,* New York: Simon and Schuster, 1963.

23. Federal Trade Commission, ''Funeral Industry Practices,'' Final Staff Report to the FTC and Proposed Trade Regulation Rule (16 CFR Part 453), Bureau of Consumer Protection, 1978. The trade regulations, however, only cover the funeral itself, which averages between $1,200 and $1,400, a bone of contention between the funeral industry and its critics, the funeral directors alleging that combining costs misrepresents their position, since they have no control over cemetery costs.

24. From ''The Politics of Regulation,'' Bill Moyers' ''Journal,'' Air date, February 24, 1980, Educational Broadcasting Corporation.

25. Federal Trade Commission, ''Funeral Industry Practices,'' p. 3.

26. Testimony of Albert H. Kramer, director of the Bureau of Consumer Protection, Federal Trade Commission, before the House Committee on Interstate and Foreign Commerce, Subcommittee on Oversight and Investigations, February 21, 1980.

27. ''The Phil Donahue Show,'' Multimedia Program Productions, Transcript no. 03181, p. 20.

28. ''The Politics of Regulation.''

29. There are three other groups, each of whose membership numbers under two thousand.

30. ''Regulation Rule: Its Effect on Small Business,'' A Report of

the House Subcommittee on Activities of Regulatory Agencies, Committee on Small Business, October 20, 1976, Washington, D.C.: U.S. Govt. Printing Office, 1976.

31. The allegations are in a Dear Colleague letter, signed by twelve members of Congress, both Republican and Democrat, dated September 14, 1979, and sent from Rep. Marty Russo's office.

32. A Dear Colleague letter, with an attached memorandum, sent by Rep. Richard L. Ottinger (Democrat, New York) and prepared by the staff of the Consumer Protection and Finance Subcommittee of the Interstate and Foreign Commerce Committee, October 29, 1979.

33. Testimony of Albert H. Kramer, p. 6.

34. Memo from Arthur Angel in response to a staff memo recommending modifications in the proposed funeral rule, sent to the commission, February 15, 1979.

35. Testimony of Albert H. Kramer, p. 3.

36. Over 92 percent of the funeral business in the country falls into the small business category, with the remainder comprising several large, publicly traded chains, along with a number of small interstate firms. Because of the oversupply of small funeral homes — 50 percent do less than one hundred funerals a year — many fear that the increased costs incurred by adding federal regulation to existing state rules will drive some of these marginal funeral homes out of business, a move eagerly anticipated by the franchises. "Rules like these mean a real opportunity to us because independent funeral directors will be more willing to join our company," said Robert L. Waltrip, chairman of Services Corp. International, the largest funeral operator in the country. Quoted in *Business Week,* October 6, 1975.

37. Congressional Record, E5144, October 22, 1979 (remarks by Rep. Morris Udall, Democrat of Arizona).

38. *Washington Post,* February 6, 1980.

39. The FTC finally approved regulations representing a considerably scaled down version of their initial foray into the funeral business eight years before. The regulations required funeral directors to supply customers with more information regarding funeral costs, but left the industry substantially free from additional regulation. Acting Commissioner David Clanton, appointed in the interim by the Republicans before James Miller III became chairman in October 1981, said he was "pleased the commission was able to reach consensus . . . that provides the information consumers need." *Washington Post,* July 23, 1981.

40. Sherrill, p. 18.

41. Agriculture, Environment and Consumer Protection Appropriations for Fiscal Year 1975, Hearings before a Senate subcommittee of the Committee on Appropriations, 93rd Congress, 2d Session, H.R. 15472, pp. 1190–95. All subsequent quotes in this section refer to this citation unless otherwise specified.

42. Departments of State, Justice, and Commerce, the Judiciary and

Related Agencies Appropriations for Fiscal Year 1979, Hearings before a Senate subcommittee of the Committee on Appropriations, 95th Congress, 2d Session, H.R. 12934, P.L. 1699. Further evidence of prior congressional intervention in FTC activity beyond the confines of the confirmation process is cited in Robert A. Katzmann's *Regulatory Bureaucracy: The Federal Trade Commission and Antitrust Policy,* Cambridge, Mass.: MIT Press, 1980. Examples cited by Katzmann include: a House subcommittee urging the FTC to step up food-pricing investigations; another House subcommittee (Monopolies and Commercial Law) pressing the Senate Interior Committee for commission action in the Exxon investigation, the costliest antitrust matter in the agency's history (pp. 147, 156–57).

43. Departments of State, Justice, and Commerce, the Judiciary and Related Agencies Appropriations for Fiscal Year 1979, Hearings before a Senate subcommittee on appropriations, 96th Congress, 2d Session, pp. 392–93.

44. Departments of State, Justice, and Commerce, the Judiciary and Related Agencies Appropriations for Fiscal Year 1981, Hearings before a House subcommittee on appropriations, 96th Congress, 2d Session, 1980, pp. 162–86.

45. The used car rule was vetoed by a 286 to 133 vote in the House, and a 69 to 27 vote in the Senate. Like the funeral rule, the used car rule focused on disclosure, requiring dealers to inform consumers of any major known defects at the time of their purchase. A unanimous vote of the U.S. court of appeals later declared the legislative veto in this case unconstitutional. It was appealed to the Supreme Court, where at this writing it is still pending. The used car dealers were represented in their lobbying efforts by the National Automobile Dealers Association, whose Political Action Committee ranks fourth in contributions to political campaigns, led by the American Medical Association — also pressuring the FTC to withdraw its efforts to regulate the professions — the United Auto Workers and the National Association of Realtors.

Chapter 6. Political Meltdown (pages 189 – 235)

1. The U.S. Geological Survey reported, in 1975, that a severe earthquake, measuring 7.5 on the Richter scale, could occur along the Hosgri fault line.

2. William J. Lanouette, "Unsettling Decision," *National Journal,* March 27, 1982, p. 558.

3. Ibid.

4. Represented by the Center for Law in the Public Interest, the in-

tervenors joined together in their efforts to petition the Nuclear Regulatory Commission. The intervenors include San Luis Obispo Mothers for Peace, Scenic Shoreline Preservation Conference, Inc., Ecology Action Club, Sandra Silver, Gordon Silver, Elizabeth Apfelberg, and John J. Forster. Their most recent effort, comprehensive in its scope, opposes PG & E's request to the NRC to reconsider the agency's decision to revoke the utility's operating license. See United States of America, Nuclear Regulatory Commission, *Before the Commission,* "In the matter of Pacific Gas and Electric Company (Diablo Canyon Nuclear Power Plant, Units 1 and 2), Docket Nos. 50–275 O.L. and 50–323 O.L., "Joint Intervenors" Request for Directed Certification and Response in Opposition to PG and E's Motion for Reconsideration.

5. "In the Matter of PG and E (Diablo Canyon)," NRC Docket nos. 50–275, 50–323, ALAB–655, June 16, 1981. The board is known as the Atomic Safety and Licensing Board.

6. Ibid. See also comments on the Diablo case in congressional hearings: "Licensing Speed-up, Safety Delay: NRC Oversight," *Ninth Report by the Committee on Government Operations,* Washington, D.C.: U.S. Govt. Printing Office, October 20, 1981.

7. Lanouette, p. 558.

8. *Washington Post,* November 20, 1981, p. A14.

9. Ibid.

10. *Inside NRC,* November 30, 1981, p. 5.

11. *Washington Post,* November 20, 1981, p. A14.

12. *Inside NRC,* November 30, 1981, p. 5.

13. Marble Hill, in Indiana; South Texas, near Houston; Zimmer, in Ohio; and Midland, in Michigan.

14. *Inside NRC,* November 30, 1981, p. 6.

15. *Inside NRC,* June 12, 1980, p. 12.

16. In the past, the NRC has suspended plant operations, but an actual license had never been suspended before Diablo.

17. *Washington Post,* November 20, 1981, p. A14.

18. *Inside NRC,* November 30, 1981, p. 6.

19. Lanouette, p. 558.

20. *Washington Post,* November 20, 1981, p. A14.

21. Ibid. Perhaps the radical cast to organizations like this one in the antinuclear movement have precipitated remarks like those of Secretary of Energy James Edwards, who attributed opposition to nuclear power in the U.S. to "subversive elements." *Orangeburg* (S.C.) *Times & Democrat,* June 17, 1981, p. 16C.

22. *Inside NRC,* December 28, 1981, p. 4.

23. *Inside NRC,* December 1, 1981, p. 9.

24. Lanouette, p. 558.

25. *Inside NRC,* November 30, 1981, p. 6.

26. The nuclear utility industry created a nonprofit organization in

Notes

1979, known as the Institute of Nuclear Power Operations (INPO), "to assist nuclear utilities in achieving a high level of excellence in safety of nuclear power operations." Every U.S. utility with "an operating license, a construction permit, or a limited work authorization for a nuclear power plant is a member of the institute," as well as some of the major domestic nuclear suppliers and engineering firms. For more information, see Institute of Nuclear Power Operations, *1981 Annual Report,* Atlanta, Georgia.

27. The question of nuclear energy really involves four separate subjects: 1) reactor safety, 2) handling radioactive waste, 3) proliferation, and 4) low-level radiation exposure. Although all of them are very serious, this chapter deals only with reactor safety, and with the regulatory environment in which this issue is processed. Many of the chapter's conclusions with regard to that environment, however, could be applicable to the other areas.

28. Having exhausted all administrative remedies within the NRC, the Natural Resources Defense Council has brought suit challenging the agency's licensing of the Erwin facility. Petition to review an order of the NRC, U.S. Court of Appeals for the District of Columbia Circuit, *Natural Resources Defense Council, Inc. v. U.S. Nuclear Regulatory Commission and United States of America,* February 26, 1982, nos. 80–1863 and 80–1864.

29. Daniel Ford, "Three Mile Island — The Paper Trail," *New Yorker,* April 13, 1981, p. 57. Ford wrote a book on the Atomic Energy Commission, *Cult of the Atom — Secret Papers of the AEC,* New York: Simon and Schuster, 1982.

30. *Report of the President's Commission on the Accident at Three Mile Island, the Need for Change: The Legacy of TMI,* Washington, D.C.: October 1979, p. 19. The report also added that "the existence of a vast body of regulations by NRC tends to focus industry attention narrowly on the meeting of regulations rather than on a systematic concern for safety" (p. 20).

31. Nuclear Regulatory Commission Special Inquiry Group, *Three Mile Island: A Report to the Commissioners and to the Public,* Vols. 1 and 2, Washington, D.C.: 1980.

32. *Washington Post,* October 26, 1976.

33. Ford, p. 47.

34. Many argue that the problem at the NRC was not the lack of safety regulations on the books, but rather that there were too many safety regulations to be workable: it was their implementation that caused the problem.

35. *Inside NRC,* June 16, 1980, p. 12.

36. Office of the Press Secretary, the White House, "Statement by the President," October 8, 1981, p. 1.

37. *Fortune,* February 22, 1982, pp. 100–118. *Barron's* also wrote about the nuclear fizzle (August 24, 1981, p. 4). Charles Komanoff, an economist, explored the subject of the costs of nuclear power plants in a

Notes

lengthy study, *Power Plant Cost Escalation — Nuclear and Coal Capital Costs, Regulation and Economics,* New York: Van Nostrand Reinhold, 1982. Citing Komanoff, as well as data from utilities across the country, the *Wall Street Journal* ran a long article attributing the sharp rise in the cost of electricity to the addition of nuclear facilities by the utilities. The $2.5 billion price tag for the Shoreham nuclear power plant on Long Island has resulted in an average 30 percent rate increase — called rate shock — for the customers of the Long Island Lighting Co. *Wall Street Journal,* August 11, 1982, p. 1.

38. *Fortune,* February 22, 1982, p. 100.

39. *New York Times,* May 29, 1982, pp. 36–42. The particular setbacks itemized by the *New York Times* included: an announcement by the Tennessee Valley Authority that it would consider canceling plans for eight nuclear reactors; prospects for foreign sales of nuclear reactors decreased with an announcement by Mexico that it had suspended its plans to buy twenty reactors by the end of the century; and the rejection by the NRC of the Reagan administration's request to start construction of the Clinch River Breeder Reactor at Oak Ridge, Tennessee.

40. Suzanne Weaver (Garment), "Inhaber and the Limits of Cost-Benefit Analysis," *Regulation,* July/August 1979, pp. 14–16.

41. Stephen H. Hanauer, "Pressure-Suppression Containments," NRC memo, September 20, 1981, p. 1.

42. Joseph M. Hendrie, Letter dated September 25, 1972, p. 1.

43. This was the first hard evidence concerning the extent of the damage to the reactor, indicating that at least 90 percent of the total thirty-seven thousand fuel rods had been damaged by the excessive heat — perhaps near 5,080 degrees Fahrenheit, which is the melting point of the uranium oxide in the fuel rods. The findings also revealed serious financial implications: namely, that the cleanup could take an additional five years, and cost another $1 billion. *Washington Post,* July 22, 1982, pp. A1 and A15.

44. Nuclear Regulatory Commission, Office of Policy Evaluation, "Safety Goals for Nuclear Power Plants: A Discussion Paper," NUREG–0880, February 1982, p. xviii.

45. Ibid.

46. Ibid., p. xxi.

47. The figures were revealed in a series of articles by Milton Benjamin in the *Washington Post,* November 2, 1982, p. A3, and November 1, 1982, p. A1. The study was performed by the Department of Energy's Sandia National Laboratories.

48. The agency is also hampered by vaguely worded regulations, purposely written that way to give maximum flexibility to the regulators, but offering little concrete guidance at the same time. The fire regulations, for example, state that "fire protection and fighting systems shall be designed to assure that their rupture or inadvertent operation does not significantly impair the safety capability of these structures, systems and components."

Notes

10 Code of Federal Regulations, Chapter 1 — Nuclear Regulatory Commission, Pt. 50, App. A, p. 361. Does it say anything about prohibiting the use of candles to locate cables, as in the case of the Browns Ferry fire? Could even the most careful of regulation writers have predicted the possibility of such a practice?

49. Robert Perry, et al., "Development and Commercialization of the Light Water Reactor," The Rand Corporation, June 1977, p. 59.

50. *New York Times,* July 6, 1982, p. A10.

51. *New York Times,* March 29, 1982.

52. Shared by private insurance companies ($160 million), the utilities ($375 million), and the federal government ($25 million).

53. Ralph Nader with Harvey Rosenfield, "Atomic Power Today," Washington, D.C.: Critical Mass Energy Project, 1982, p. 4.

54. *General Public Utilities Corporation, Jersey Central Power & Light Company, Metropolitan Edison Company, Pennsylvania Electric Company v. United States of America,* U.S. District Court, Eastern District of Pennsylvania, Complaint, p. 9.

55. Ibid., p. 21.

56. Ibid., p. 27.

57. Ibid., p. 37.

58. The discovery process allows outside groups to submit questions to the NRC, as well as to other parties to the proceeding.

59. For further documentation on the proposed and final rules involving public participation, see Nuclear Regulatory Commission, "Rules of Practice for Domestic Licensing Proceedings: Modifications to the NRC Hearing Process," *Federal Register,* June 8, 1981, pp. 30349–52; and Nuclear Regulatory Commission, "Expediting the NRC Hearing Process," 46 Fed. Reg. 58,279–81 (1981).

60. *Inside NRC,* July 13, 1981, p. 12.

61. Nuclear Regulatory Commission, "Licensing Requirements for the Storage of Spent Fuel in an Independent Spent Fuel Storage Installation: Minor Clarifying and Conforming Amendments," 46 Fed. Reg. 58,281 (1981).

62. Elizabeth Rolph, *Nuclear Power and the Public Safety — A Study in Regulation,* Lexington, Mass.: D. C. Heath, 1979, p. 75. Rolph's book is an excellent study of the period: readable, comprehensive, and analytical. Another fine study, which was published several years later, is David Okrent, *Nuclear Reactor Safety: On the History of the Regulatory Process,* Madison: University of Wisconsin Press, 1981.

63. *Calvert Cliffs Coordinating Committee v. United States Atomic Energy Commission,* 449 F. 2d 1109 (1971).

64. Houston Industries eventually proposed plans canceling its Allen's Creek facility, requesting permission from the Texas Public Utility Commission to pass along to customers its $362 million investment in the project. *Wall Street Journal,* June 17, 1982, p. 12.

65. Ironically, although the NRC is now limiting the rights of inter-

venors, the agency has in the past supported what is known as "intervenor funding," public financing of outside groups who are challenging the NRC. The NRC has included intervenor funding in its budget requests to Congress, with Congress eliminating intervenor funding from the agency's requests, citing budgetary constraints.

66. Fritz F. Heimann, "The Regulation of Nuclear Power," Lecture at the Massachusetts Institute of Technology, May 9, 1980, p. 2.

67. Testimony of Ellyn R. Weiss, House Subcommittee on Energy and the Environment, Committee on Interior and Insular Affairs, April 9, 1981, p. 8.

68. *In re Vermont Yankee Nuclear Power Corp.* (Vermont Yankee Nuclear Power Station), ALAB–56, 4 A.E.C. 930 (1972), and *Vermont Yankee Nuclear Power Corp. v. NRDC,* 435 U.S. 519 (1978).

69. Ellyn R. Weiss, Letter to Commissioner John F. Ahearne, June 22, 1981.

70. Congressional Budget Office, "Delays in Nuclear Reactor Licensing and Construction: The Possibilities for Reform," March 1979, p. 23.

71. Ibid., p. 13.

72. Ibid., p. xi.

73. Rolph, p. 64.

74. *Inside NRC,* April 6, 1981, p. 3.

75. *New York Times,* September 5, 1982, p. 34.

76. *New York Times,* September 11, 1982, p. 22.

77. Commissioner John Ahearne advocates eliminating the *sua sponte* rule on the grounds that the hearing should only examine "contested issues." He cites an early AEC decision indicating that "Boards are neither required nor expected to look for new issues. . . . Normally there is a presumption that the parties themselves have properly shaped the issues, particularly because the hearing follows comprehensive reviews by the regulatory staff and the Advisory Commission of Reactor Safeguards." *Consolidated Edison Co.* (Indian Point Unit 3), CLI–74–28, 8 AEC 7, 9 (1974). Cited in a memorandum by John Ahearne, "The NRC Hearing Process," April 1, 1981, p. 4.

78. Union of Concerned Scientists and the Natural Resources Defense Council, "Comments on Proposed Rules of Practice for Domestic Licensing Proceedings: Expediting the NRC Hearing Process," presented to the NRC, p. 7. Another set of interesting recommendations for reforming the hearing process representing the nuclear industry's point of view comes from Marcus A. Rowden, "Achieving a More Effective Licensing Process — Basic Reform within Existing Law," Atomic Industrial Forum, November 1981.

79. *Patriot,* May 19, 1982, p. 1.

80. In the case of TMI, various schemes have been floated, with no end in sight. One of them, announced by Governor Richard Thornburgh of

Pennsylvania, involved a cost-sharing plan in which the $760 million tab would be split among the utility, the manufacturers and suppliers, and the two states, Pennsylvania and New Jersey. *Inside NRC,* August 10, 1981, p. 3.

81. In fact, the undamaged reactor at Three Mile Island cannot be restarted until the government assesses the "psychological stress" experienced by the community as a result. This directive came about through a ruling issued by the U.S. Court of Appeals for the District of Columbia on May 14, 1982, requiring the NRC for the first time to weigh psychological effects before allowing a plant to operate. The decision was written by Judge J. Skelley Wright. *People against Nuclear Energy v. United States Nuclear Regulatory Commission and the USA,* 678 F. 2d 222 (1982). The decision was reversed by the Supreme Court on April 19, 1983.

82. Testimony of Peter Bradford, House Subcommittee on Energy and the Environment, Committee on Interior and Insular Affairs, May 22, 1982, p. 9.

83. As of June 1982, nearly thirty cases were in litigation, brought by public interest groups or individuals affiliated with them. Many of these cases were filed prior to Palladino's appointment to the commission.

84. *Washington Post,* March 6, 1982, p. 48.

85. *Report of the President's Commission,* p. 56.

Chapter 7. The Risks of Laissez Faire (pages 237 – 256)

1. Liability for the nuclear industry was limited by the Price-Anderson Act of 1957.

2. Questions were raised about the financial health of the asbestos industry by the *Wall Street Journal,* which pointed out that the asbestos cases represented just the "latest shock for the battered asbestos industry." In addition to its legal problems, the asbestos industry has also faced reduced consumption of asbestos by half since 1973, as well as a series of attempts on the part of asbestos makers in the last several years either to "go out of business entirely" or to "disassociate themselves from their product." *Wall Street Journal,* August 30, 1982, p. 15.

3. This figure is derived from research commissioned by the company from a private consulting firm, Epidemiological Research of Boston. The firm also found that Johns-Manville would ultimately have to deal with fifty-two thousand lawsuits. *Newsweek,* September 6, 1982, p. 55.

4. Ibid.

5. Ibid., p. 57.

6. Lawyers receive seventy-seven cents for every sixty-six cents

awarded to product liability suit winners, according to Senator Robert Kasten (Republican, Wisconsin). *Wall Street Journal,* September 9, 1982, p. 26.

7. Ibid.

8. *Wall Street Journal,* June 9, 1982, p. 31.

9. *Wall Street Journal,* June 14, 1982, p. 1.

10. *Newsweek,* September 6, 1982, p. 57.

11. *New York Times,* August 28, 1982, p. 1.

12. Ibid., p. 43. Prior efforts to get Congress to remove asbestos lawsuits from the courts have been stalled, largely over the issue of who would pay compensation.

13. Ibid.

14. American Bar Association, American Trial Lawyers Association, National Association of Attorneys General, and the American Law Institute.

15. The plan would be administered by the states and funded by the federal government; claims would be filed through the state court systems. The legal changes would involve liberalizing state statutes of limitations, which, by making the time of exposure critical, often limit legal action. In addition, many worker compensation laws prevent victims from going to court. *New York Times,* September 28, 1982, p. A20.

16. *Wall Street Journal,* May 14, 1982, p. 14.

17. *Business Week,* March 1, 1982, p. 92.

18. *Washington Post,* May 16, 1982, pp. F1 and F6.

19. Michael Wines, "Verdict Still out on Deregulation's Impact on U.S. Air Travel System," *National Journal,* March 6, 1982, p. 406.

20. *Wall Street Journal,* May 14, 1982, p. 14.

21. Ibid.

22. Ibid. An interesting explanation for the reasons behind airline deregulation is included in Stephen Breyer, *Regulation and Its Reform,* Cambridge, Mass.: Harvard University Press, 1982, ch. 11.

23. *National Journal,* March 6, 1982, p. 406.

24. *Business Week,* February 22, 1982, p. 95.

25. *Washington Post,* May 16, 1982, pp. F1 and F6.

26. The *Wall Street Journal* reported an impromptu debate over cocktails in a New York hotel at the time of airline deregulation. One of industry's representatives, Melvin Brenner, then a senior vice president at TWA, argued that airlines would "load routes with extra capacity and slash fares, resulting in a financial blood bath and bankruptcy for the weakest." In a reversal of roles, his counterpart in the Transportation Department argued that airline officials act rationally and would avoid such dangerous decision making. *Wall Street Journal,* May 14, 1982, p. 14.

27. *Washington Post,* May 16, 1982, pp. F1 and F6.

28. *Wall Street Journal,* March 21, 1983, p. 23.

29. *Washington Post,* February 22, 1982, p. A9.

30. *New York Times,* August 27, 1982, p. A10.

31. Ibid. In the words of Richard B. Thornburg of the National Beer Wholesalers Association.

32. Without federal regulations that would pre-empt state standards, the companies would have to operate according to the standards of the strictest states. In an interesting twist to the adversarial relationship that has plagued the regulatory environment, the alcohol industry now finds itself on the same side as its long-time opponent in the public interest community, the Center for Science in the Public Interest; both are trying to stave off a return to marketplace.

33. *Wall Street Journal*, September 23, 1982, p. 37.

34. Ibid.

35. *Wall Street Journal*, August 24, 1982, p. 54.

36. Ibid.

37. *National Journal*, July 31, 1982, p. 1340.

38. As reported in the *Washington Post*, October 4, 1982.

Chapter 8. There's No Such Thing as a Free Market (pages 257 – 276)

1. Robert B. Reich, "Made and Litigated in the U.S.A.," *Business Week*, October 27, 1980.

2. EPA Emissions Trading Policy Statement, 47 Fed. Reg. 15,076 (1982).

3. Reminiscent of the short-lived Safe Harbor Leasing tax gift to the corporations, in which rich companies could buy the tax credits of failing companies and wind up paying virtually no taxes. Under this system, one company could sell pollution credits to a newly expanding factory, the latter thus avoiding the installation of costly pollution control equipment, while even a company about to go out of business could sell its "pollution rights" to "another polluter for whatever the traffic will bear." Bruce Ackerman and Donald Elliott, "Air-Pollution Rights," *New York Times*, September 11, 1982, p. 23.

4. The Carter administration, for example, relaxed export controls to enable manufacturers to sell 2.3 million pajamas treated with the flame retardant TRIS (a carcinogenic compound, No. 2, No. 3–dibromopropyl phosphate) to Third World countries, despite the fact that they were banned in this country after studies showed that TRIS was a carcinogen. Under similar pressures from industries whose products have run into regulatory trouble in the United States, the Reagan administration has sought to ease export controls on hazardous products, or drugs that have either been banned by the FDA or not yet been approved. The rationale for selling drugs abroad is justified on the basis of risk-benefit ratios — the drug may have benefits

that outweigh its hazards in countries where the medical problems may justify a higher degree of risk taking. The drug Entero-Vioform, which treats dysentery, has been linked to side effects that include blindness and paralysis. Nevertheless, the government of India requested its producer, Ciba-Geigy, to continue selling the drug on the grounds that the dysentery problem itself was life threatening and justified the risk of side effects. At the same time, the government of Bangladesh banned the drug. The only problem with this rationalization is that most Third World patients taking the drug are probably unaware of its side effects; that the drug has been banned elsewhere; and that safer alternative treatments may be available. See an excellent article by Michael DeCourcy Hinds, *New York Times,* August 22, 1982, p. E9.

5. This was called a "deadly standard" by *Newsweek,* in an informative article on the effects of hazardous chemical exports in Third World countries. *Newsweek,* August 17, 1981, pp. 53–55. The article cites the case of one mother in rural Brazil who applied a chemical called ektafos to her children's heads to rid them of fleas and lice, then watched helplessly as they died. Thousands of cases of pesticide poisoning go unreported due to the ignorance of medical personnel in these areas while the problem continues unabated.

6. *New York Times,* September 10, 1982, pp. A1 and A16.

7. The booster was a Minuteman rocket purchased from NASA for $365,000.

8. *Washington Post,* April 26, 1982, p. A24.

9. Testimony of Louis Harris, House Subcommittee on Health and the Environment, Committee on Energy and Commerce, October 15, 1981, pp. 3 and 5.

10. Ibid. Even the Chamber of Commerce, long-time critic of federal regulation, reported the results of a survey commissioned from the Opinion Research Corporation whose findings were similar to Harris's. The chamber's survey concluded that 70 percent of the public felt that air quality goals should be based on health considerations and the protection of recreation areas and natural resources, and that those standards should be enforced by the federal government. When the chamber study introduced cost factors into the questionnaire, it was found that 60 percent opposed closing those factories until they met air quality standards. See Chamber of Commerce, Special Resources and Environmental Fact Sheet, "Clean Air: What Do Americans Want?" December 1981.

11. Louis Harris, "Views of Government Regulation of Business," The Harris Survey, August 10, 1981, p. 1.

12. Ibid.

13. Ibid.

14. The hopeful part of the survey was that 62 percent said they wanted to know more about how federal regulations are made. *Washington Post,* May 31, 1982, p. A15.

15. "Offset trading," for example, allows new facilities to open in areas where the air is too contaminated to meet basic health standards, by getting other businesses to take additional control actions.

16. *Washington Post,* September 21, 1982, p. A17.

17. For further discussion of this topic, see Joseph G. Perpich, "Industrial Involvement in the Development of NIH Recombinant DNA Research Guidelines and Related Federal Policies," *Recombinant DNA Technical Bulletin* 59 (June 1982); and Joseph G. Perpich, "Genetic Engineering and Related Technologies: Scientific Progress and Public Policies," *Technology in Society,* Summer 1983.

Bibliography

Ackerman, Bruce A., and William T. Hassler. *Clean Coal/Dirty Air.* New Haven: Yale University Press, 1981.
Aharoni, Yair. *The No-Risk Society.* Chatham, N.J.: Chatham House Publishers, Inc., 1981.
American Bar Association. *Federal Regulation: Roads to Reform.* Washington, D.C.: American Bar Association, 1978.
American Enterprise Institute. *Government Regulation: Proposals for Procedural Reform.* Washington, D.C.: AEI, 1979.
———. *Major Regulatory Initiatives during 1978: The Agencies, the Courts, and the Congress.* Washington, D.C.: AEI, 1978.
———. *Regulation and Regulatory Reform: A Survey of Proposals of the 95th Congress.* Washington, D.C.: AEI, 1978.
Argyris, Chris, et al. *Regulating Business: The Search for an Optimum.* San Francisco: Institute for Contemporary Studies, 1978.
Baram, Michael S. *Alternatives to Regulation: Managing Risks to Health, Safety and the Environment.* Lexington, Mass.: Lexington Books, 1982.
Bardach, Eugene, and Robert A. Kagan. *Going by the Book: The Problem of Regulatory Unreasonableness.* Philadelphia: Temple University Press, 1982.
———, eds. *Social Regulation: Strategies for Reform.* San Francisco: Boyd and Fraser, 1981.
Breyer, Stephen. *Regulation and Its Reform.* Cambridge, Mass.: Harvard University Press, 1982.
Brownstein, Ronald, and Nina Easton. *Reagan's Ruling Class: Portraits of the President's Top 100 Officials.* Washington, D.C.: The Presidential Accountability Group, 1982.
Clark, Timothy B., Marvin H. Kosters, and James C. Miller III. *Reforming Regulation.* Washington, D.C.: American Enterprise Institute for Public Policy Research, 1980.
Committee for Economic Development. *Redefining Government's Role in the Market System.* New York: Kearney Press, 1979.
Conservation Foundation. *State of the Environment 1982.* Washington, D.C.: Conservation Foundation, 1982.
Cooper, Phillip J. *Public Law and Public Administration.* Palo Alto: Mayfield Publishing Company, 1983.
Crandall, Robert W., and Lester B. Lave, eds. *The Scientific Bases of Health and Safety Regulation.* Washington, D.C.: The Brookings Institution, 1981.
Davis, Kenneth Culp. *Administrative Law and Government.* St. Paul: West Publishing Company, 1975.

Bibliography

————. *Discretionary Justice — A Preliminary Inquiry.* Baton Rouge: Louisiana State University Press, 1969.

Dimock, Marshall K. *Law and Dynamic Administration.* New York: Praeger Publishers, 1980.

Dunlop, John T. *Business and Public Policy.* Cambridge, Mass.: Harvard University Press, 1980.

Ferguson, Allen R., ed. *Attacking Regulatory Problems: An Agenda for Research in the 1980's.* Cambridge, Mass.: Ballinger Publishing Company, 1981.

Freedman, James O. *Crisis and Legitimacy: The Administrative Process and American Government.* Cambridge: Cambridge University Press, 1978.

Fritschler, A. Lee. *Smoking and Politics — Policymaking and the Federal Bureaucracy.* 3d ed. Englewood Cliffs, N.J.: Prentice-Hall, 1983.

————, and Bernard H. Ross. *Business Regulation and Government Decision-Making.* Cambridge, Mass.: Winthrop Publishers, 1980.

Gatti, James, ed. *The Limits of Government Regulation.* New York: Academic Press, 1981.

General Accounting Office. *Improved Quality, Adequate Resources, and Consistent Oversight Needed If Regulatory Analysis Is to Help Control Costs of Regulation.* Washington, D.C.: U.S. Govt. Printing Office, GAO/PAD-83-6, Nov. 2, 1982.

Green, Mark, and Norman Waitzman. *Business War on the Law: An Analysis of the Benefits of Federal Health/Safety Enforcement.* Washington, D.C.: The Corporate Accountability Research Group, Ralph Nader, 1981.

Jacoby, Neil H. *Corporate Power and Social Responsibility.* New York: Macmillan Publishing Company, Inc., 1973.

Kagan, Robert A. *Regulatory Justice: Implementing a Wage-Price Freeze.* New York: Russell Sage Foundation, 1978.

Katzmann, Robert A. *Regulatory Bureaucracy: The Federal Trade Commission and Antitrust Policy.* Cambridge, Mass.: MIT Press, 1980.

Kohlmeier, Louis M., Jr. *The Regulators: Watchdog Agencies and the Public Interest.* New York: Harper and Row, 1969.

Krasnow, Erwin G., Lawrence D. Longley, and Herbert A. Terry. *The Politics of Broadcast Regulation.* New York: St. Martin's Press, 1982.

Krislov, Samuel, and Lloyd D. Musolf. *The Politics of Regulation.* Boston: Houghton Mifflin Co., 1964.

Landis, James M. *The Administrative Process.* New Haven: Yale University Press, 1938.

Lave, Lester B. *The Strategy of Social Regulation: Decision Frameworks for Policy.* Washington, D.C.: The Brookings Institution, 1981.

Leone, Robert A. *Government Regulation of Business: Developing the Managerial Perspective.* Boston: Harvard Business School, 1981.

Lindblom, Charles E. *Politics and Markets: The World's Political-Economic Systems.* New York: Basic Books, Inc., 1977.

Bibliography

MacAvoy, Paul W., ed. *The Crisis of the Regulatory Commissions: An Introduction to a Current Issue of Public Policy.* New York: W. W. Norton, 1970.

————, ed. *Unsettled Questions on Regulatory Reform.* Washington, D.C.: American Enterprise Institute, 1978.

McGraw, Thomas K. *Regulation in Perspective: Historical Essays.* Cambridge, Mass.: Harvard University Press, 1981.

Mitnick, Barry M. *The Political Economy of Regulation: Creating, Designing and Removing Regulatory Forms.* New York: Columbia University Press, 1980.

National Institute of Allergy and Infectious Diseases. *Recombinant DNA Technical Bulletin.* Washington, D.C.: National Institutes of Health, 1982.

Noll, Roger G. *Reforming Regulation: An Evaluation of the Ash Council Proposals.* Washington, D.C.: The Brookings Institution, 1971.

Office of Management and Budget. *Improving Government Regulations: Current Status and Future Directions.* Washington, D.C.: U.S. Govt. Printing Office, 1980.

Owen, Bruce M., and Ronald Braeutingam. *The Regulation Game: Strategic Use of the Administrative Process.* Cambridge, Mass.: Ballinger, 1978.

Pertschuk, Michael. *Revolt against Regulation: The Rise and Pause of the Consumer Movement.* Berkeley: University of California Press, 1982.

Poole, Robert W., Jr. *Instead of Regulation: Alternatives to Federal Regulatory Agencies.* Lexington, Mass.: Lexington Books, 1981.

Quirk, Paul J. *Industry Influence in Federal Regulatory Agencies.* Princeton, N.J.: Princeton University Press, 1981.

Schiff, Frank W. *Looking Ahead: Identifying Key Economic Issues for Business and Society in the 1980's.* Worcester, Mass.: Heffernan Press, Inc., 1980.

Schultze, Charles L. *The Public Use of Private Interest.* Washington, D.C.: The Brookings Institution, 1977.

Schwartz, Bernard. *The Professor and the Commissions.* New York: Alfred Knopf, 1959.

Steiner, George A., and John F. Steiner. *Business, Government and Society — A Managerial Perspective.* New York: Random House, 1980.

Stokes, McNeill. *Conquering Government Regulations: A Business Guide.* New York: McGraw-Hill, 1982.

Stone, Alan. *Economic Regulation and the Public Interest — The Federal Trade Commission in Theory and Practice.* Ithaca: Cornell University Press, 1977.

U.S. Chamber of Commerce. *Quality of Regulators: From Minimal Qualifications to Affirmative Qualifications.* Washington, D.C.: U.S. Chamber of Commerce, 1981.

Bibliography

U.S. Congress. House. Committee on Energy and Commerce. 97th Congress, 1st Session. *Presidential Control of Agency Rulemaking.* Washington, D.C.: U.S. Govt. Printing Office, June 15, 1981.

———. House. Committee on Interstate and Foreign Commerce, Subcommittee on Oversight and Investigations. 94th Congress, 2d Session. *Federal Regulatory Reform.* Washington, D.C.: U.S. Govt. Printing Office, October 1976.

———. Senate. Committee on Governmental Affairs and the Committee on the Judiciary. 96th Congress, 2d Session. *Reform of Federal Regulation,* pts. 1 and 2. Washington, D.C.: U.S. Govt. Printing Office, June 1980.

———. Senate. Committee on the Judiciary. 97th Congress, 1st Session. *The Regulatory Reform Act.* Washington, D.C.: U.S. Govt. Printing Office, November 30, 1981.

United States Regulatory Council. *Regulation: The View from Janesville, Wisconsin, and a Regulator's Perspective.* Washington, D.C.: U.S. Govt. Printing Office, March 1980.

Vaughn, Robert G. *Conflict-of-Interest Regulations in the Federal Executive Branch.* Lexington, Mass.: Lexington Books, D. C. Heath and Company, 1979.

Weaver (Garment), Suzanne. *Decision to Prosecute: Organization and Public Policy in the Antitrust Division.* Cambridge, Mass.: MIT Press, 1977.

Weidenbaum, Murray L. *Business, Government and the Public.* Englewood Cliffs, N.J.: Prentice-Hall, Inc., 1981.

———. *The Future of Business Regulation.* New York: AMACOM, 1979.

Weiss, Leonard W., and Michael W. Klass, eds. *Case Studies in Regulation — Revolution and Reform.* Boston: Little, Brown, 1981.

Welborn, David M. *Governance of Federal Regulatory Agencies.* Knoxville: University of Tennessee Press, 1977.

White, Lawrence J. *Reforming Regulation: Processes and Problems.* Englewood Cliffs, N.J.: Prentice-Hall 1981.

Wilson, James Q. *The Politics of Regulation.* New York: Basic Books, 1980.

Woll, Peter. *Administrative Law — The Informal Process.* Berkeley and Los Angeles: University of California Press, 1963.

———. *American Bureaucracy.* New York: W. W. Norton, 1963.

Woolsey, Suzanne H., and Michael N. Sohn, eds. *Regulatory Impact Analysis: Achieving Client Objectives under Cost/Benefit Assessments and Other Regulatory Reform Initiatives.* New York: Harcourt Brace Jovanovich, 1981.

Index

Index

ABOUT THE AUTHORS

Susan J. Tolchin is Professor of Public Administration at George Washington University in Washington, D.C. Martin Tolchin is a prize-winning congressional correspondent in the Washington bureau of the *New York Times*. Together they have written two previous books — *To the Victor: Political Patronage from the Clubhouse to the White House* (1971) and *Clout: Womanpower and Politics* (1974).

DATE DUE

DATE DUE	BORROWER'S NAME	ROOM NUMBER